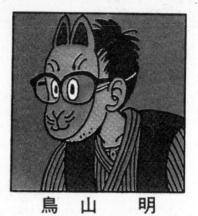

鳥　山　明

ABOUT the CREATOR

Widely known all over the world for his playful,
innovative storytelling and humorous, distinctive
art style, **Dragon Ball** creator Akira Toriyama is
also known in his native Japan for the wildly popular
Dr. Slump, his previous manga series about the
adventures of a mad scientist and his android
"daughter." His hit series **Dragon Ball** ran from
1984 to 1995 in Shueisha's weekly **Shônen Jump**
magazine. He is also known for his design work
on video games such as **Dragon Warrior**,
Chrono Trigger and **Tobal No.1**. His recent
manga works include **Cowa**, **Kajika** and **Sand
Land**. He lives with his family in Tokyo, Japan.

DRAGON BALL VOL. 6

This graphic novel, number 6 in a series of 42, contains
the monthly comic series DRAGON BALL PART 3 #4
through #9 in their entirety.

STORY AND ART BY
AKIRA TORIYAMA

ENGLISH ADAPTATION BY
GERARD JONES

Translation/Mari Morimoto
Touch-Up Art & Lettering/Wayne Truman
Cover Design/Hidemi Sahara
Graphics & Layout/Sean Lee
Edited by/Jason Thompson

Director of Sales & Marketing/Dallas Middaugh
Marketing Manager/Renée Solberg
Sales Representative/Mike Roberson
Assistant Sales Manager/Denya S. Jur
Editor-in-Chief/Hyoe Narita
Publisher/Seiji Horibuchi

PARENTAL ADVISORY
Dragon Ball contains images and themes that
may be unsuitable for young children. It is
recommended for ages 13 and up.

Printed in Canada

Published by Viz Communications, Inc.
P.O. Box 77010 • San Francisco, CA 94107

10 9 8 7 6 5 4 3 2 1
First printing, September 2001

Vizit us at our World Wide Web site at
www.vizkids.com!

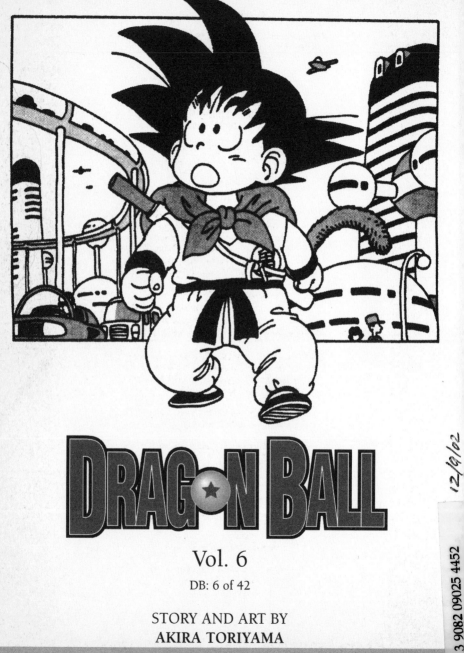

VIZ GRAPHIC NOVEL

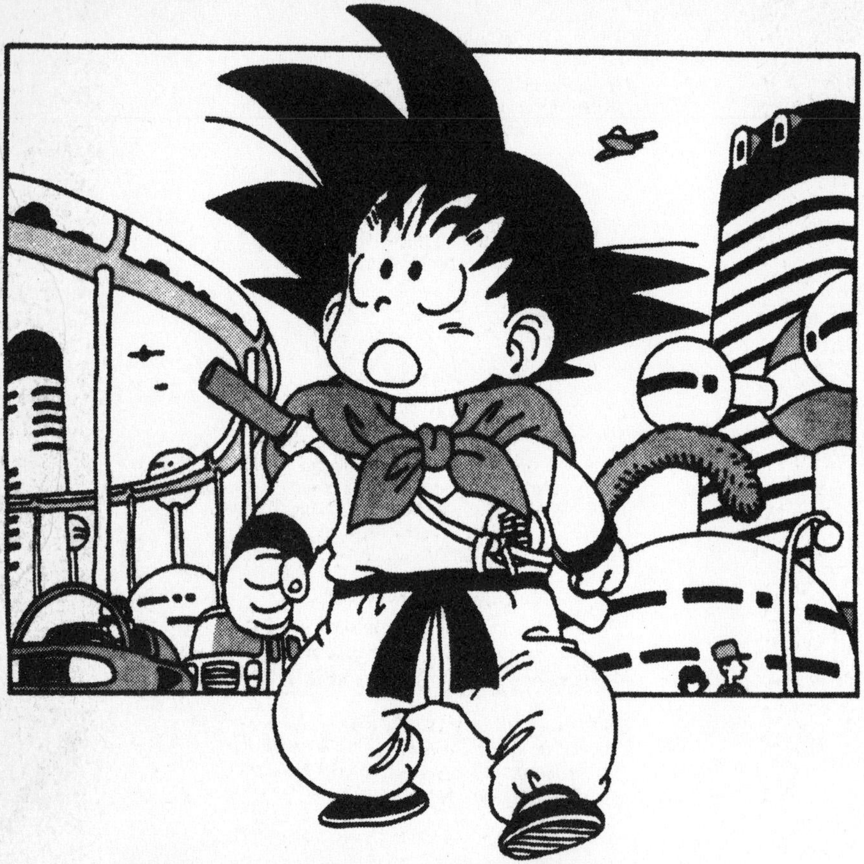

DRAGON BALL

Vol. 6

DB: 6 of 42

STORY AND ART BY

AKIRA TORIYAMA

THE MAIN CHARACTERS

Son Goku
Monkey-tailed young Goku has always been stronger than normal. His grandfather Gohan gave him the *nyoibô*, a magic staff, and Kame-Sen'nin gave him the *kinto'un*, a magic flying cloud. However, the *kinto'un* was recently destroyed by Colonel Silver, forcing Goku to find alternate means of transportation!

Oolong
Immature, shapeshifting Oolong was the only member of the group who got his wish with the Dragon Balls.

Bulma
A genius inventor, Bulma met Goku on her quest for the seven magical Dragon Balls.

Pu'ar
Yamcha's shapeshifting friend.

Yamcha
Yamcha used to be a desert bandit, but he went to the city to be Bulma's boyfriend. He uses "Fist of the Wolf-Fang" kung-fu.

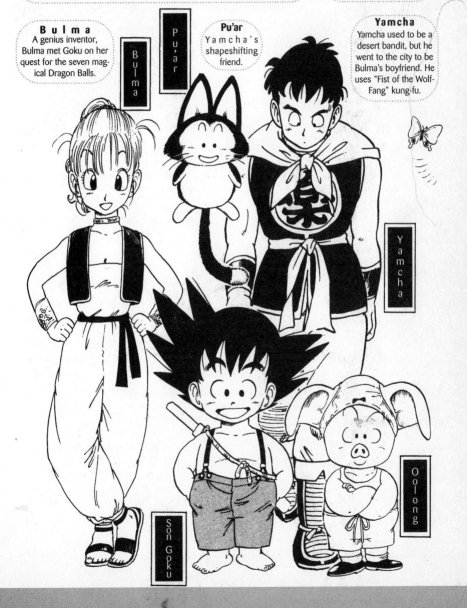

Bulma

Pu'ar

Yamcha

Son Goku

Oolong

Sergeant Major Purple

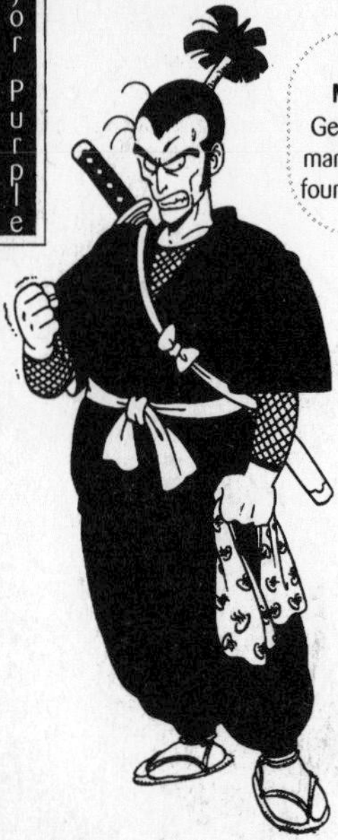

Sergeant Major Purple
General White's right-hand man, a ninja who guards the fourth level of Muscle Tower.

General White

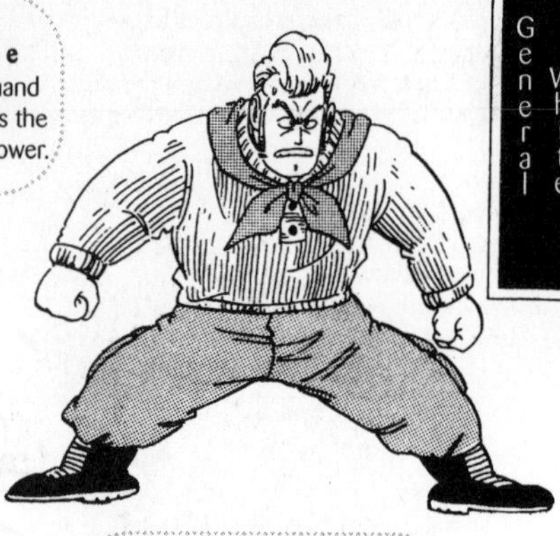

General White
The diabolical boss of Muscle Tower. He kidnapped the mayor of Jingle Village to force the peaceful villagers to help him find a Dragon Ball. Now he waits on the sixth level of his tower, mocking Goku's efforts to climb to the top…

Kame-Sen'nin (The "Turtle Hermit")
A lecherous but powerful martial artist (also known as the *muten-rôshi*, or "Invincible Old Master") who trained Goku's grandfather, Son Gohan, as well as Goku himself. He taught Goku the *kamehameha* attack.

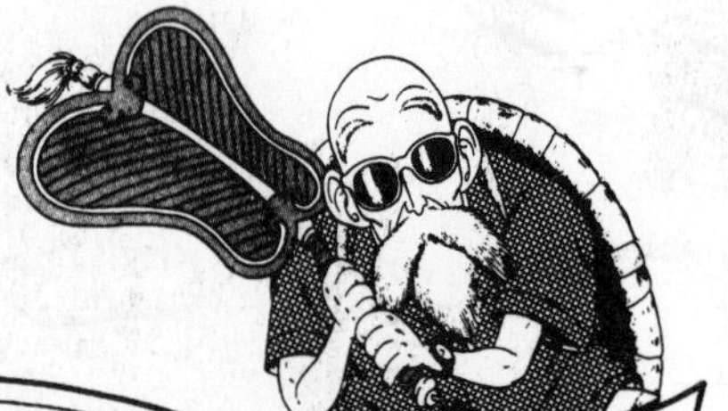

Kame-Sen'nin

Legend says that whoever gathers the seven magical "Dragon Balls" will be granted any one wish. Son Goku, a young boy from the mountains, first heard the legend from a city girl named Bulma. After many dangerous adventures with Bulma, Goku trained under the great martial artist Kame-Sen'nin and competed in the "Strongest Under the Heavens" fighting tournament. Afterwards, Goku resumed his quest for the Dragon Balls, only to find that a powerful enemy, the Red Ribbon Army, was also searching for them. Now, Goku faces a perilous challenge in Muscle Tower, the Red Ribbon Army's arctic base!

DRAGON BALL 6

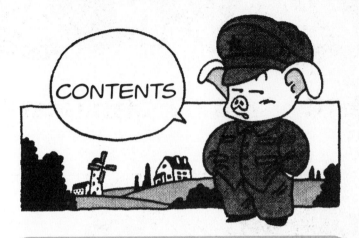

CONTENTS

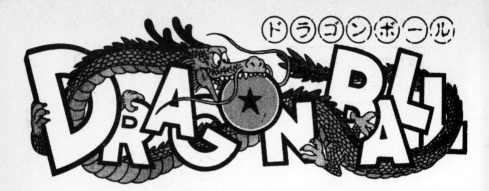

Tale 61 • The 4 1/2 Tatami Mat Flip

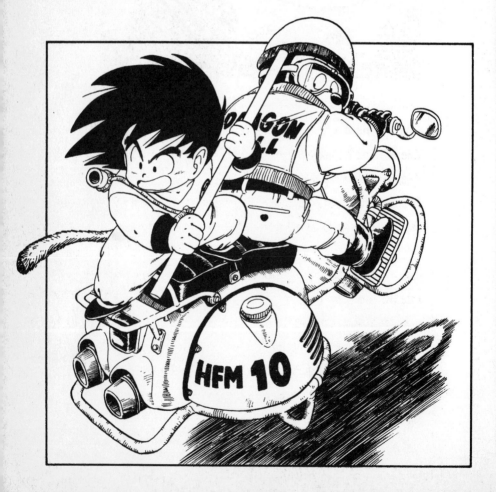

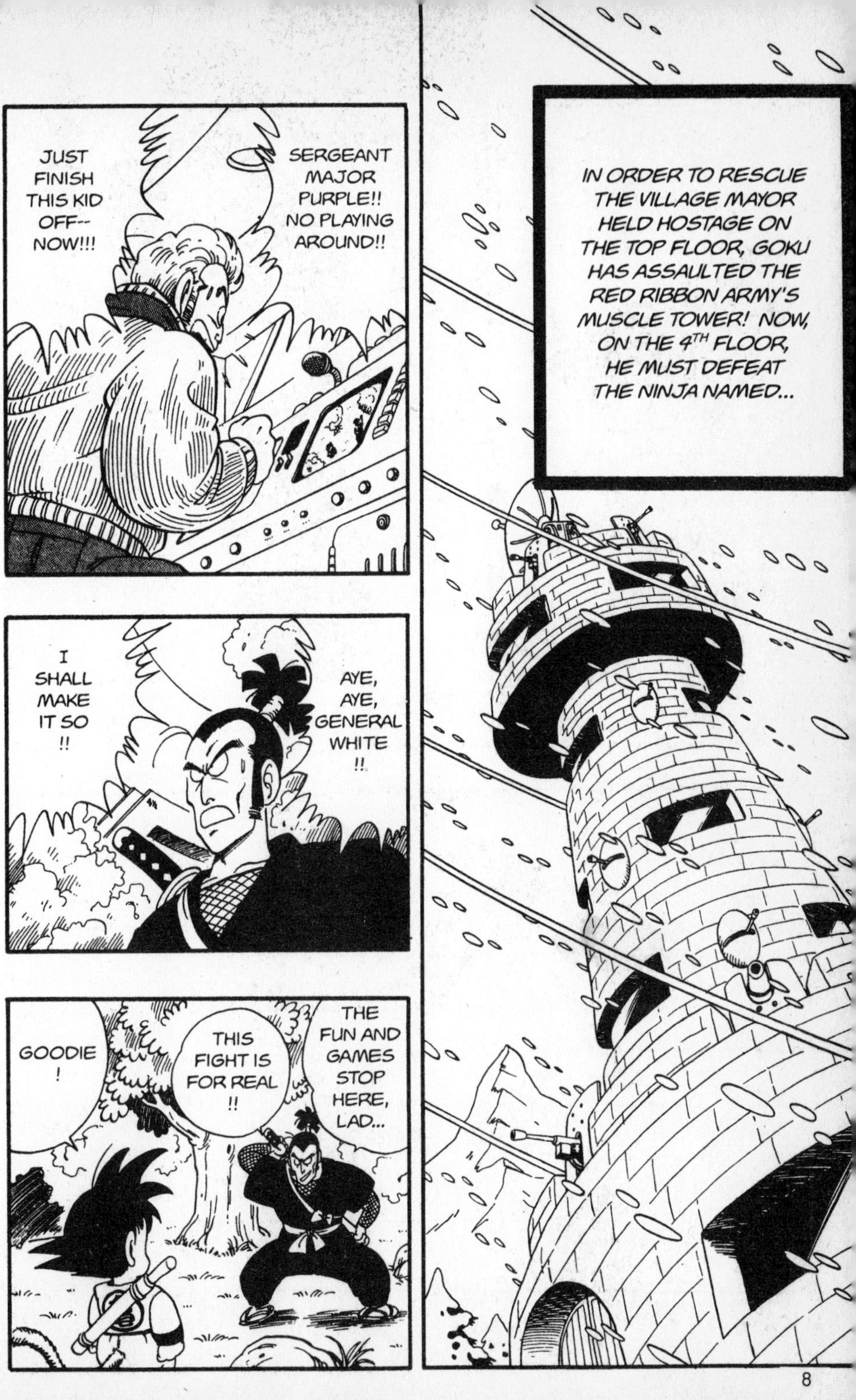
SERGEANT MAJOR PURPLE!! NO PLAYING AROUND!!
JUST FINISH THIS KID OFF-- NOW!!!
AYE, AYE, GENERAL WHITE !!
I SHALL MAKE IT SO !!
THE FUN AND GAMES STOP HERE, LAD...
THIS FIGHT IS FOR REAL !!
GOODIE !
IN ORDER TO RESCUE THE VILLAGE MAYOR HELD HOSTAGE ON THE TOP FLOOR, GOKU HAS ASSAULTED THE RED RIBBON ARMY'S MUSCLE TOWER! NOW, ON THE 4TH FLOOR, HE MUST DEFEAT THE NINJA NAMED...

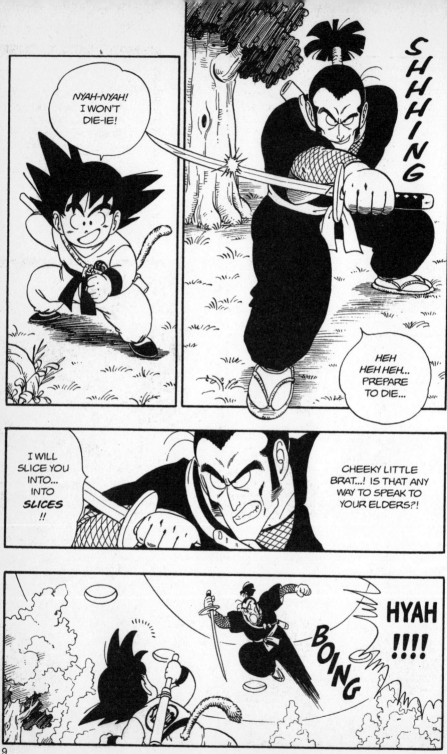

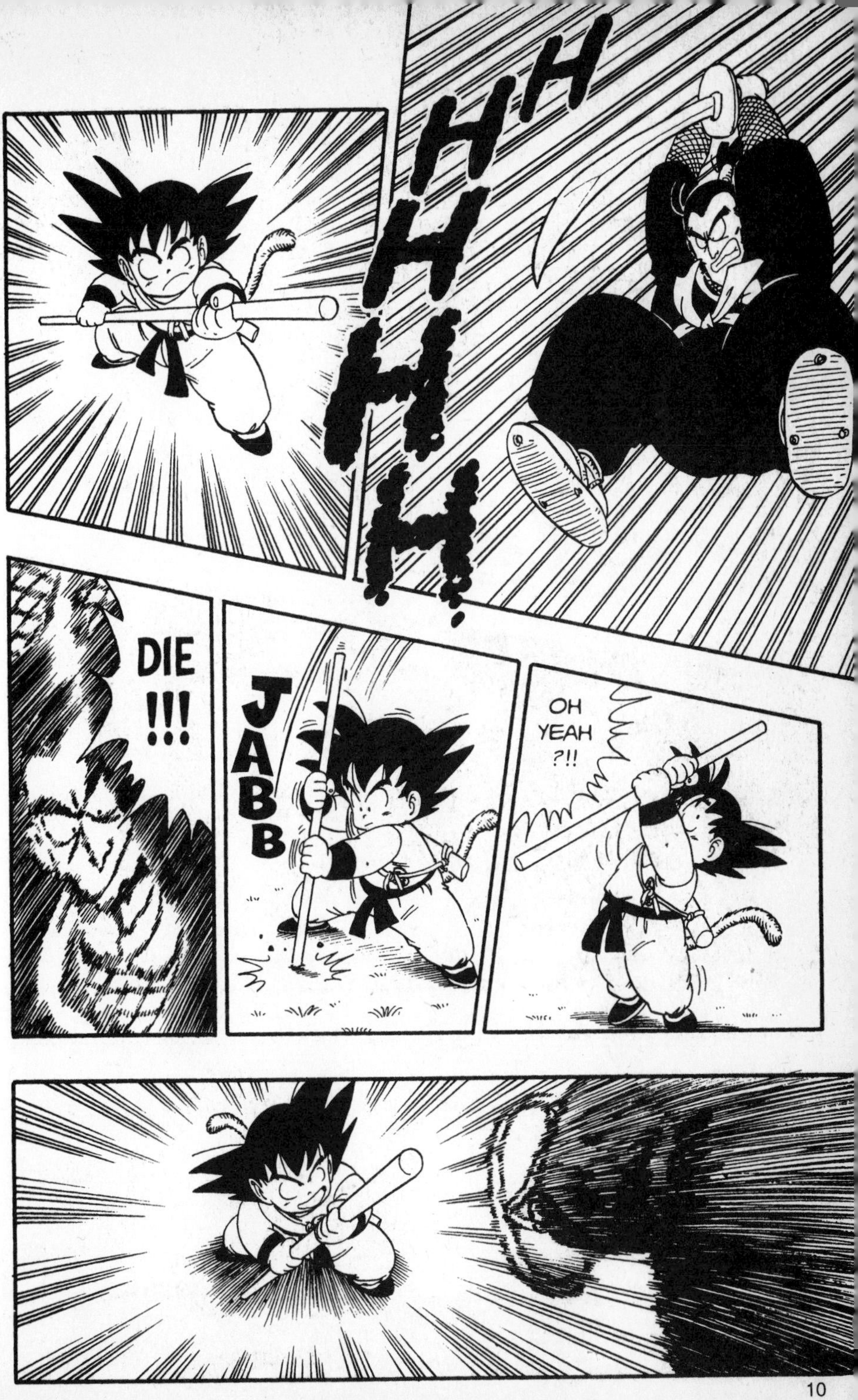
HHHHH!
OH YEAH ?!!
JABB
DIE !!!

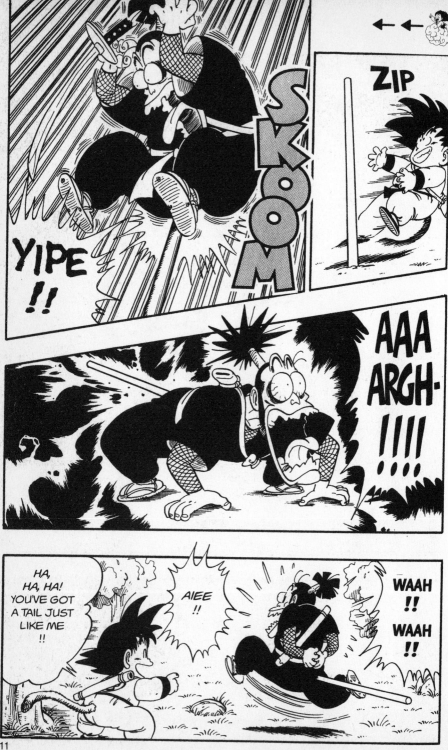

11

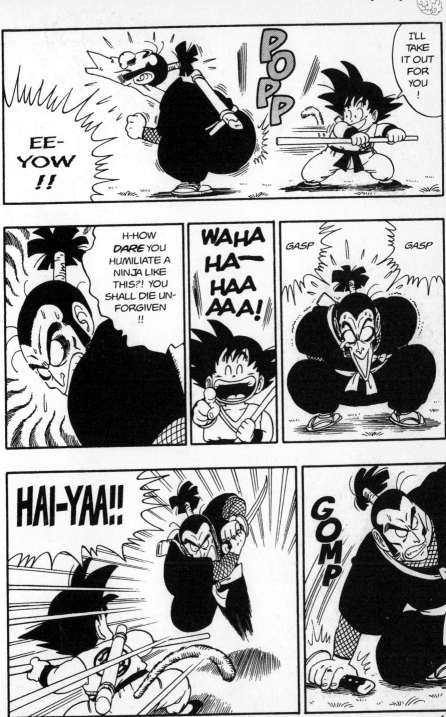

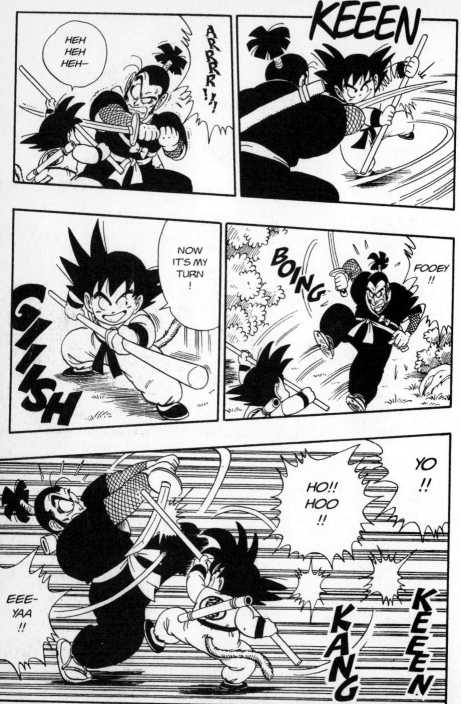

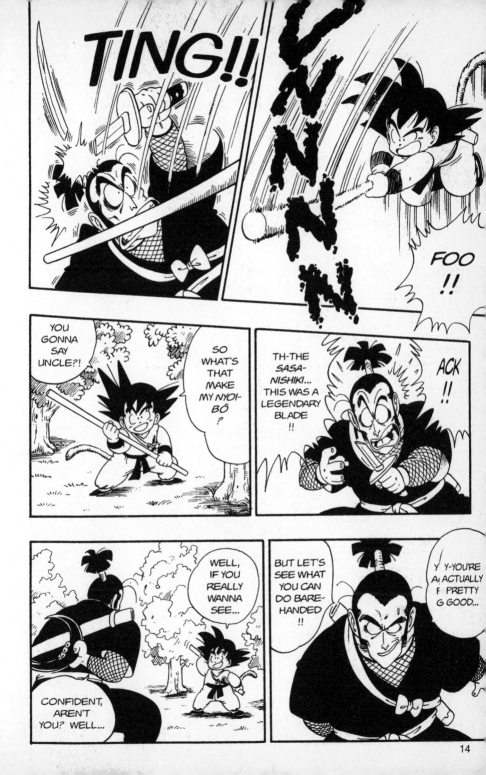

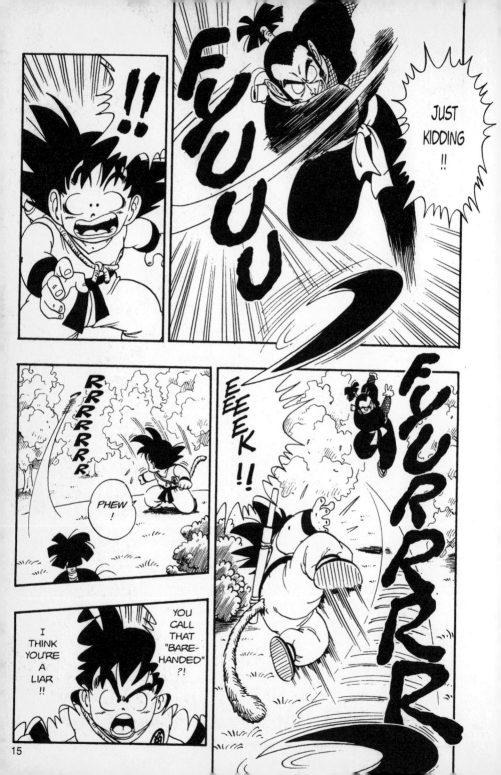

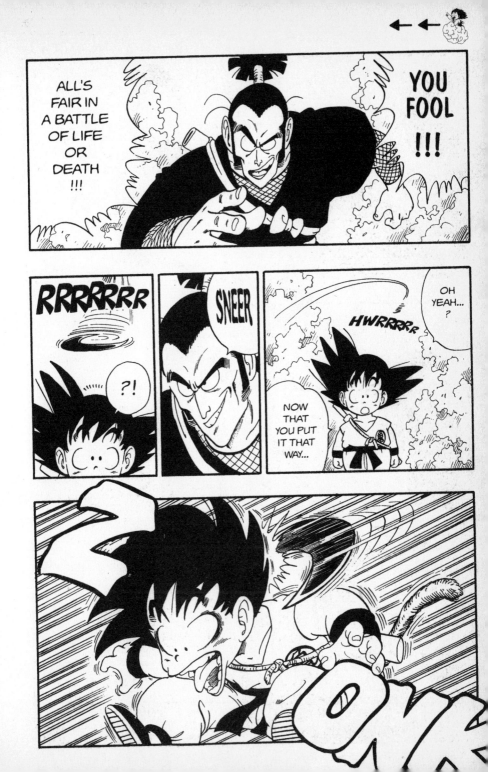

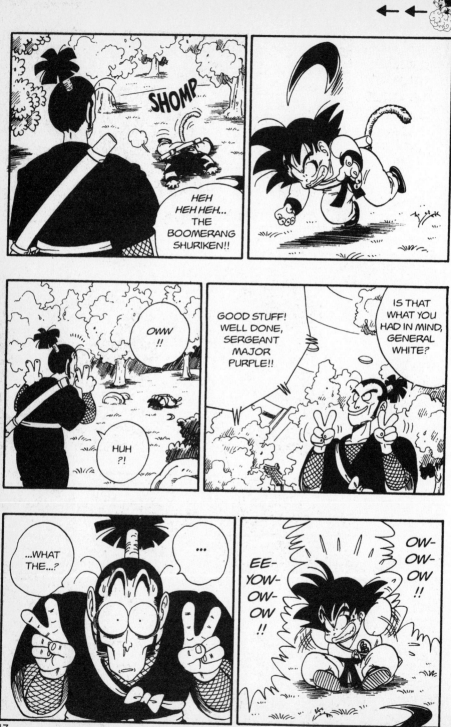

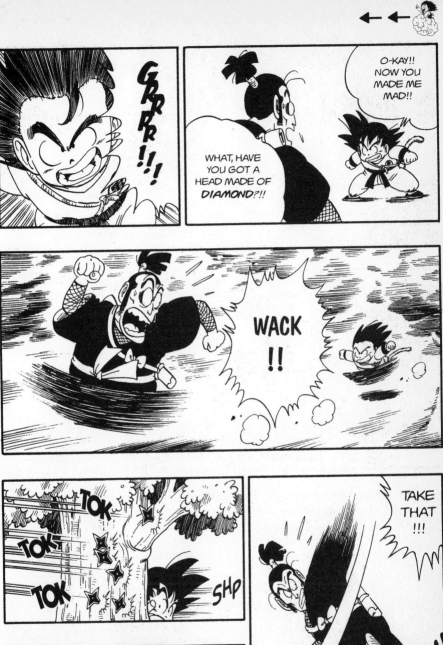
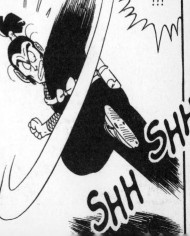
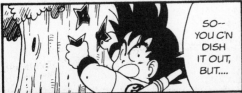

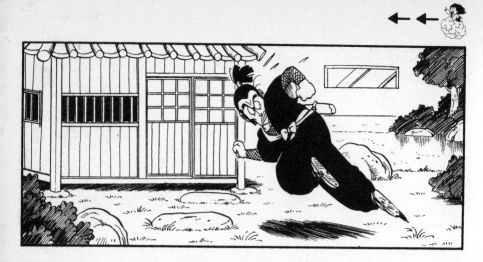

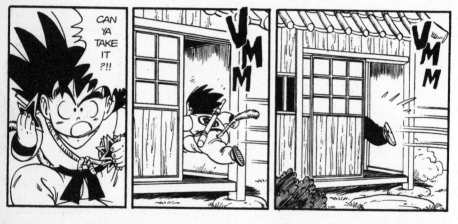

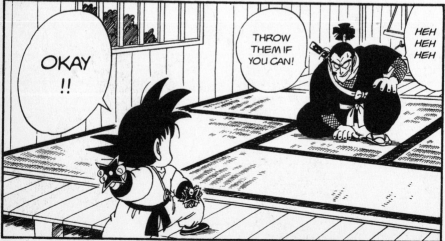

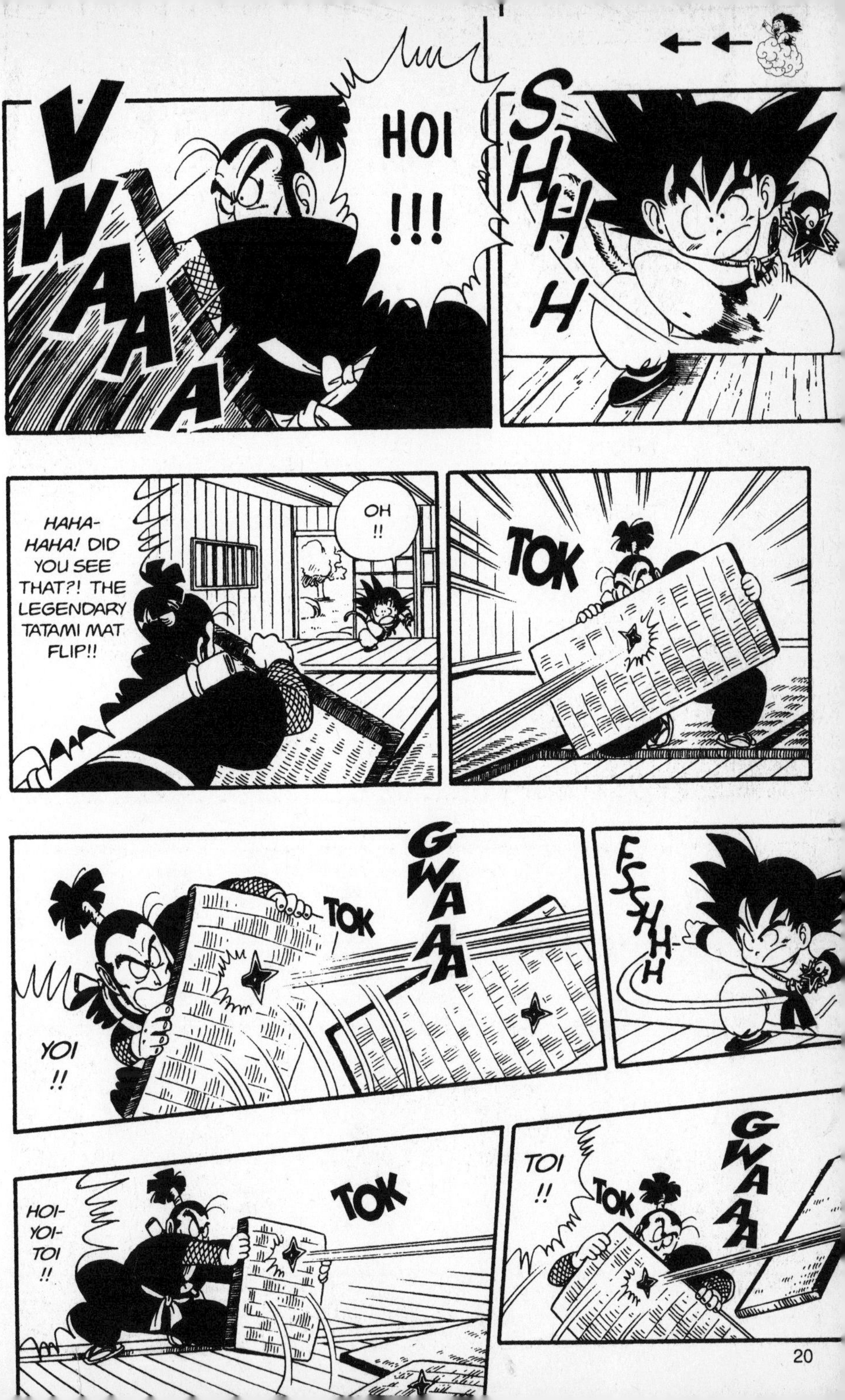
SHHHH
VWAAAA
HOI
!!!
OH
!!
TOK
HAHA-
HAHA! DID
YOU SEE
THAT?! THE
LEGENDARY
TATAMI MAT
FLIP!!
FSSHHH
GWAAA
TOK
YOI
!!
TOI
!!
TOK
GWAAA
TOK
HOI-
YOI-
TOI
!!

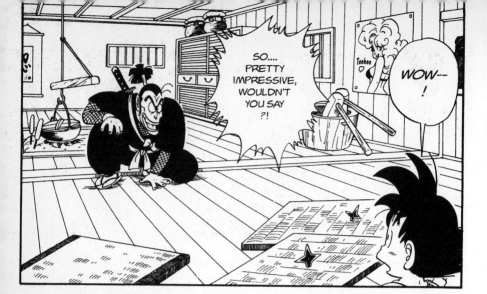

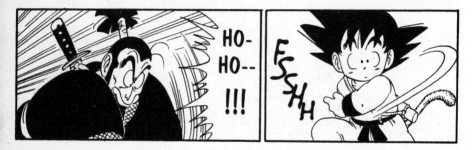

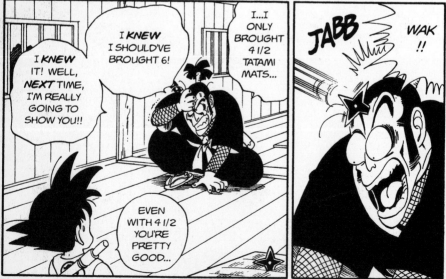

ドラゴンボール

DRAGON BALL

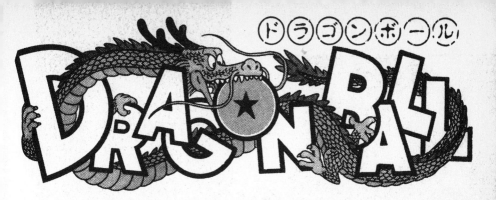

Tale 62 • The Ninja Split!

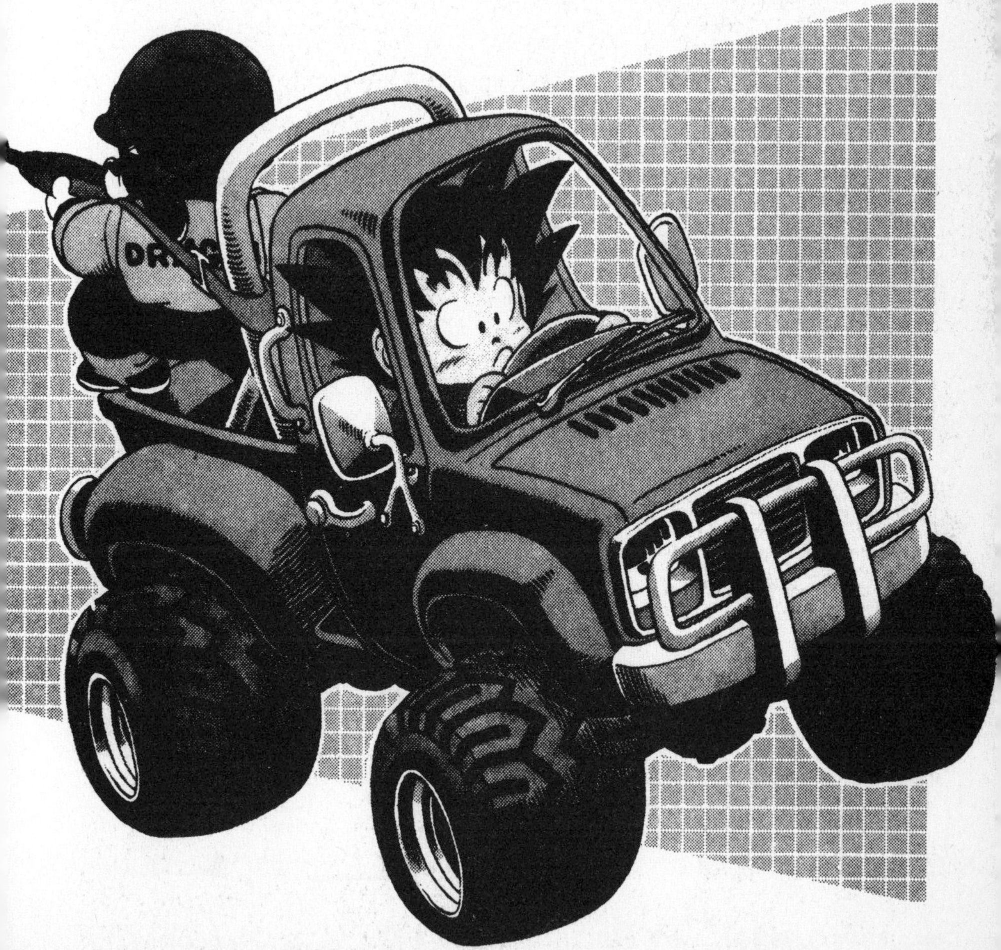

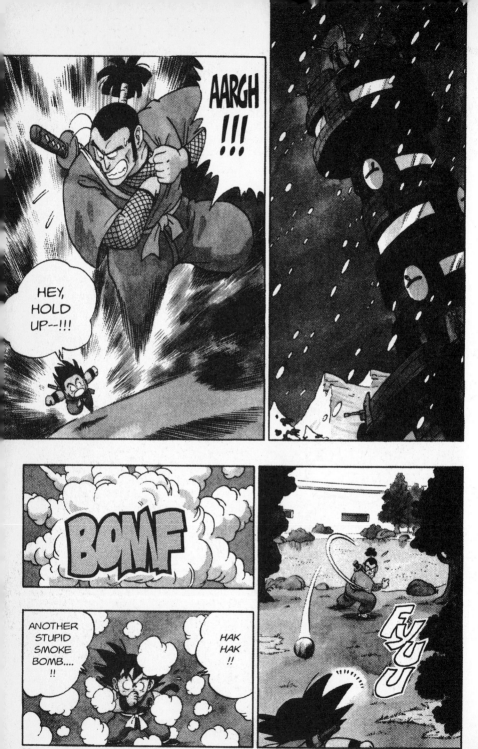

SON GOKU
HERO OF THE
ANCIENT CHINESE
FABLE **SAIYÛKI**
("JOURNEY TO THE WEST")

SON GOKU
HERO OF
DRAGON BALL

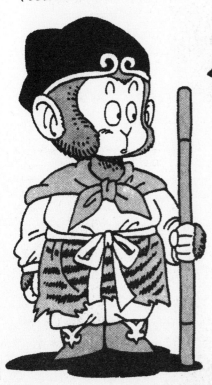

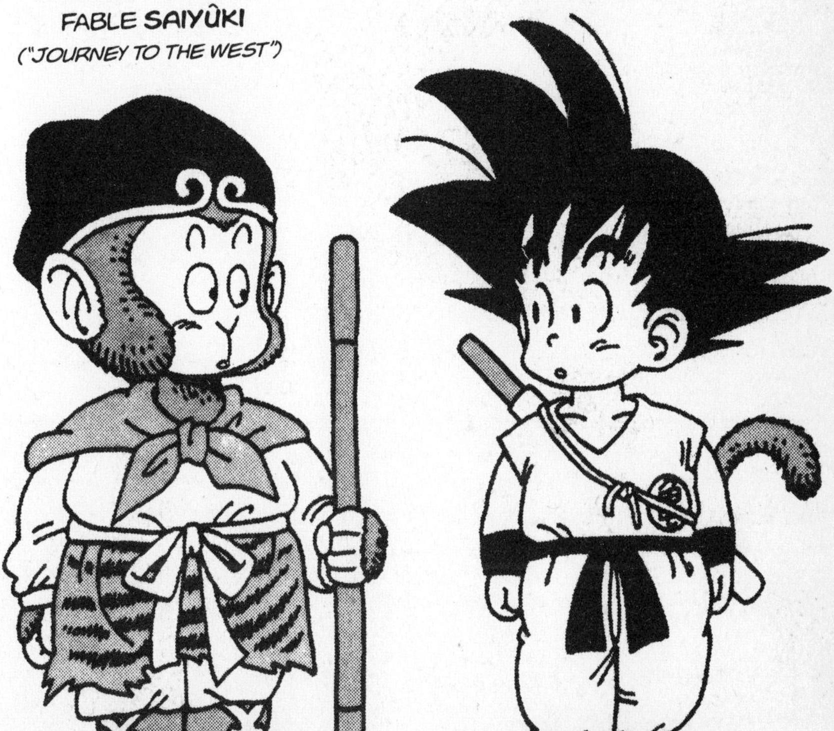

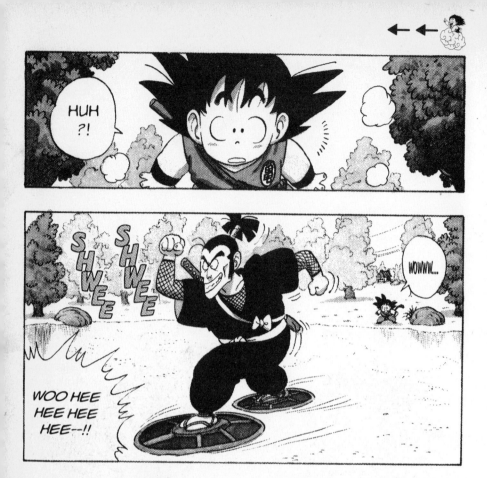

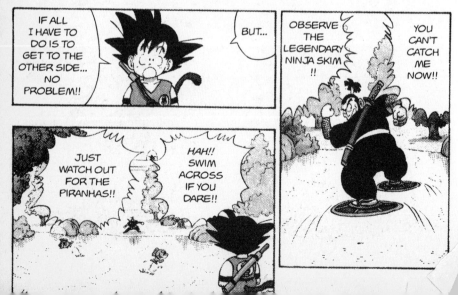

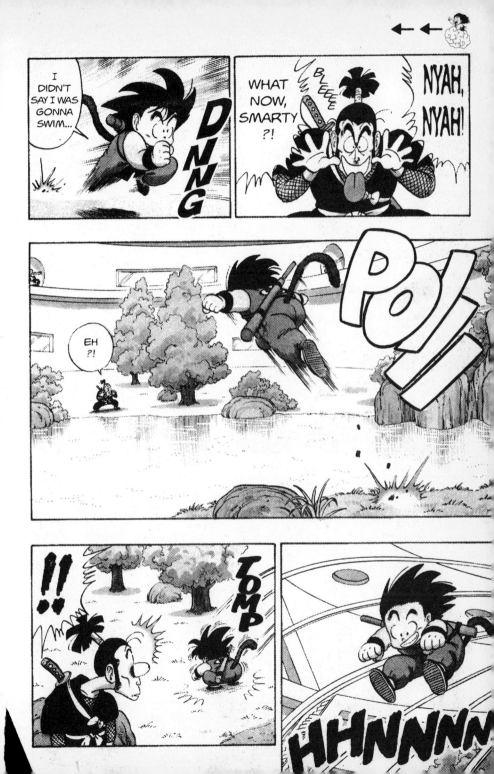

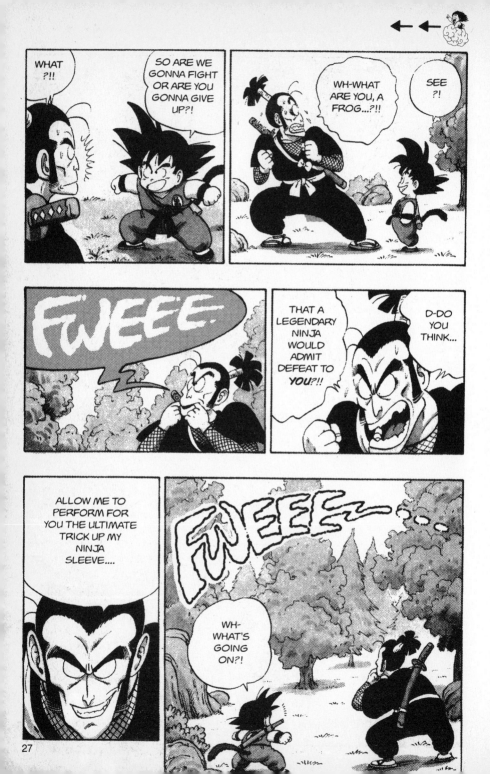

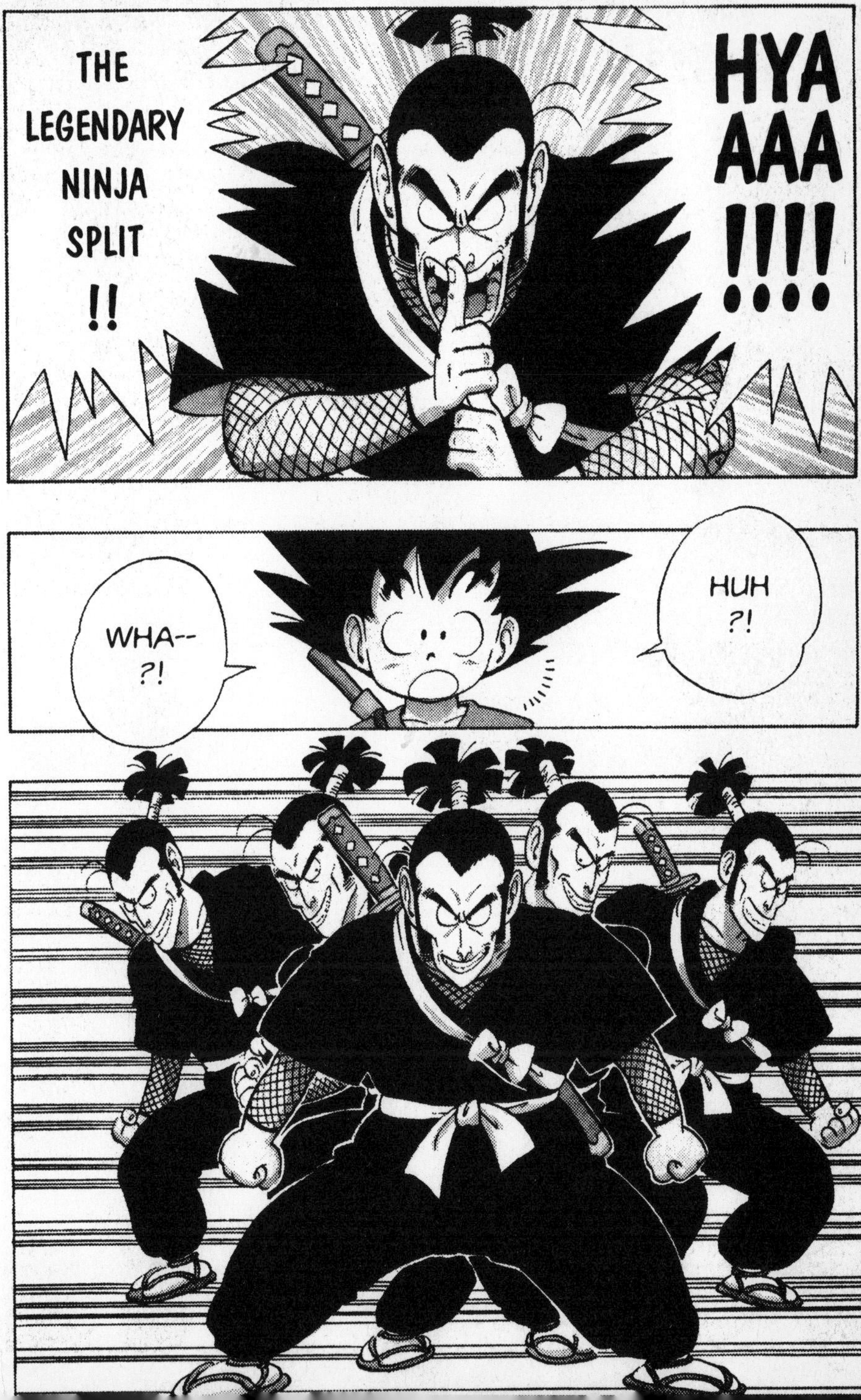
HYAAAA!!!!
THE LEGENDARY NINJA SPLIT!!
HUH?!
WHA--?!

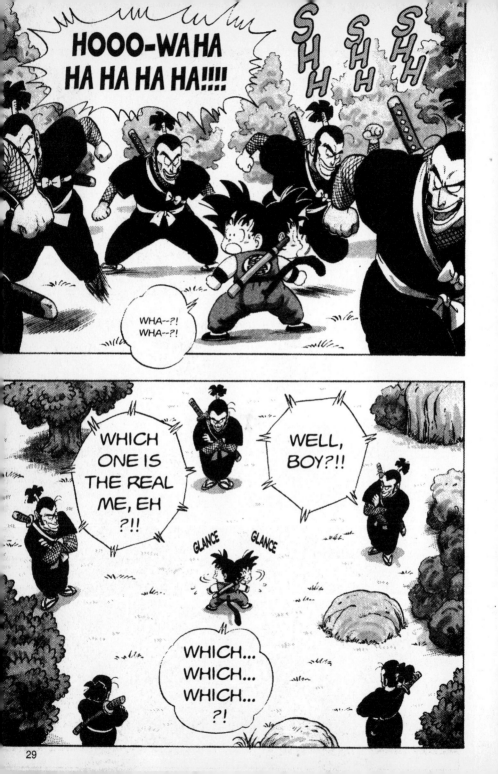

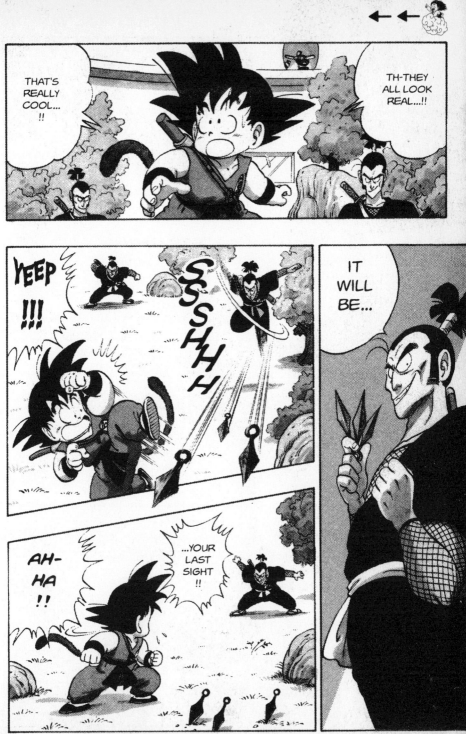

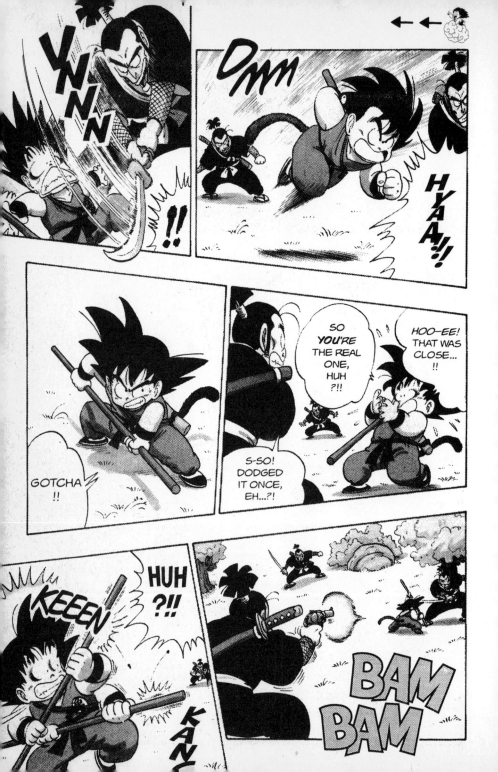

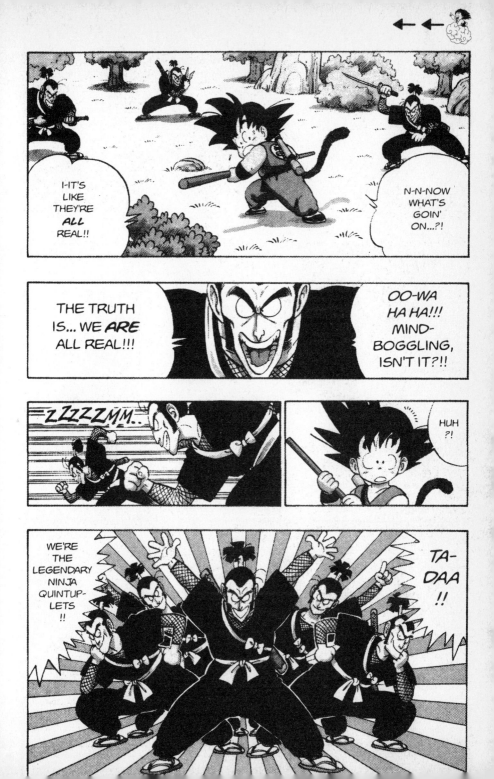

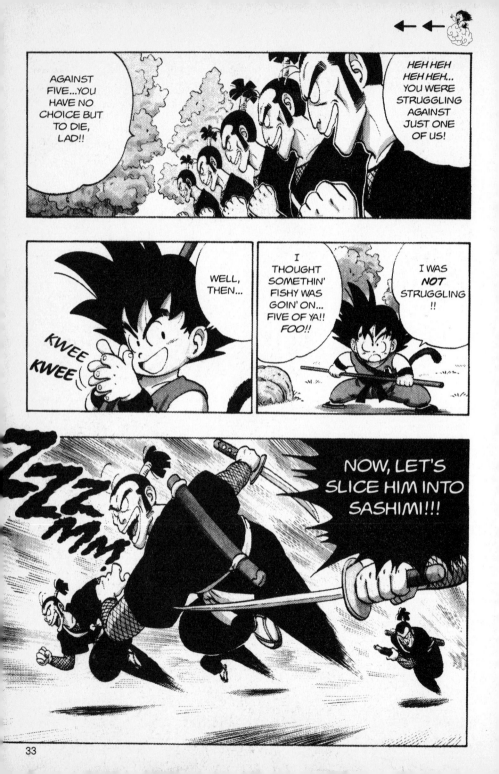

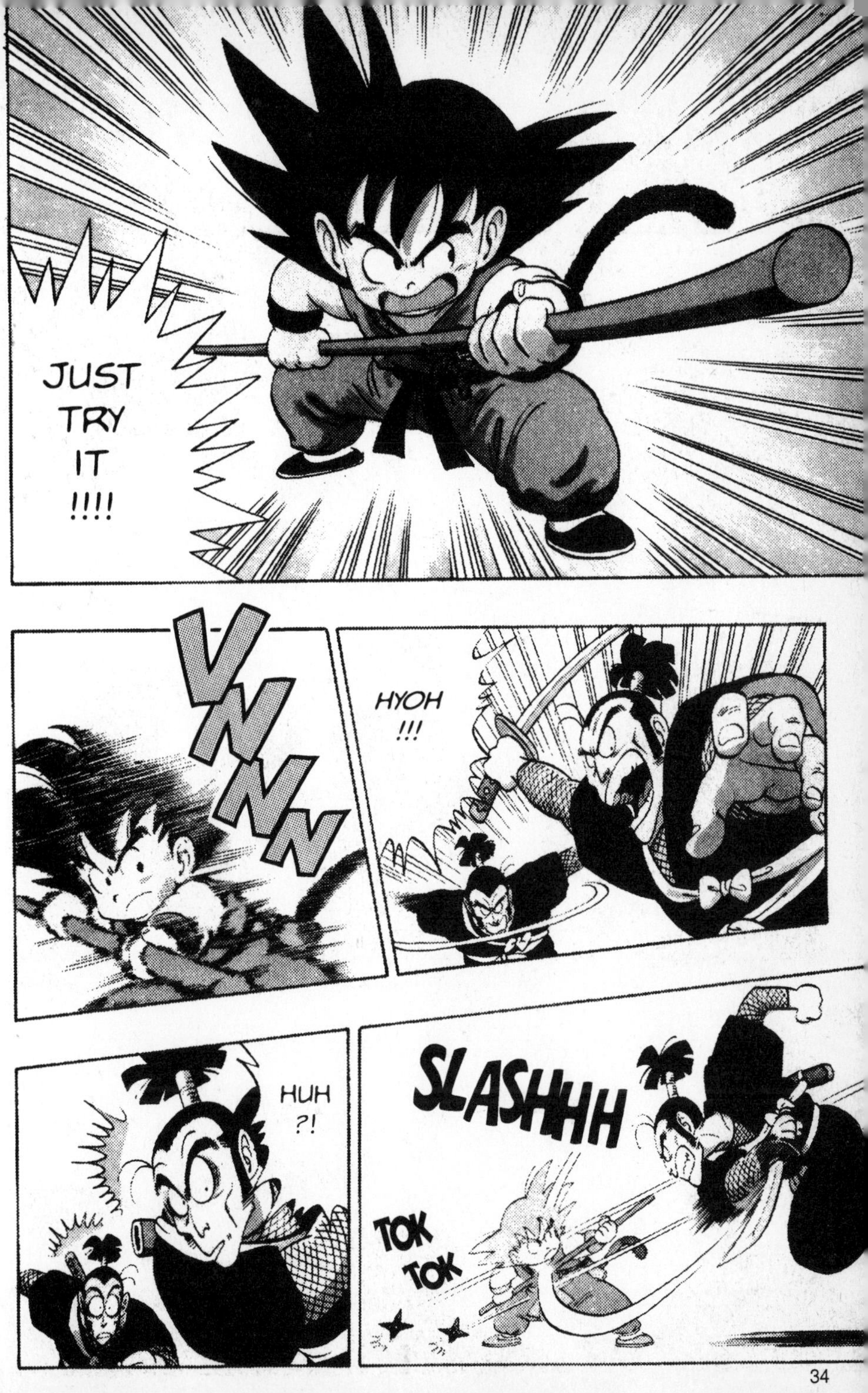
JUST TRY IT !!!!
HYOH !!!
VNNNN
SLASHHH
TOK TOK
HUH ?!

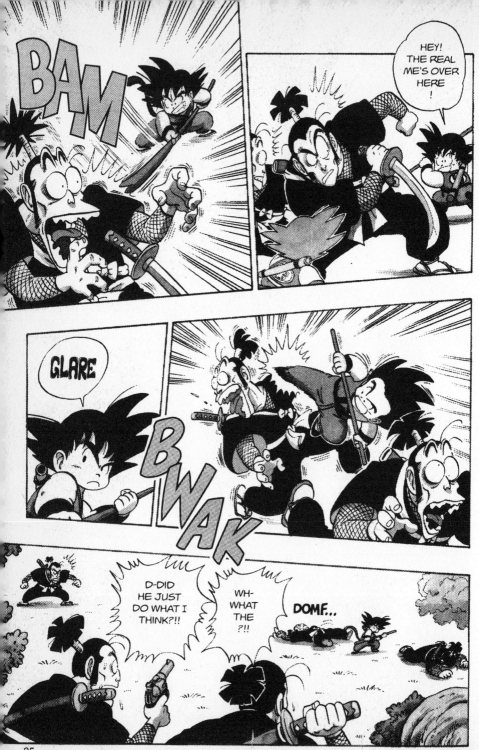

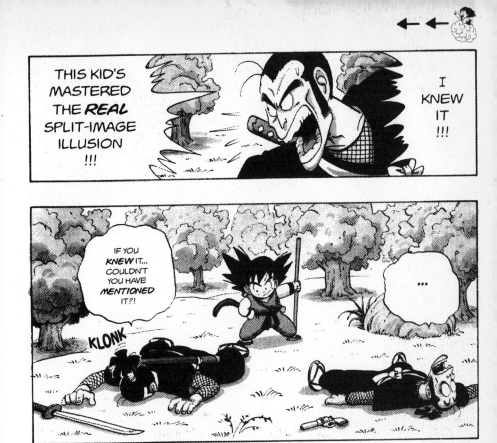

THIS KID'S MASTERED THE **REAL** SPLIT-IMAGE ILLUSION !!!

I KNEW IT !!!

IF YOU *KNEW* IT... COULDN'T YOU HAVE *MENTIONED* IT?!

...

KLONK

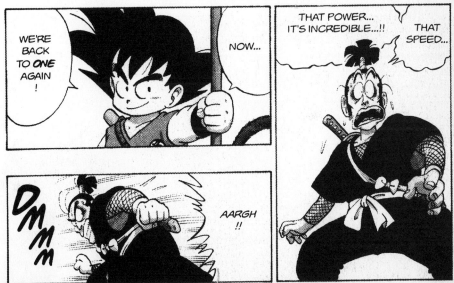

WE'RE BACK TO **ONE** AGAIN !

NOW...

THAT POWER... IT'S INCREDIBLE...!!

THAT SPEED...

DMMMM

AARGH !!

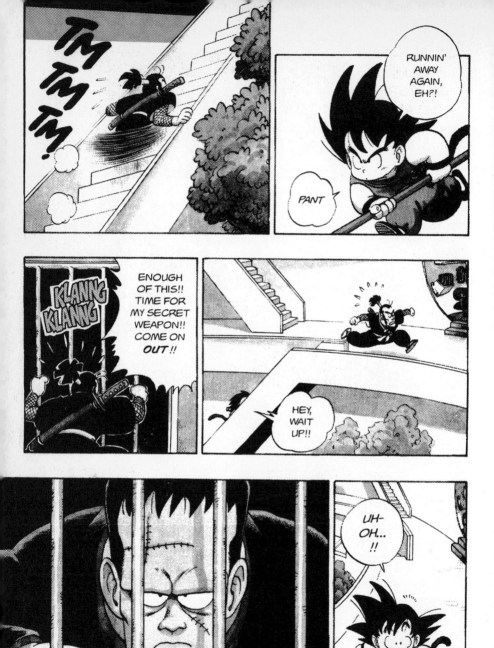

NEXT: Mechanical Man Number 8!

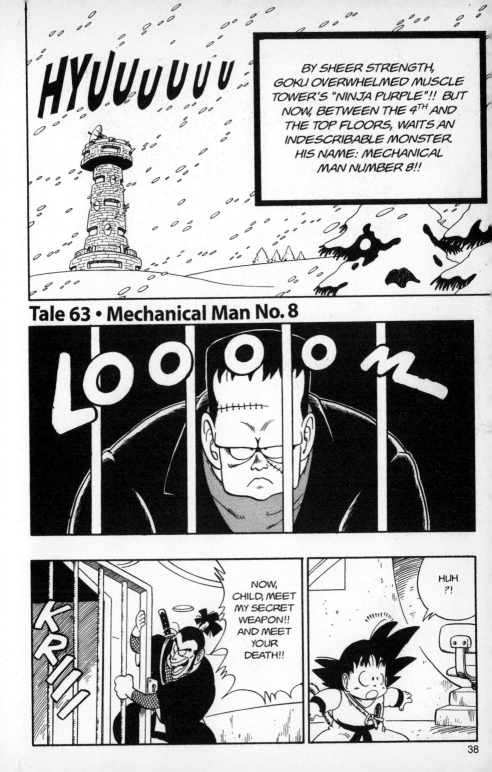

Tale 63 • Mechanical Man No. 8

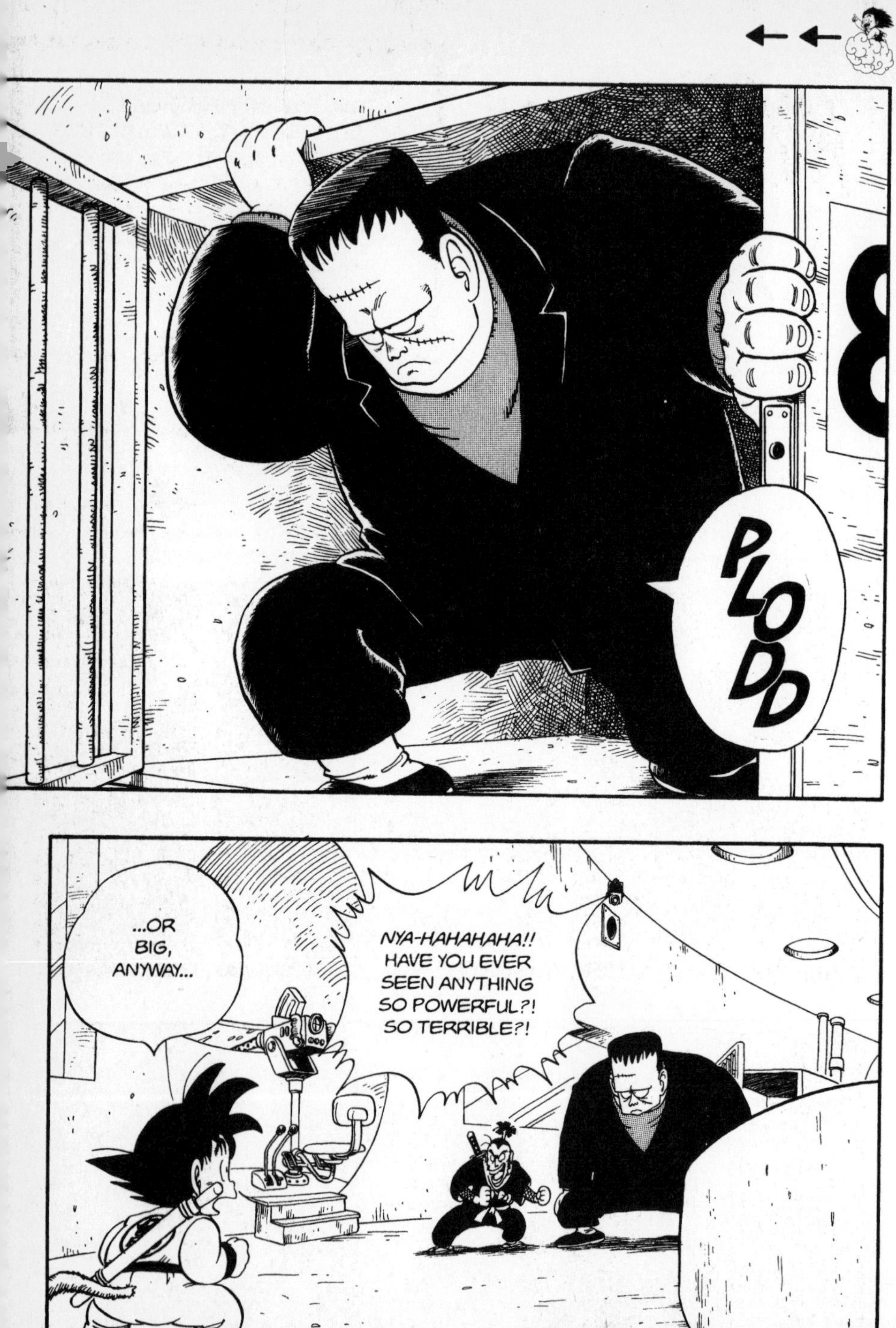
PLODD
NYA-HAHAHAHA!! HAVE YOU EVER SEEN ANYTHING SO POWERFUL?! SO TERRIBLE?!
...OR BIG, ANYWAY...

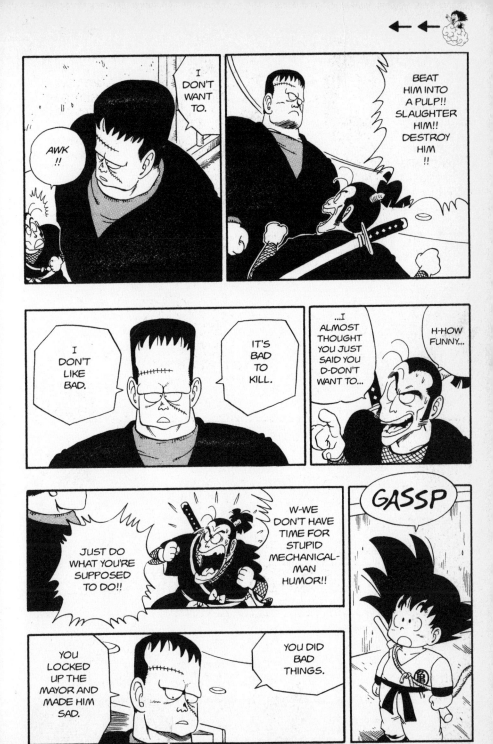

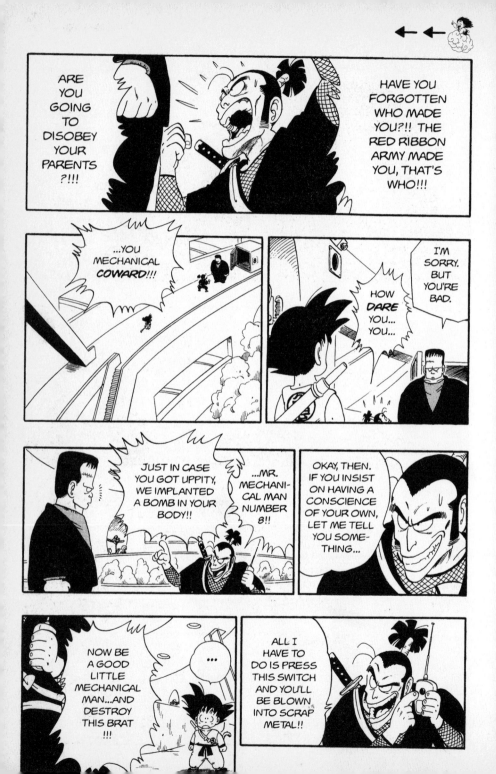

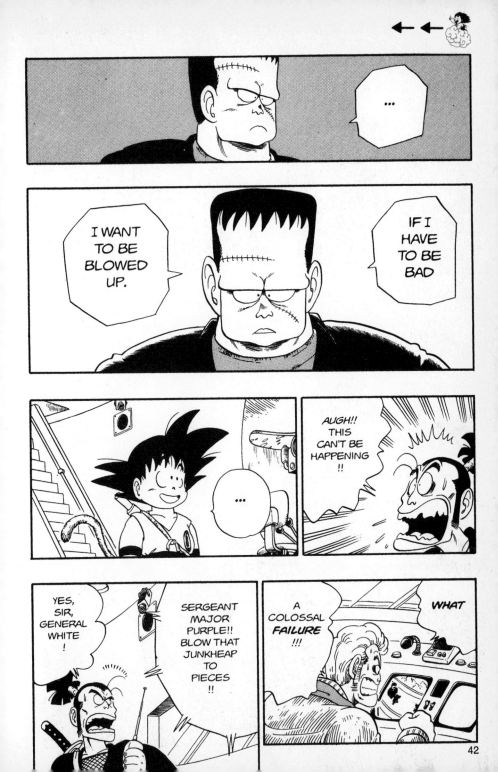

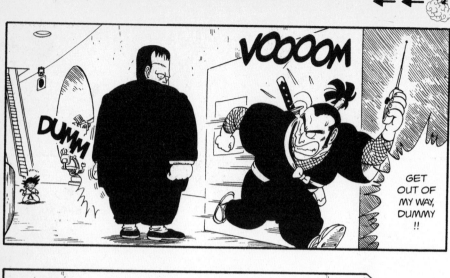

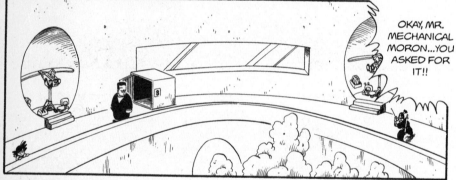

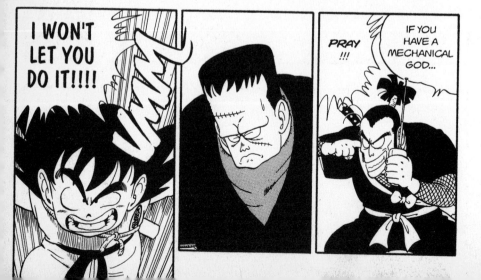

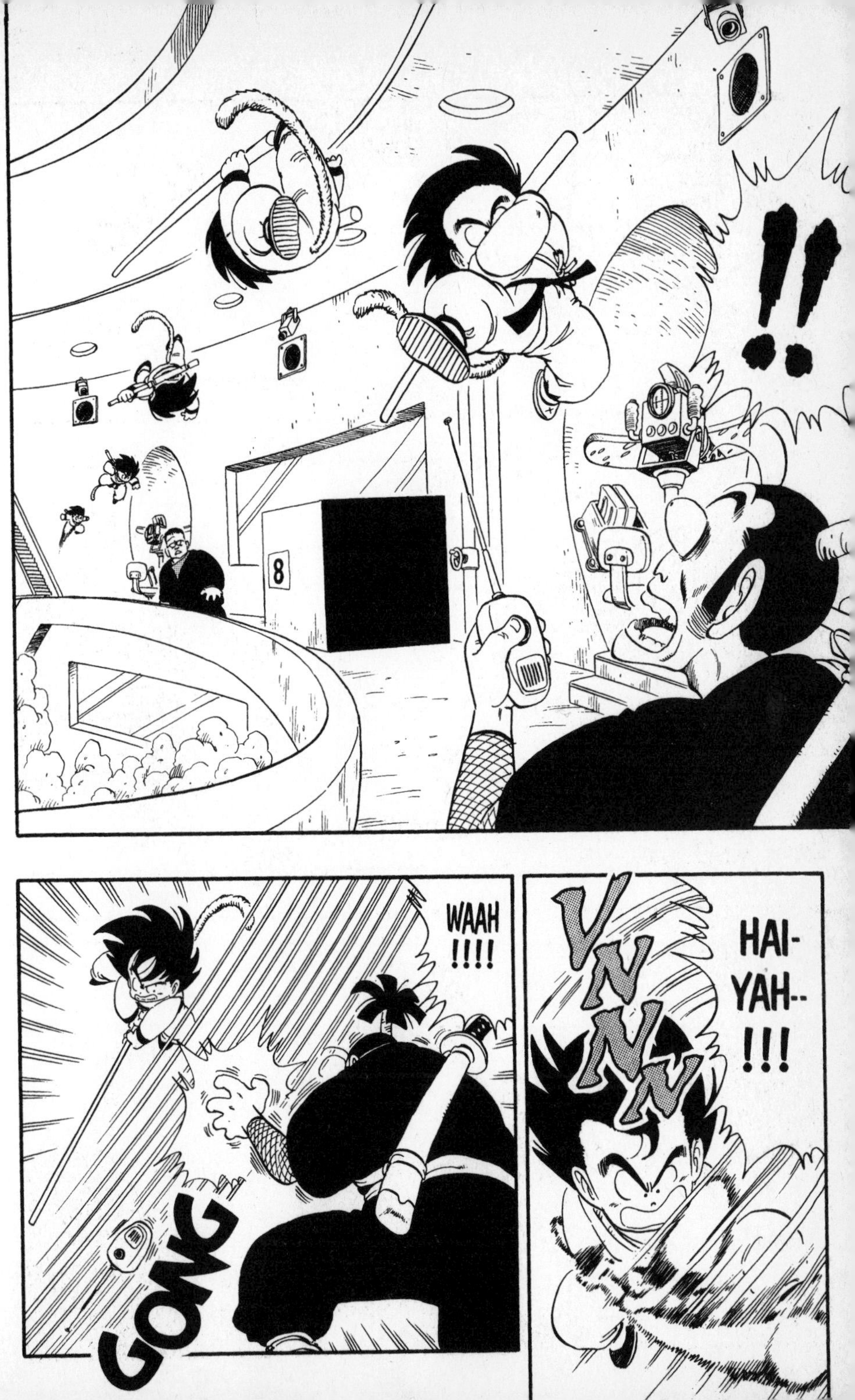
!!
HAI-YAH--!!!
VNNN
WAAH!!!!
GONG

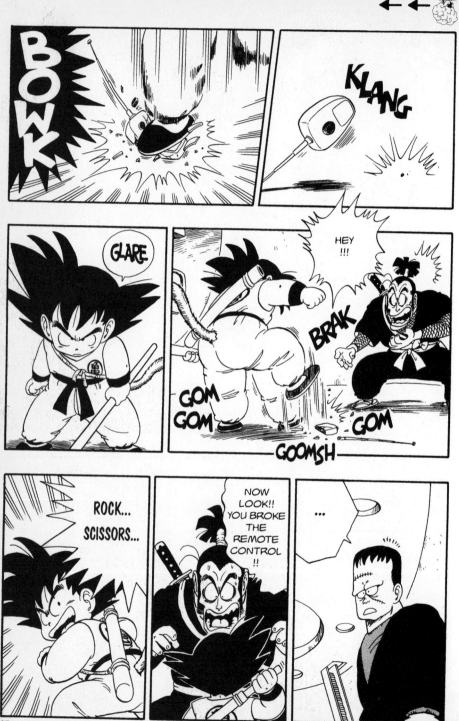

45

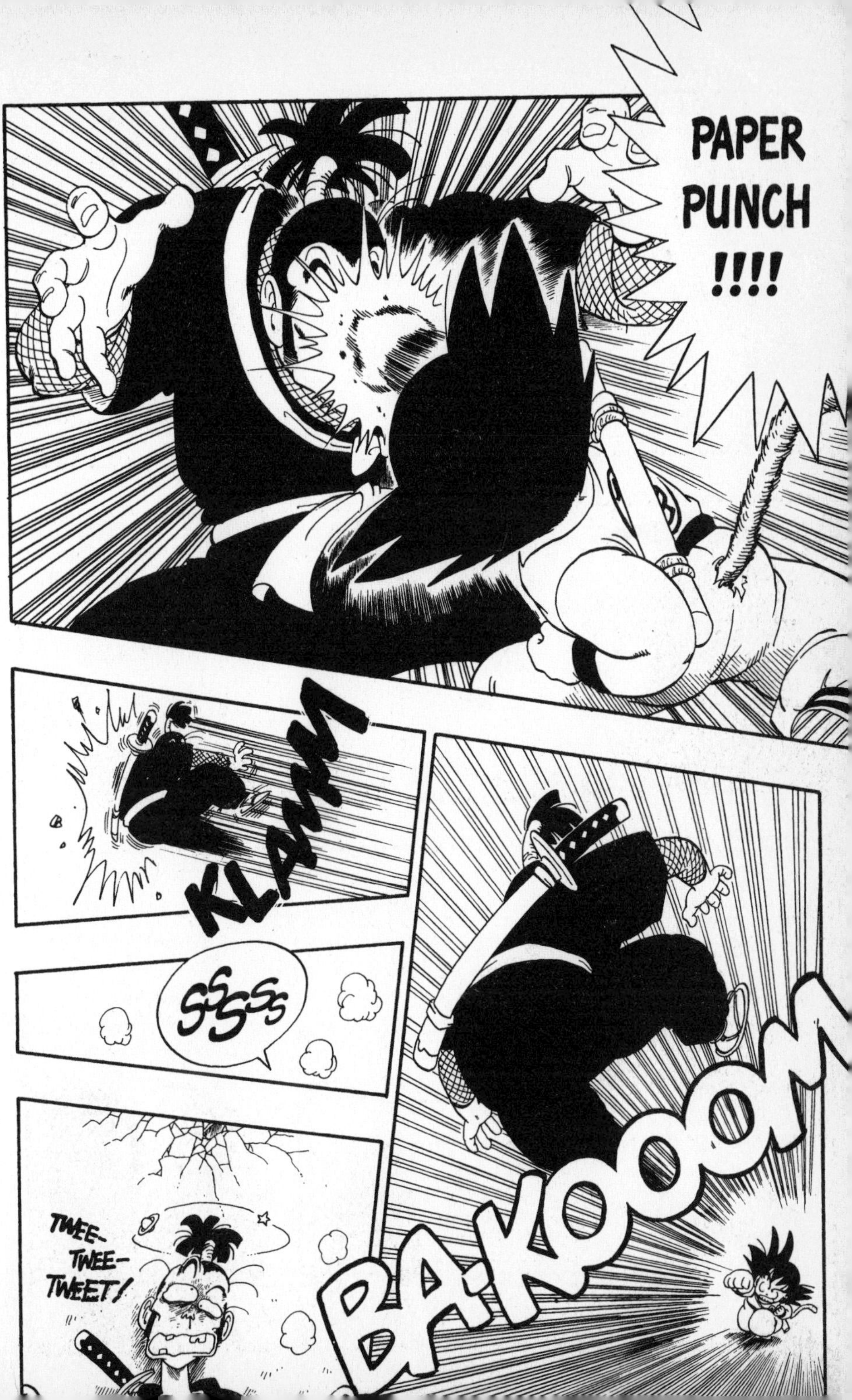
PAPER PUNCH !!!!
BA-KOOOOM
KLAMM
SSSSS
TWEE-TWEE-TWEET!

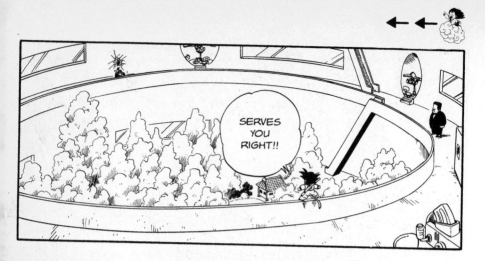

SERVES YOU RIGHT!!

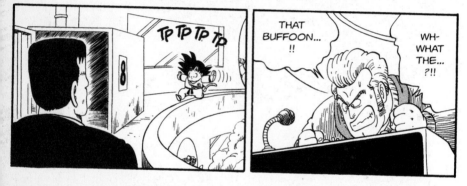

TP TP TP TP

THAT BUFFOON...!!

WH-WHAT THE...?!!

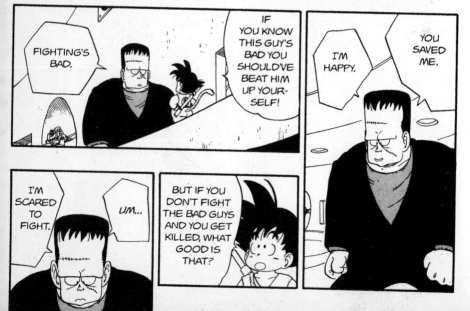

FIGHTING'S BAD.

IF YOU KNOW THIS GUY'S BAD YOU SHOULD'VE BEAT HIM UP YOUR-SELF!

I'M HAPPY.

YOU SAVED ME.

I'M SCARED TO FIGHT.

UM...

BUT IF YOU DON'T FIGHT THE BAD GUYS AND YOU GET KILLED, WHAT GOOD IS THAT?

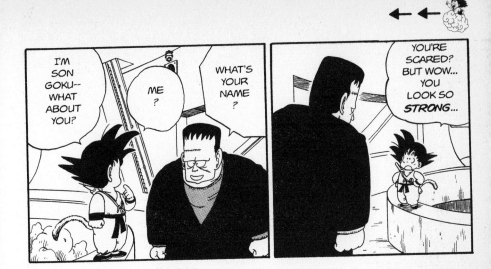

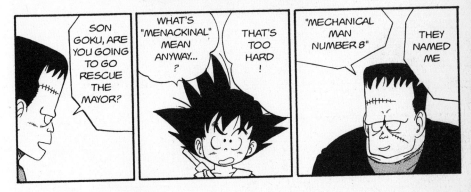

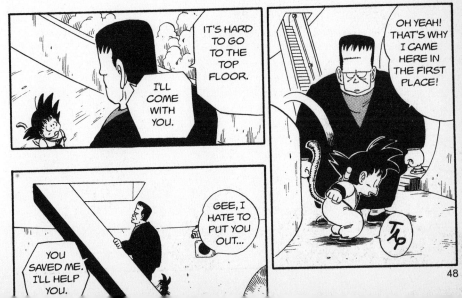

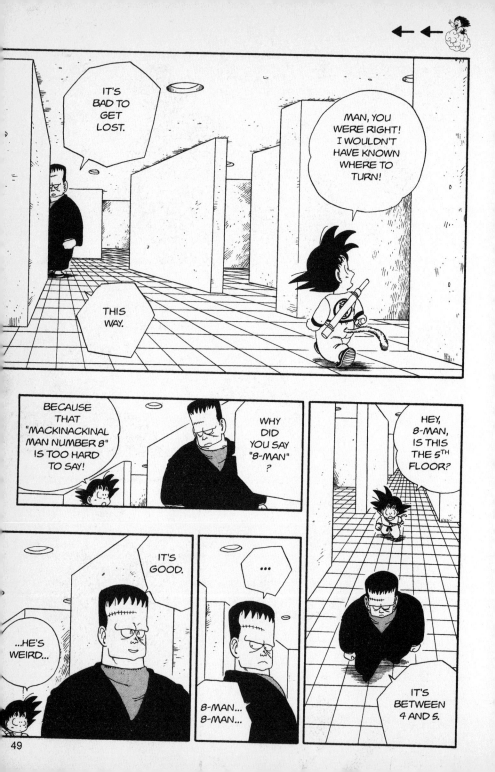

49

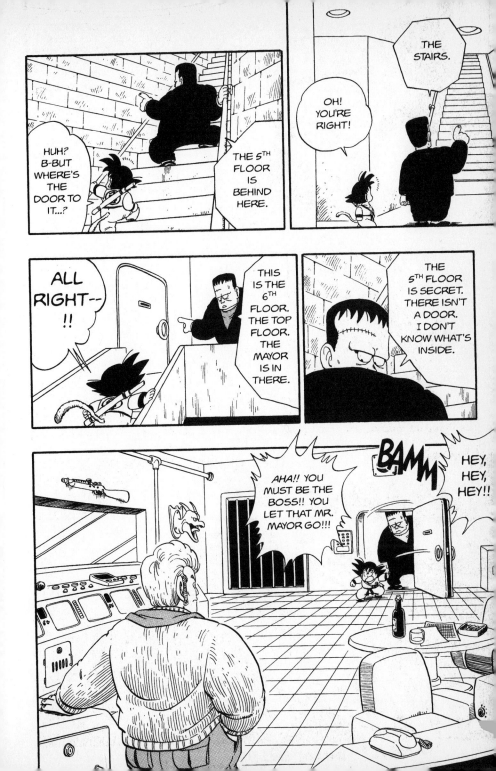

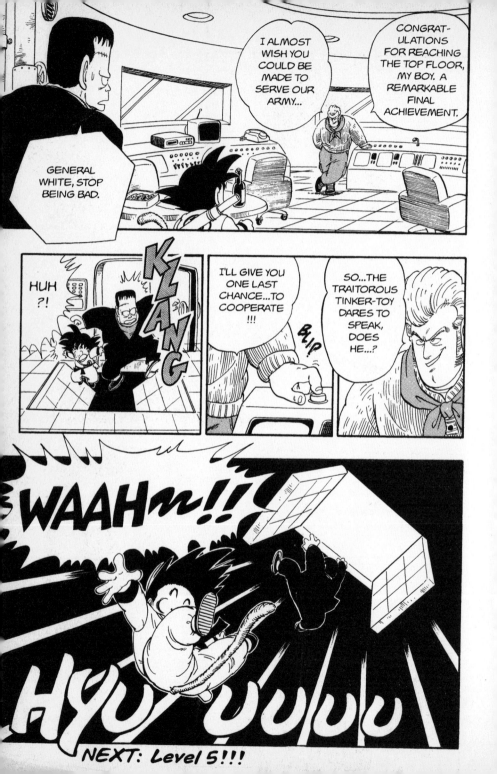

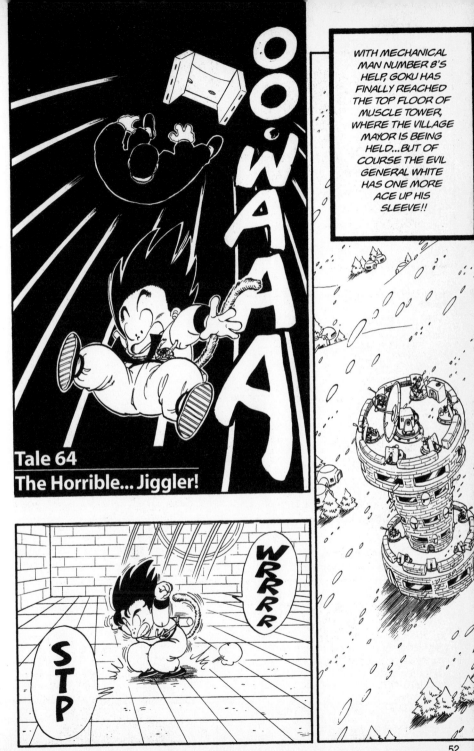

Tale 64
The Horrible... Jiggler!

WITH MECHANICAL MAN NUMBER 8'S HELP, GOKU HAS FINALLY REACHED THE TOP FLOOR OF MUSCLE TOWER, WHERE THE VILLAGE MAYOR IS BEING HELD...BUT OF COURSE THE EVIL GENERAL WHITE HAS ONE MORE ACE UP HIS SLEEVE!!

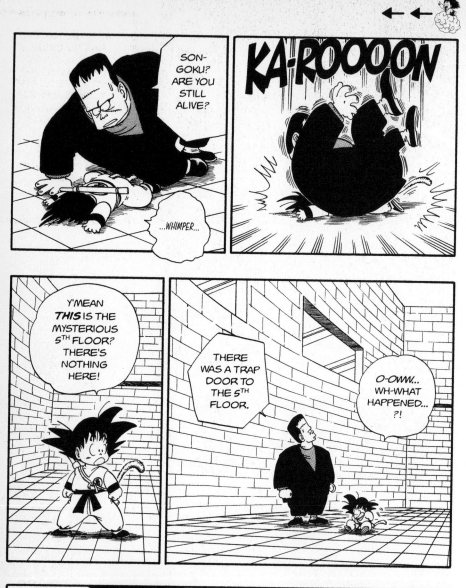

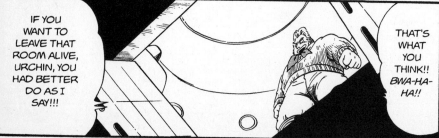

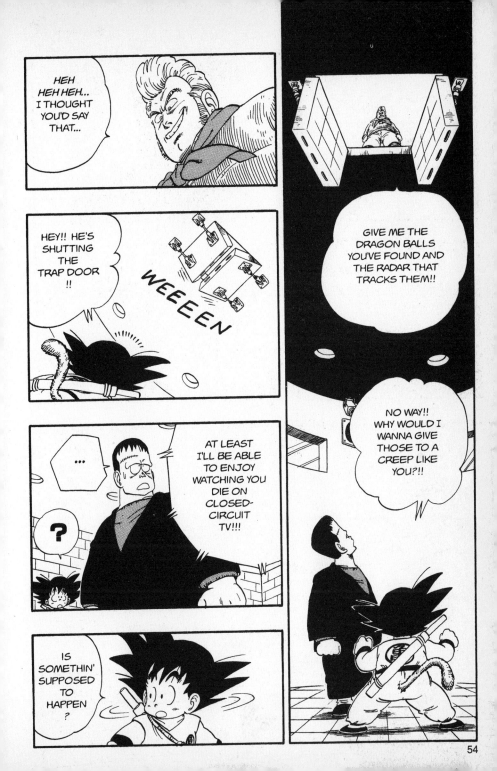

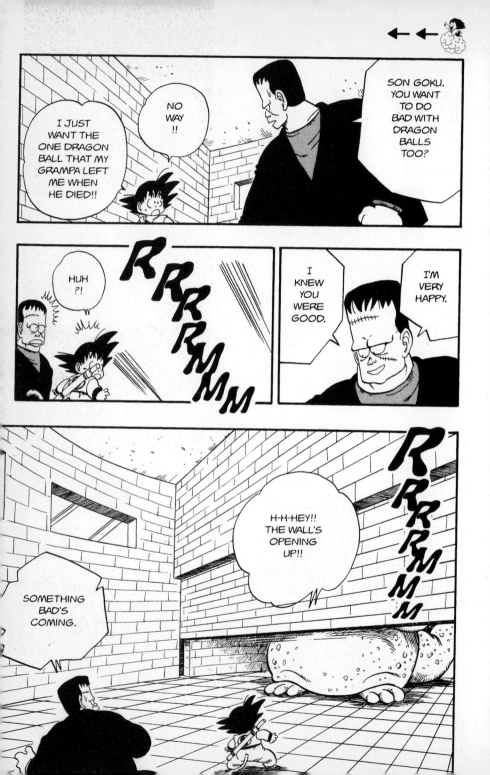

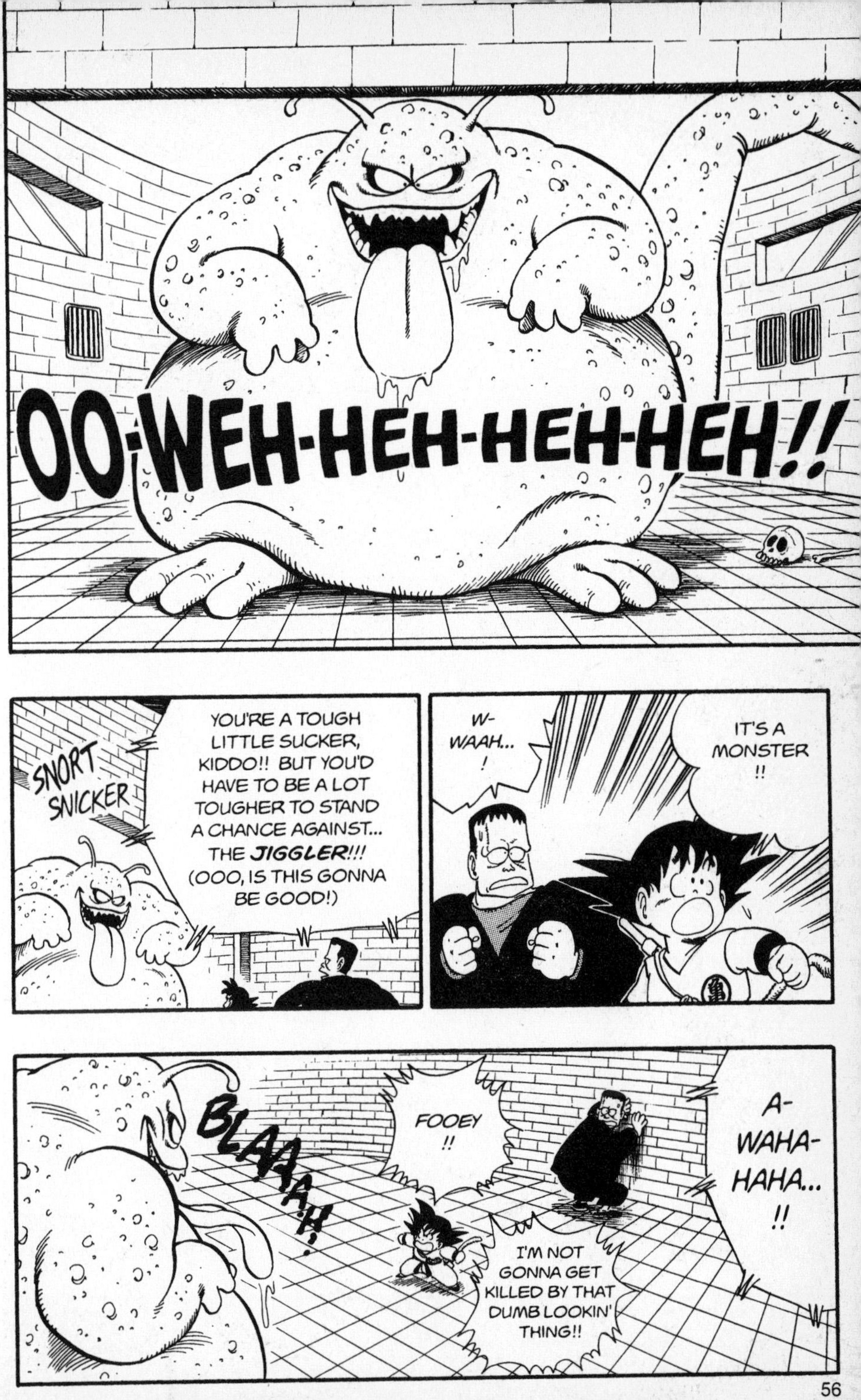
OO-WEH-HEH-HEH-HEH!!
IT'S A MONSTER !!
W-WAAH... !
YOU'RE A TOUGH LITTLE SUCKER, KIDDO!! BUT YOU'D HAVE TO BE A LOT TOUGHER TO STAND A CHANCE AGAINST... THE JIGGLER!!! (OOO, IS THIS GONNA BE GOOD!)
SNORT SNICKER
A-WAHA-HAHA... !!
FOOEY !!
BLAAAAH!
I'M NOT GONNA GET KILLED BY THAT DUMB LOOKIN' THING!!

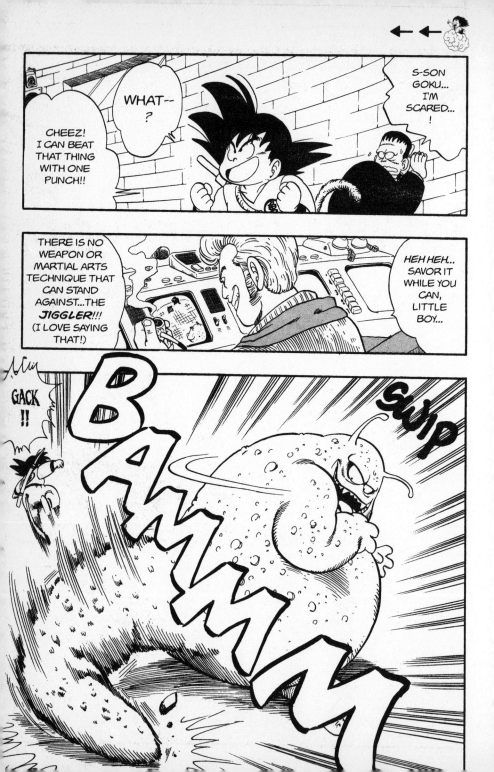

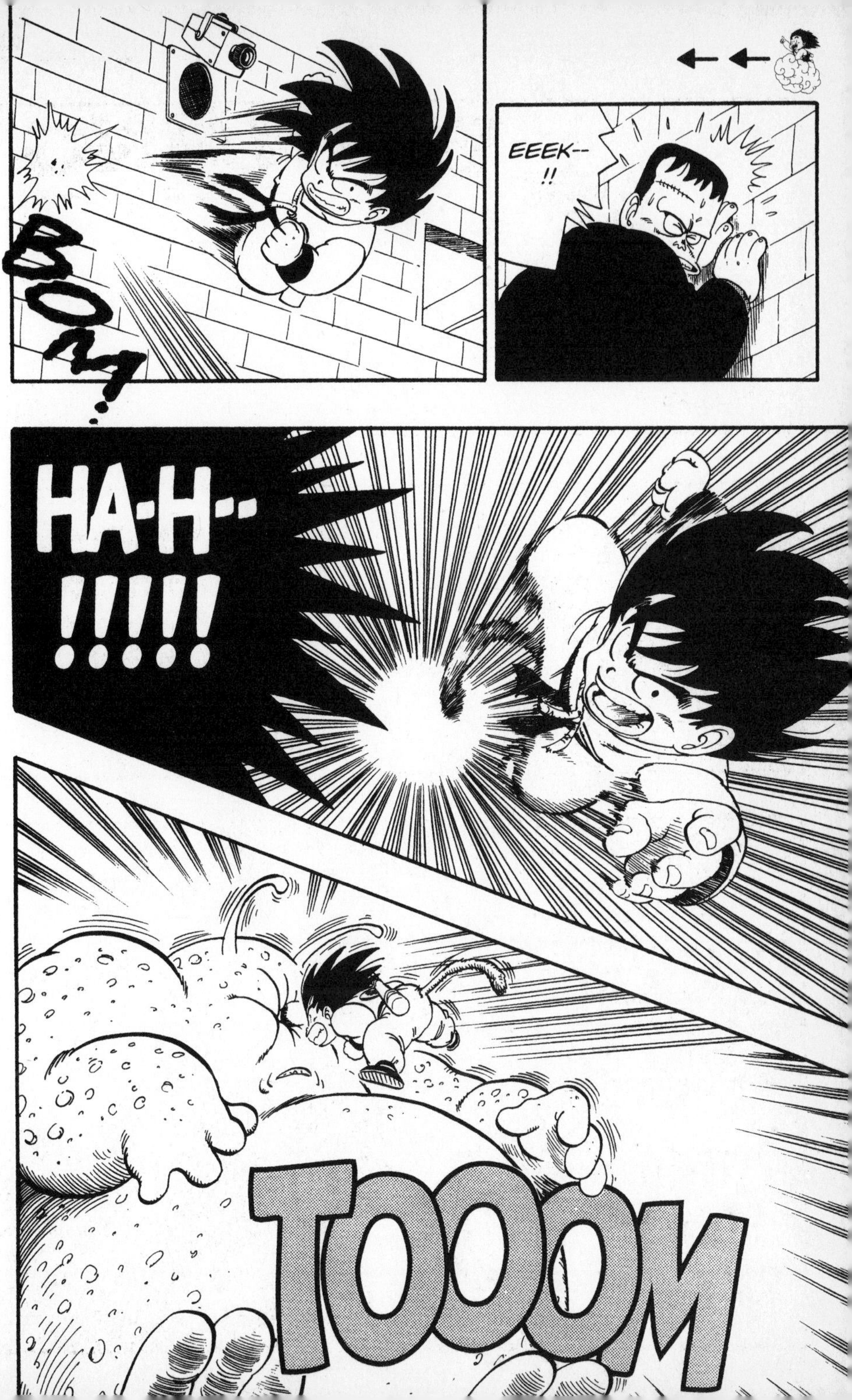
EEEK--!!
BOM
HA-H--!!!!!!
TOOOM

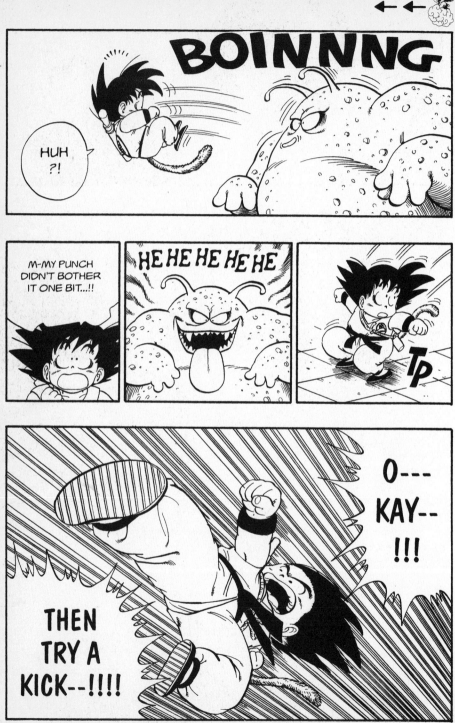

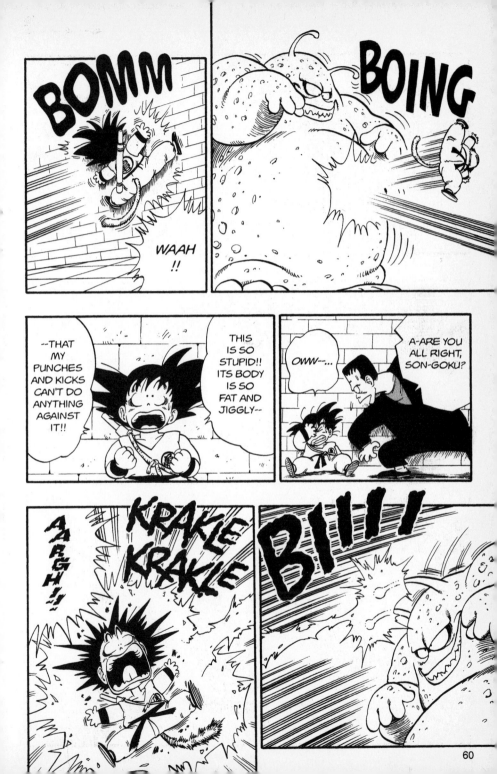

60

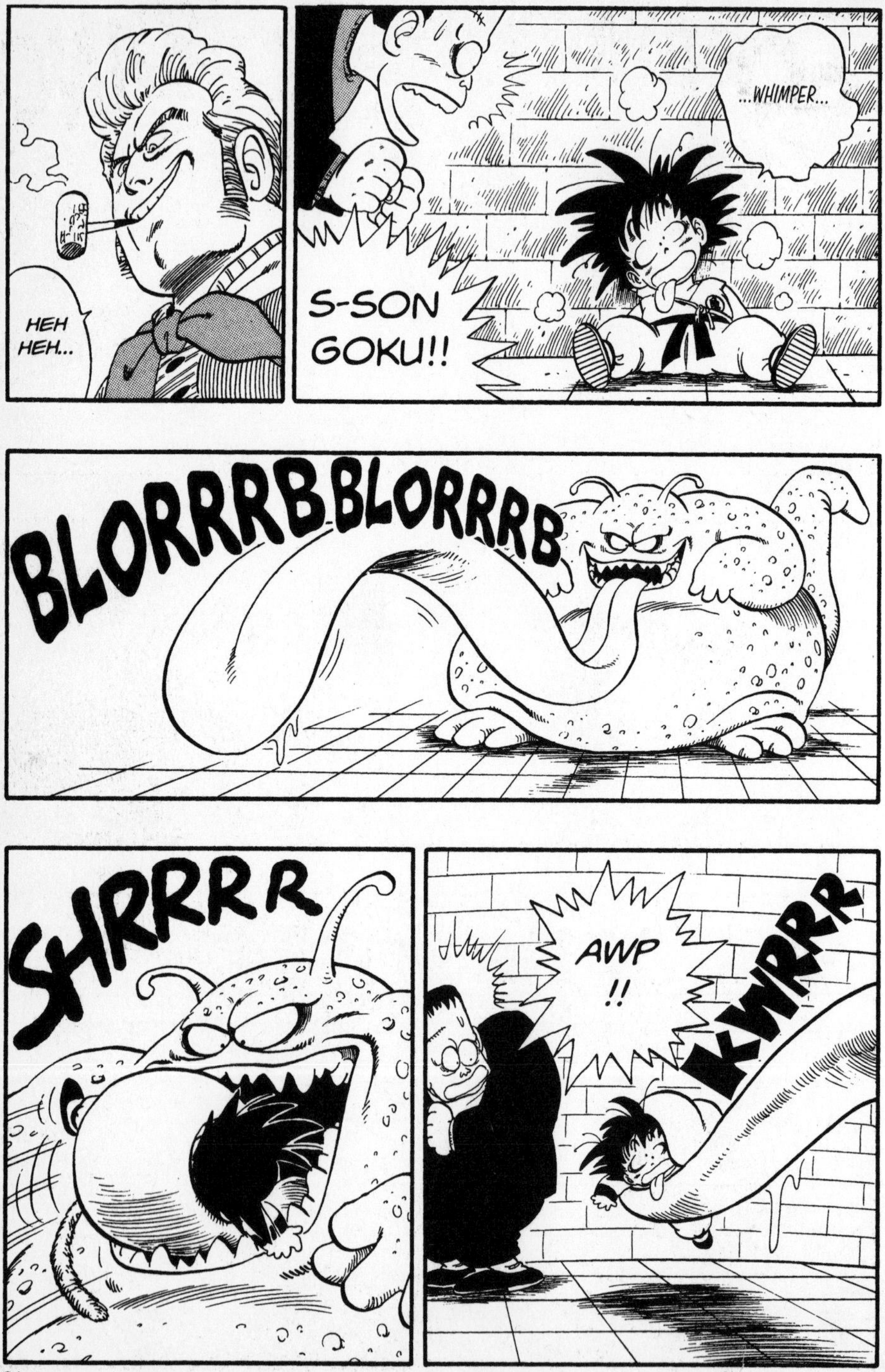
...WHIMPER...
S-SON GOKU!!
HEH HEH...
BLORRRB BLORRRB
AWP !!
KWRRR
SHRRRR

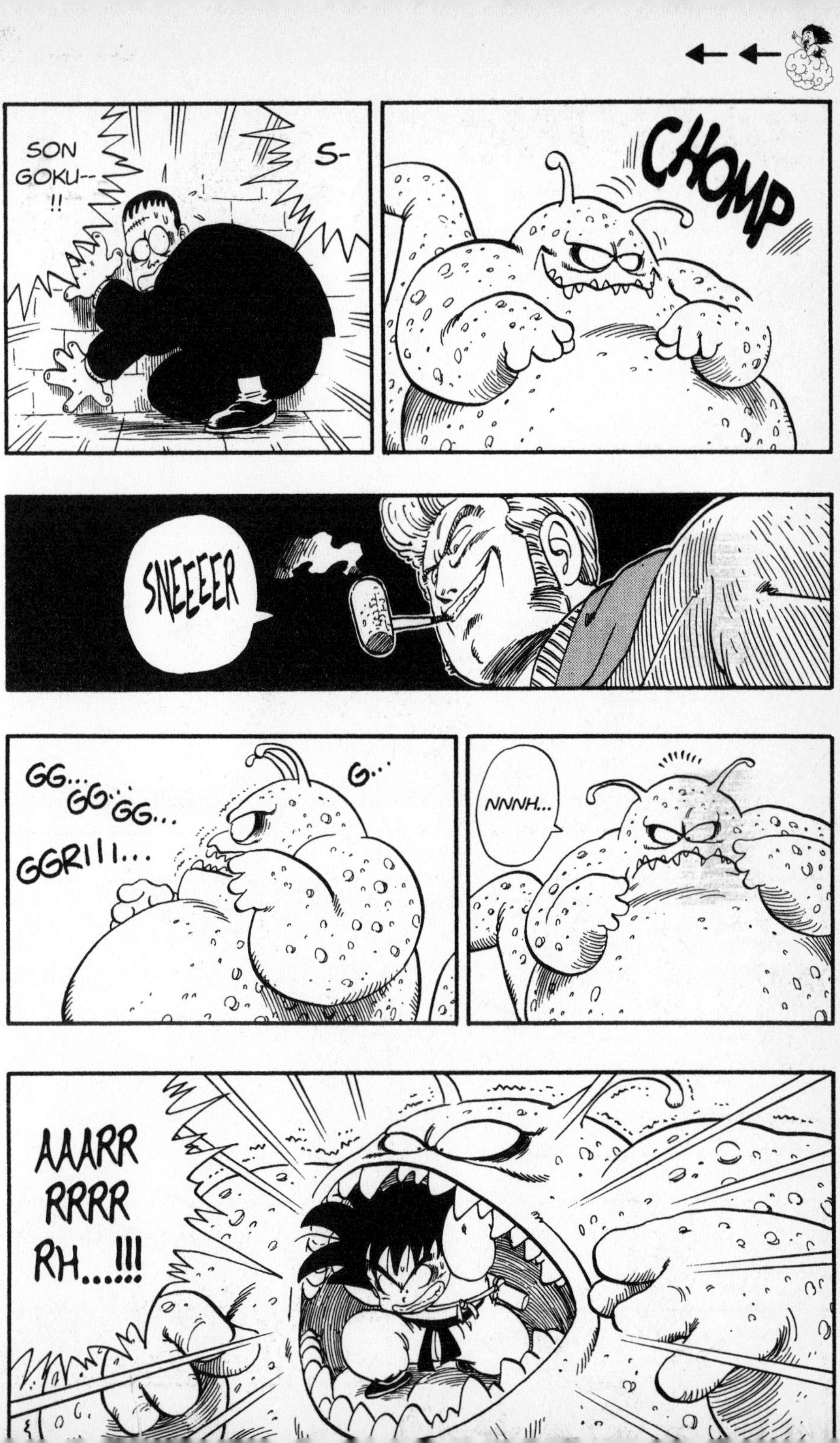
CHOMP
S-
SON GOKU--!!
SNEEEER
NNNH...
G...
GG... GG... GG...
GGRIII...
AAARR RRRR RH...!!!

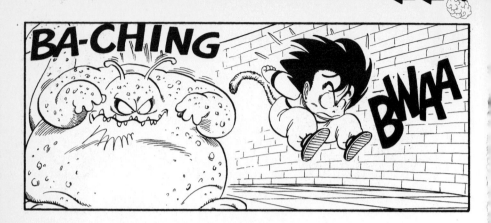

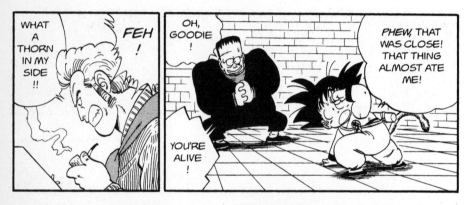

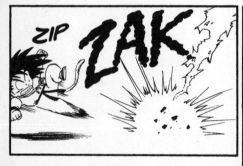

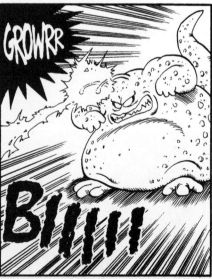

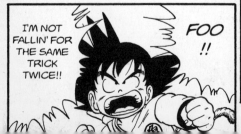

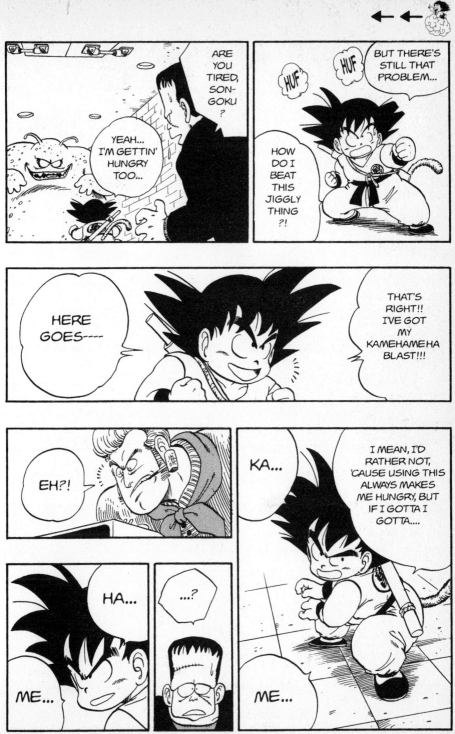

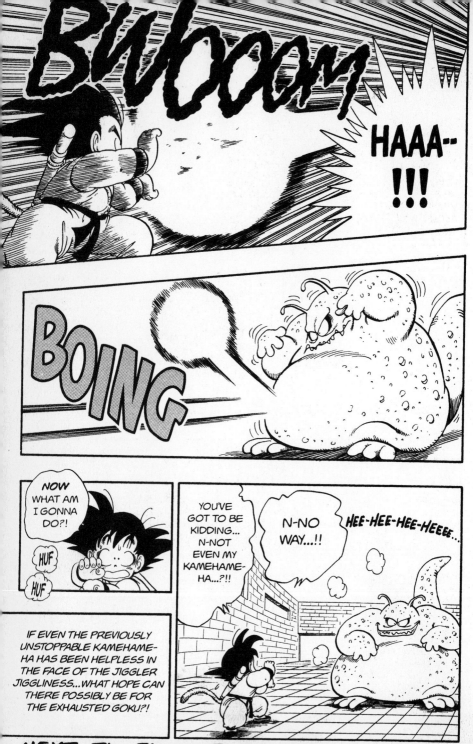

NEXT: *The Jiggler Jiggles On!*

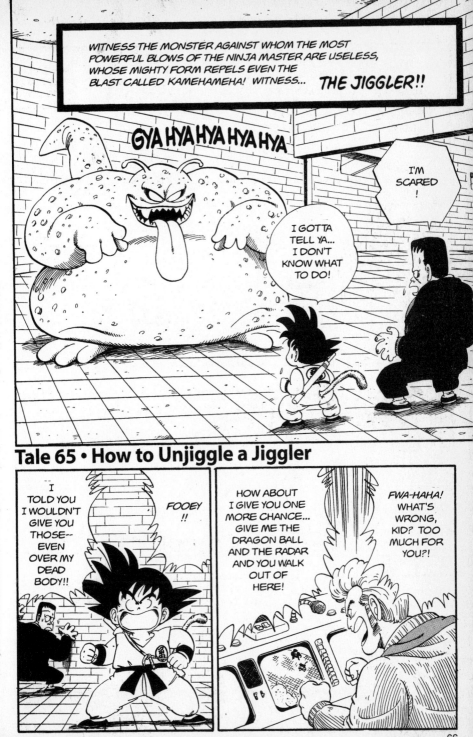

Tale 65 • How to Unjiggle a Jiggler

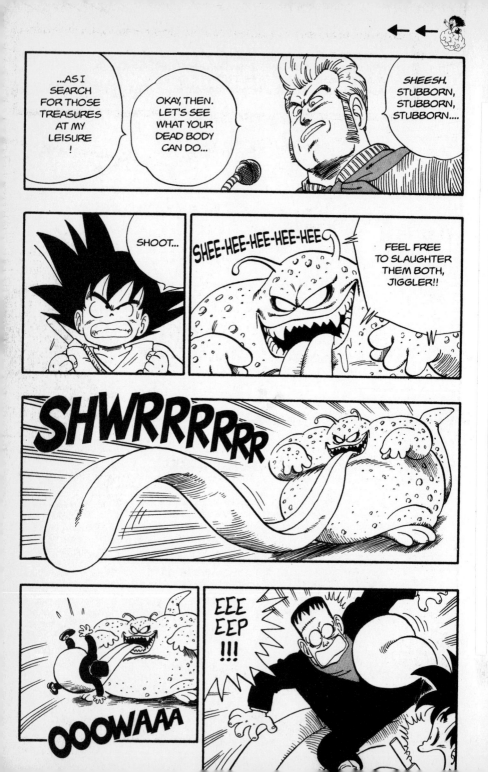

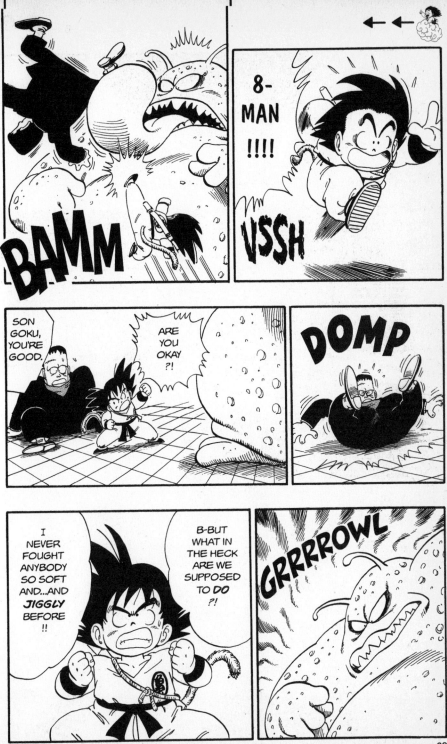

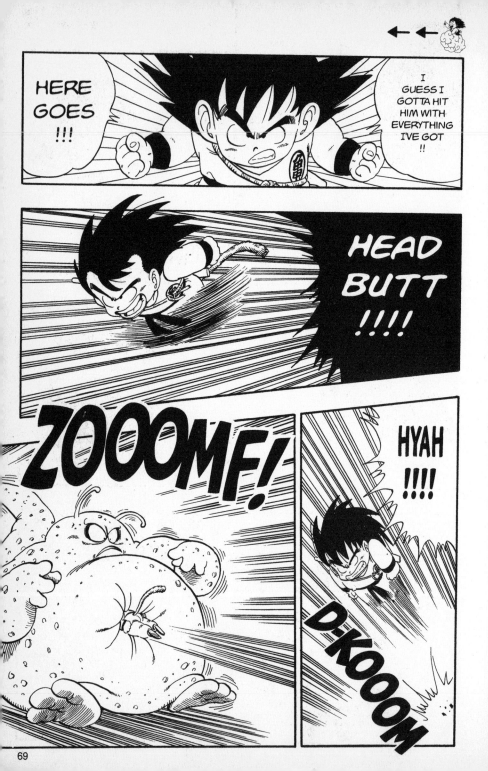

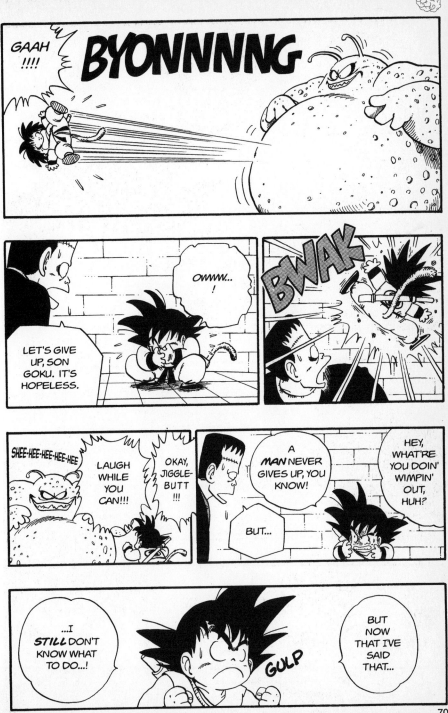

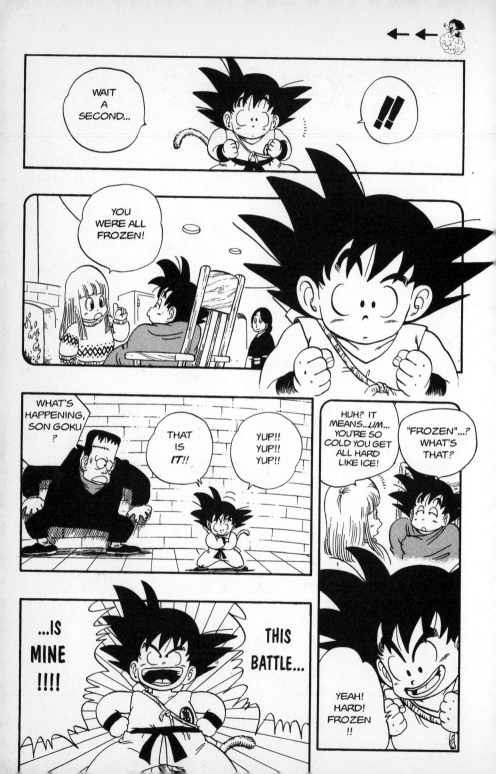

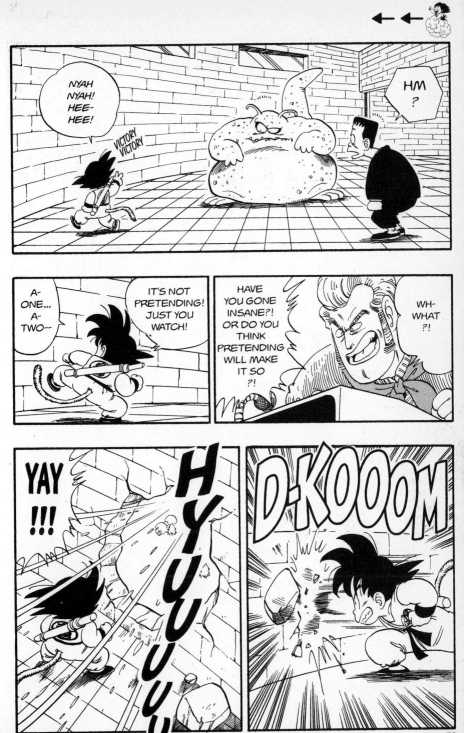

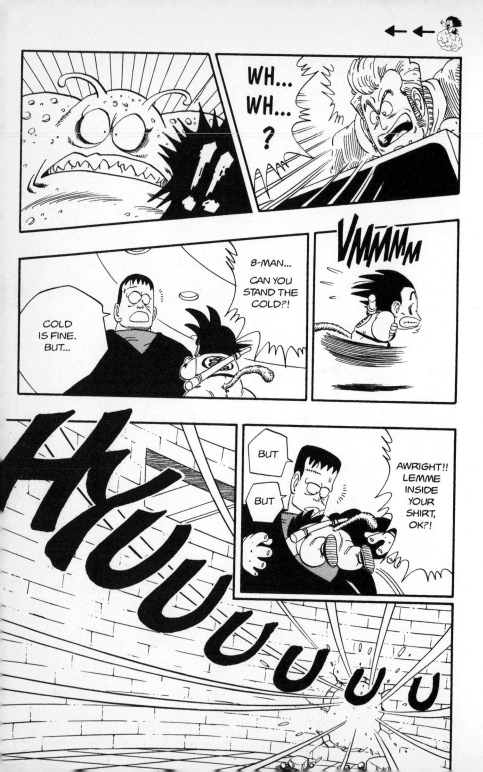

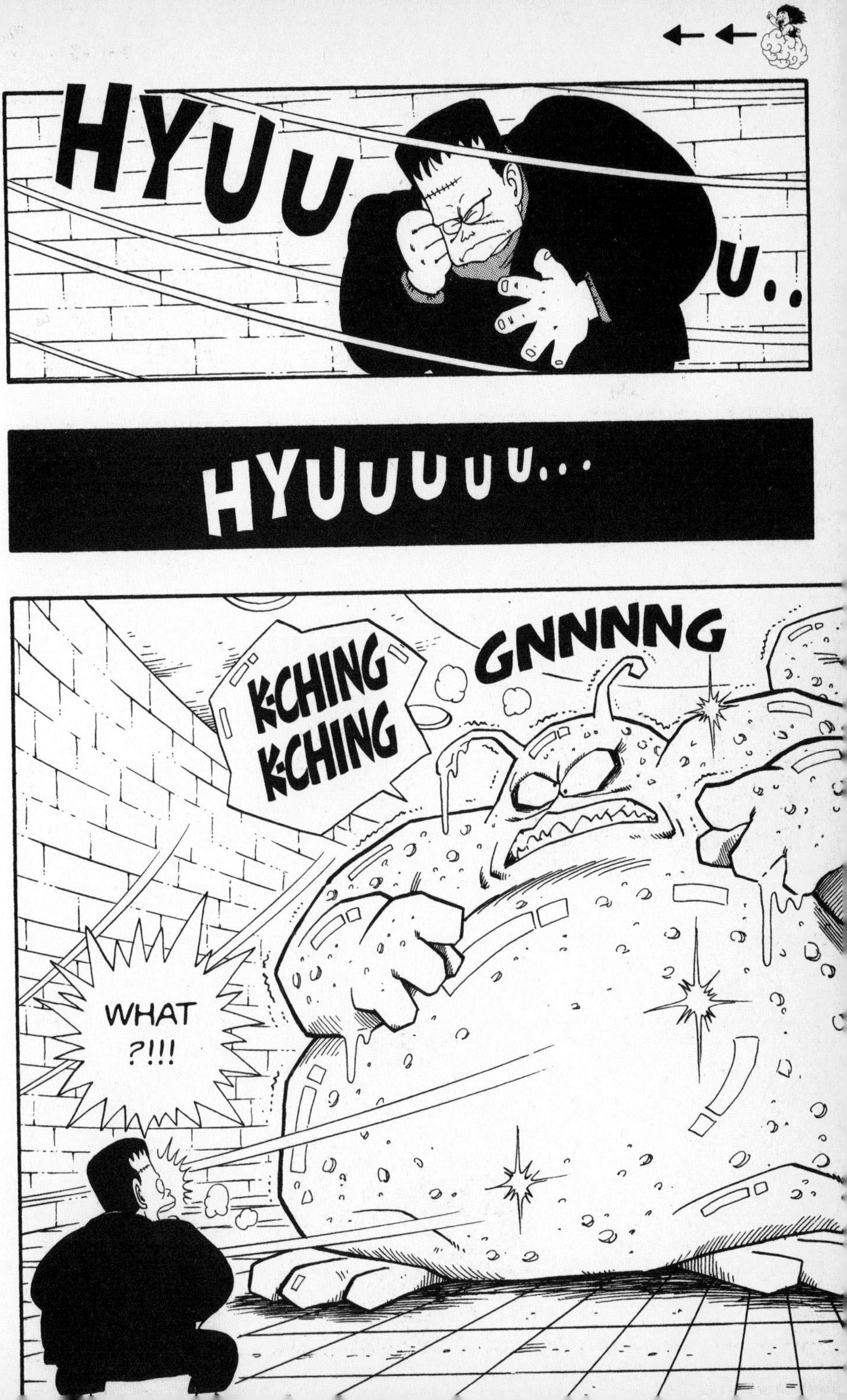
HYUU
U..
HYUUUUU...
GNNNNG
K-CHING
K-CHING
WHAT ?!!!

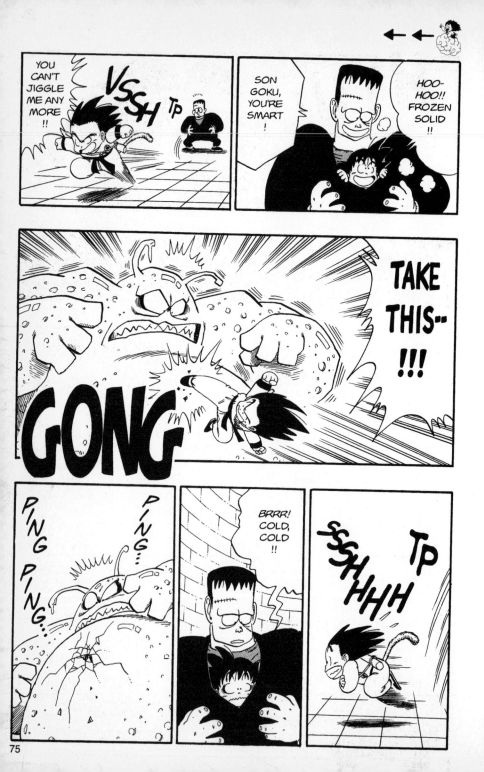

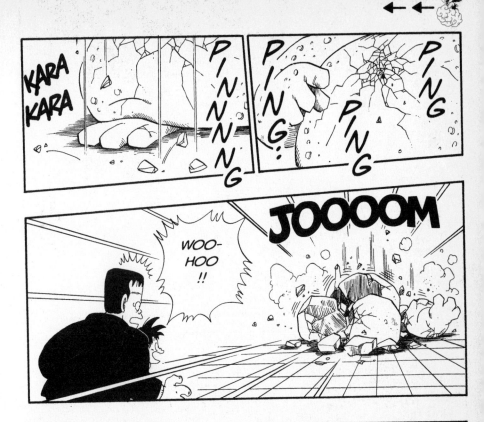

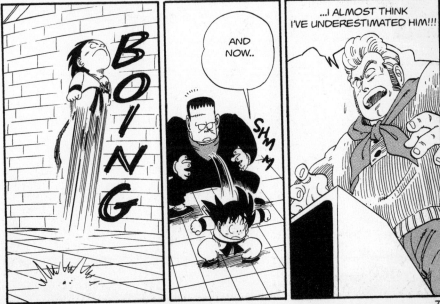

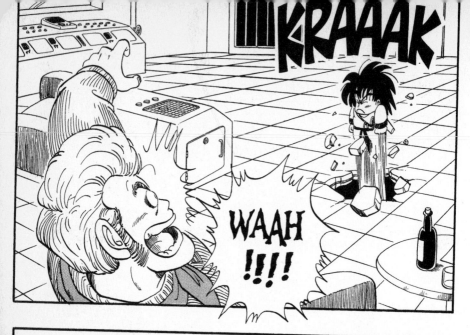

KRAAAK

WAAH!!!!

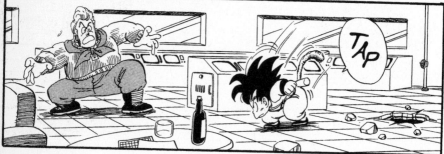

TAP

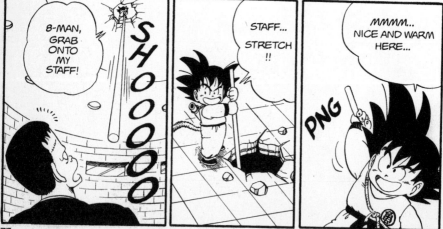

8-MAN, GRAB ONTO MY STAFF!

SHOOOOOO

STAFF... STRETCH!!

MMMM... NICE AND WARM HERE...

PNG

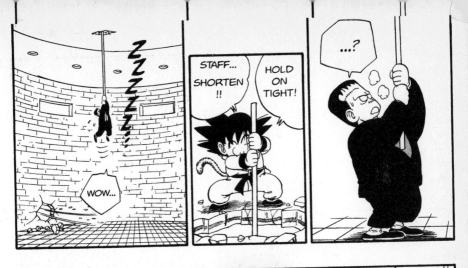

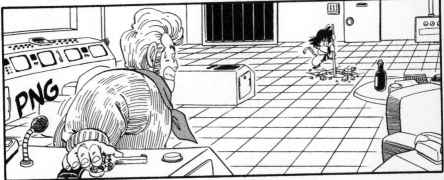

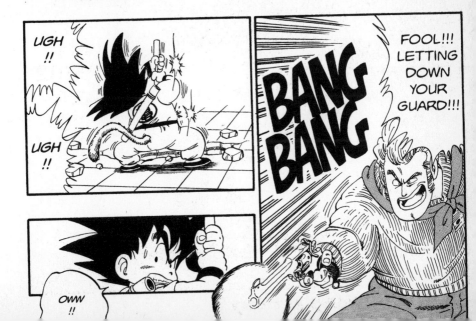

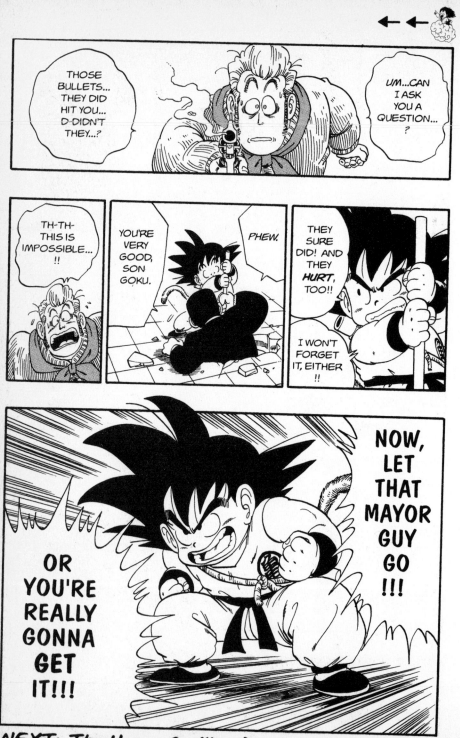

NEXT: The Heavy Artillery!

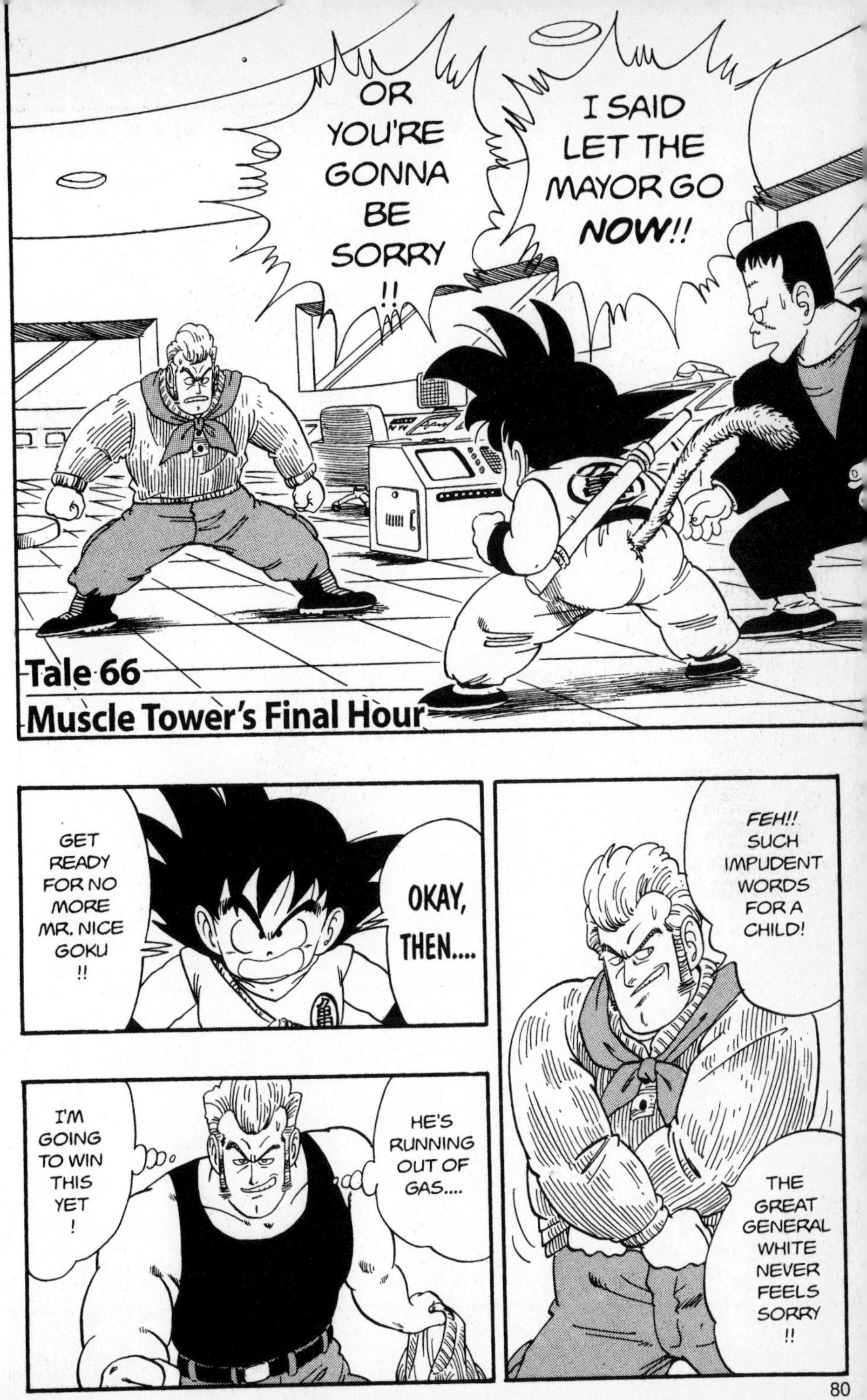
I SAID LET THE MAYOR GO NOW!!
OR YOU'RE GONNA BE SORRY!!
Tale 66
Muscle Tower's Final Hour
FEH!! SUCH IMPUDENT WORDS FOR A CHILD!
THE GREAT GENERAL WHITE NEVER FEELS SORRY!!
OKAY, THEN....
GET READY FOR NO MORE MR. NICE GOKU!!
HE'S RUNNING OUT OF GAS....
I'M GOING TO WIN THIS YET!

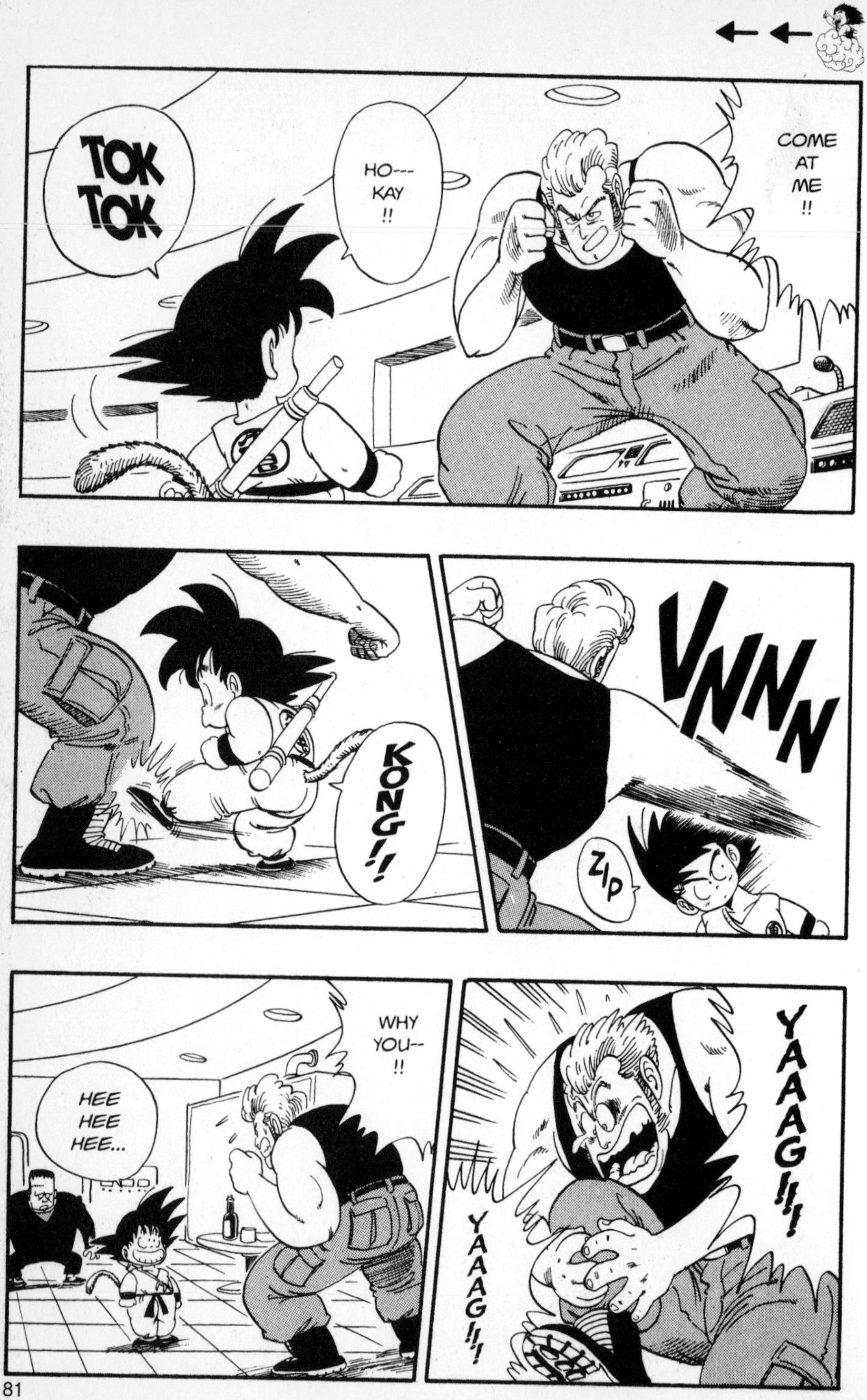
COME AT ME !!
HO--- KAY !!
TOK TOK
VNNNN
ZIP
KONG!!
YAAAAG!!!
YAAAG!!!
WHY YOU-- !!
HEE HEE HEE...

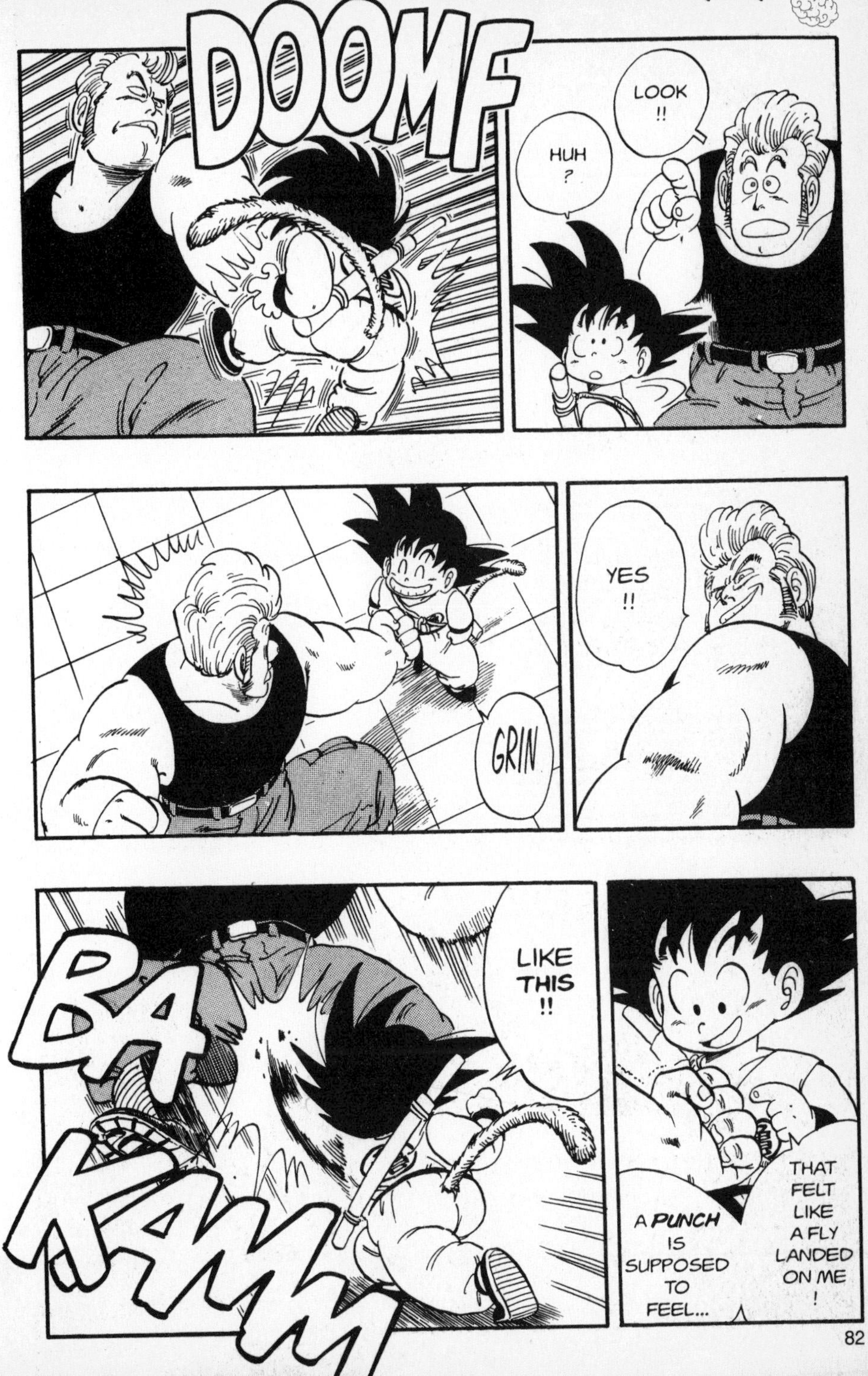
LOOK !!
HUH ?
DOOMF
YES !!
GRIN
THAT FELT LIKE A FLY LANDED ON ME !
A PUNCH IS SUPPOSED TO FEEL...
LIKE THIS !!
BA KAMM

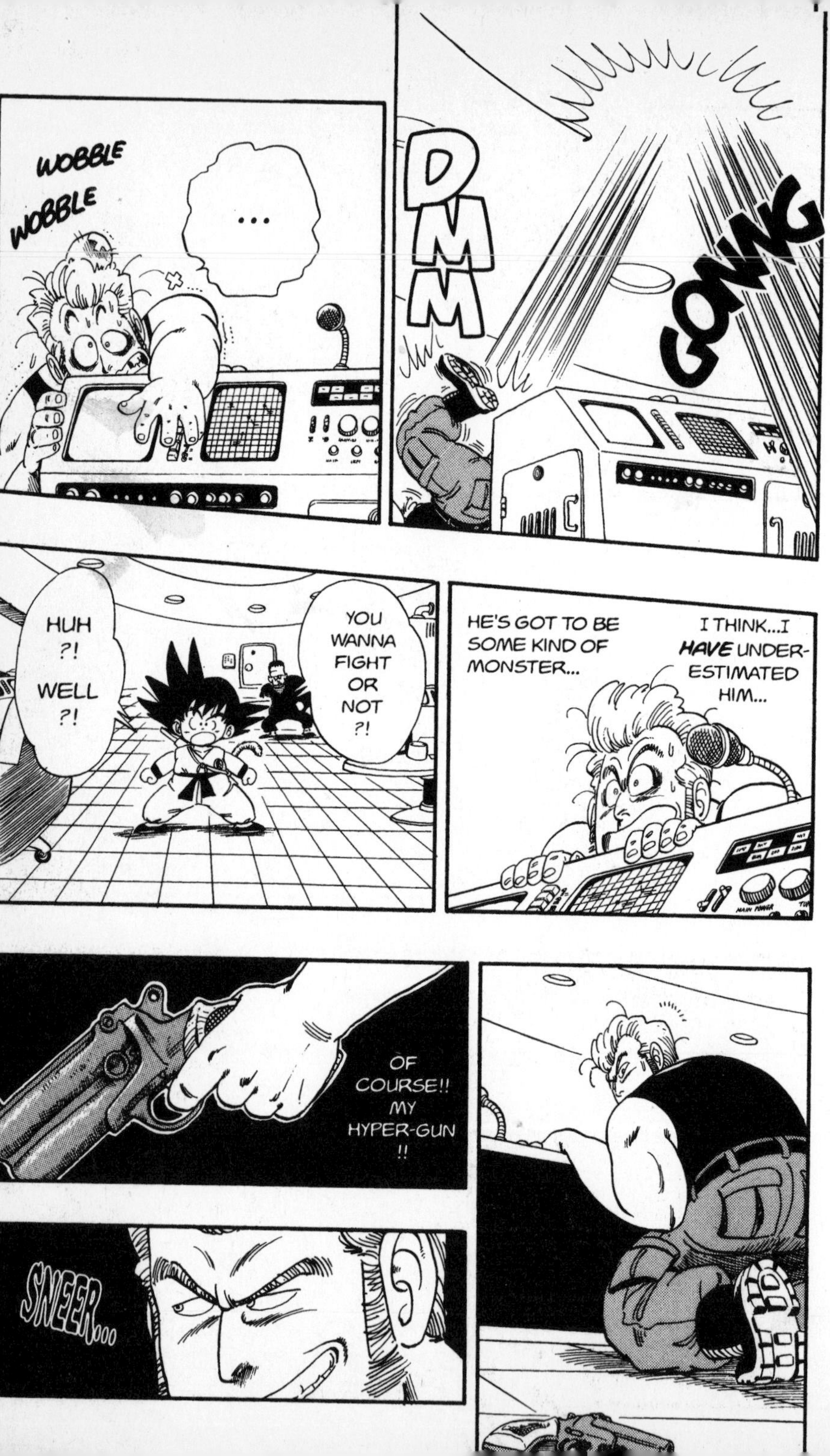
DMMM
GONNG
WOBBLE
WOBBLE
...
I THINK...I *HAVE* UNDER-ESTIMATED HIM...
HE'S GOT TO BE SOME KIND OF MONSTER...
YOU WANNA FIGHT OR NOT ?!
HUH ?! WELL ?!
OF COURSE!! MY HYPER-GUN !!
SNEER...

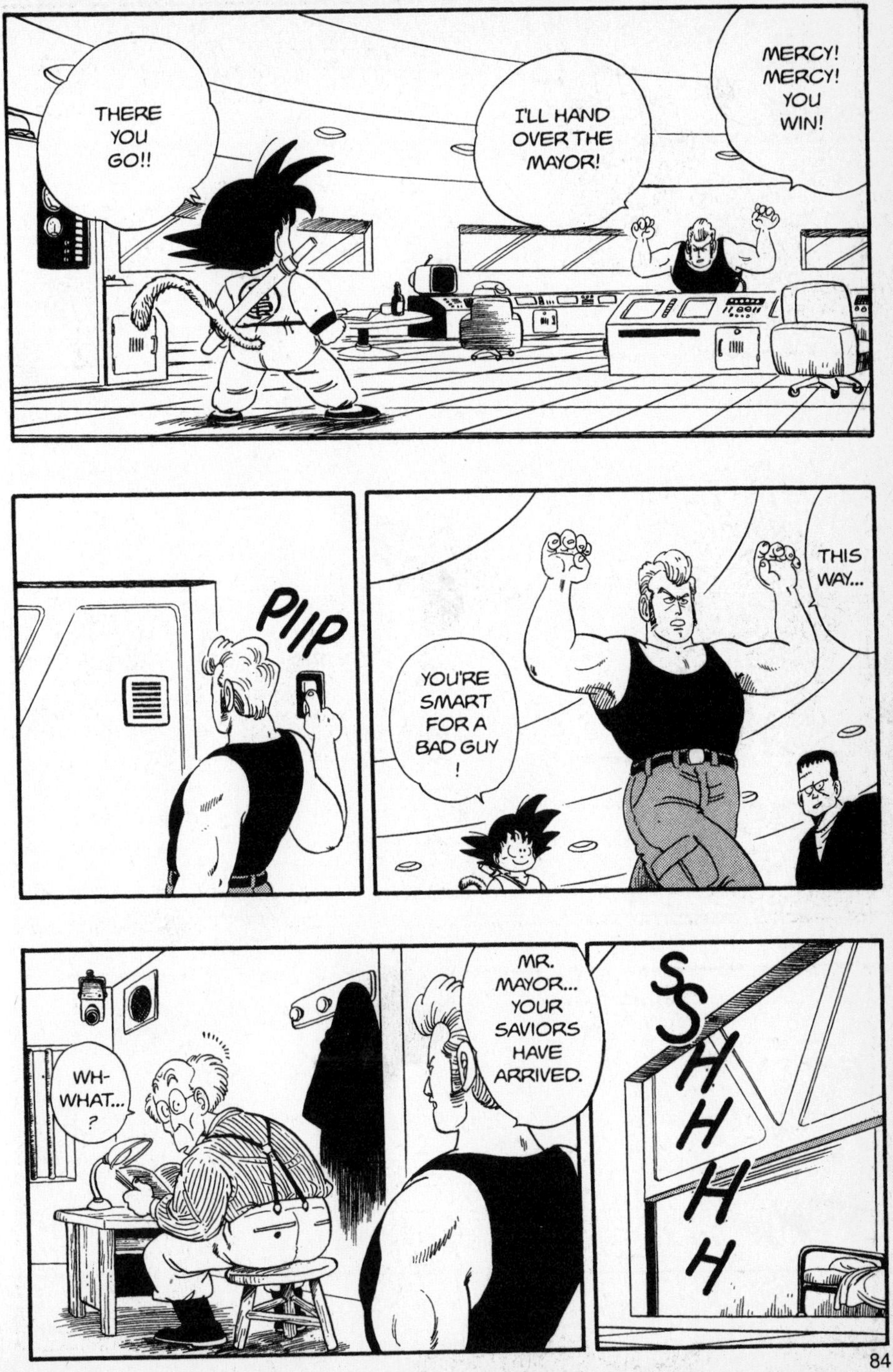
MERCY! MERCY! YOU WIN!
I'LL HAND OVER THE MAYOR!
THERE YOU GO!!
THIS WAY...
YOU'RE SMART FOR A BAD GUY!
PIIP
SSHHHH
MR. MAYOR... YOUR SAVIORS HAVE ARRIVED.
WH-WHAT...?

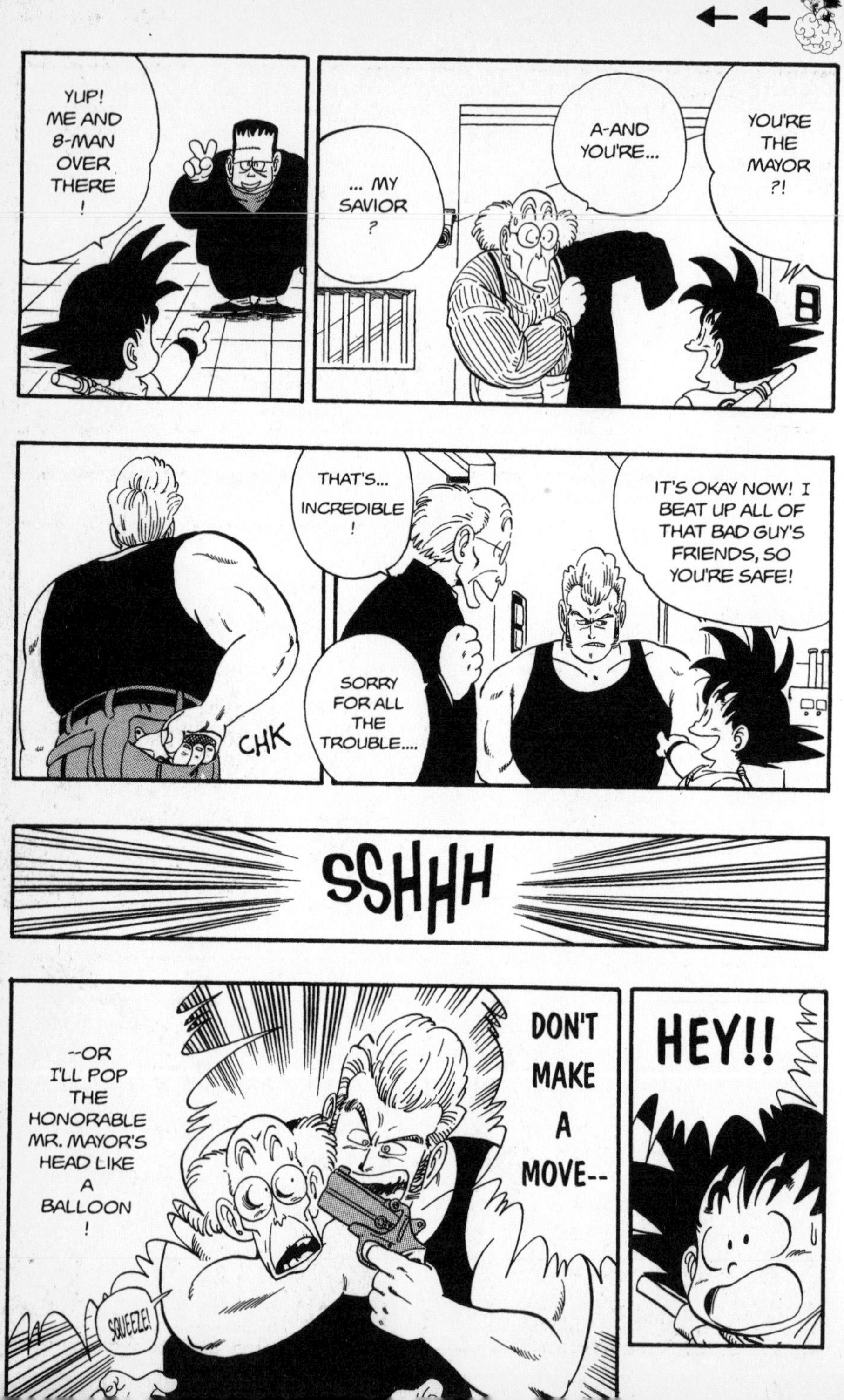
YOU'RE THE MAYOR ?!
A-AND YOU'RE...
... MY SAVIOR ?
YUP! ME AND 8-MAN OVER THERE !
IT'S OKAY NOW! I BEAT UP ALL OF THAT BAD GUY'S FRIENDS, SO YOU'RE SAFE!
THAT'S... INCREDIBLE !
SORRY FOR ALL THE TROUBLE....
CHK
SSHHH
HEY!!
DON'T MAKE A MOVE--
--OR I'LL POP THE HONORABLE MR. MAYOR'S HEAD LIKE A BALLOON !
SQUEEZE!

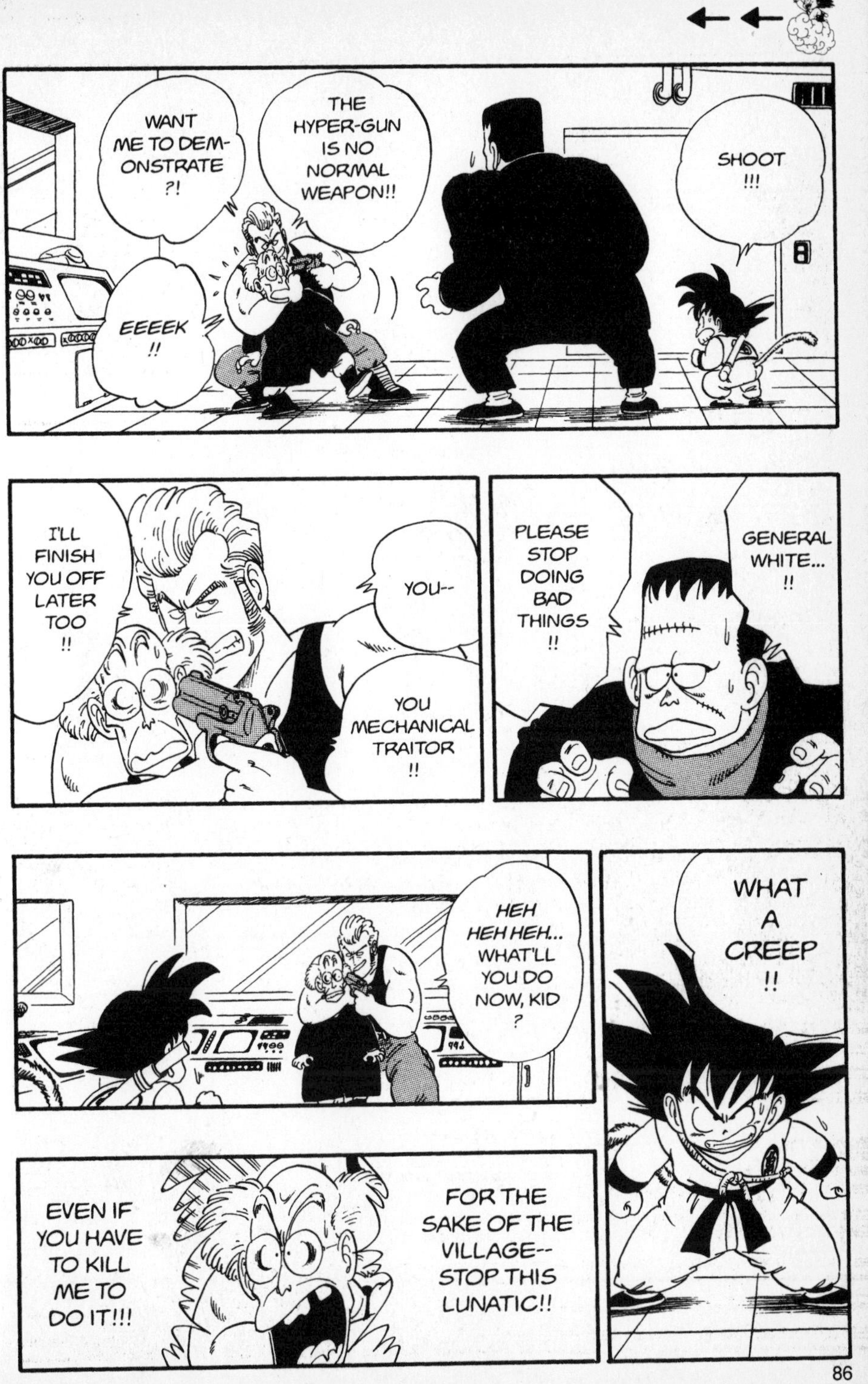
SHOOT!!!
THE HYPER-GUN IS NO NORMAL WEAPON!!
WANT ME TO DEMONSTRATE?!
EEEEK!!
GENERAL WHITE...!!
PLEASE STOP DOING BAD THINGS!!
YOU--
YOU MECHANICAL TRAITOR!!
I'LL FINISH YOU OFF LATER TOO!!
WHAT A CREEP!!
HEH HEH HEH... WHAT'LL YOU DO NOW, KID?
FOR THE SAKE OF THE VILLAGE--STOP THIS LUNATIC!!
EVEN IF YOU HAVE TO KILL ME TO DO IT!!!

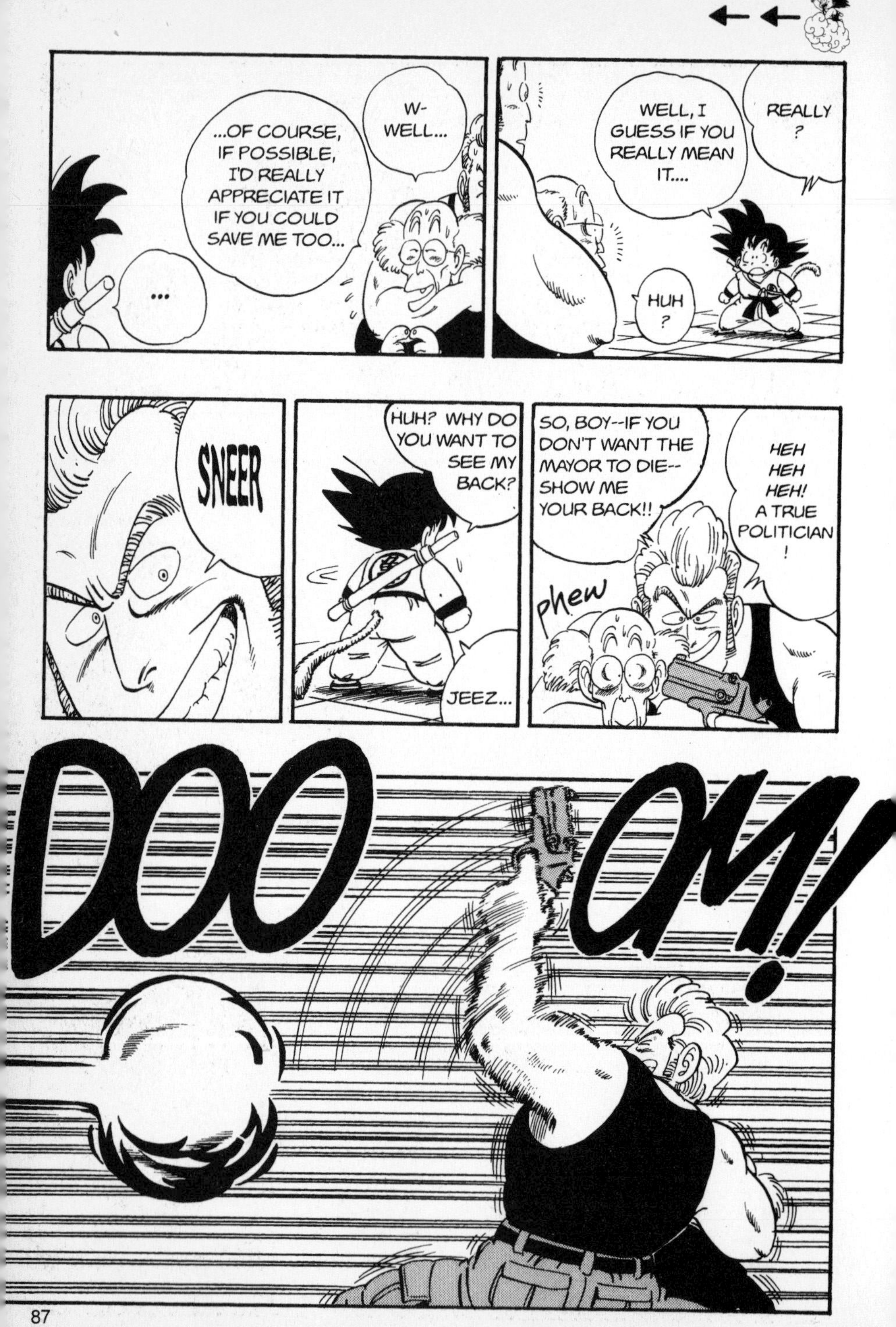
REALLY ?
WELL, I GUESS IF YOU REALLY MEAN IT....
HUH ?
W- WELL...
...OF COURSE, IF POSSIBLE, I'D REALLY APPRECIATE IT IF YOU COULD SAVE ME TOO...
...
HEH HEH HEH! A TRUE POLITICIAN !
SO, BOY--IF YOU DON'T WANT THE MAYOR TO DIE-- SHOW ME YOUR BACK!!
phew
HUH? WHY DO YOU WANT TO SEE MY BACK?
JEEZ...
SNEER
DOO OM!

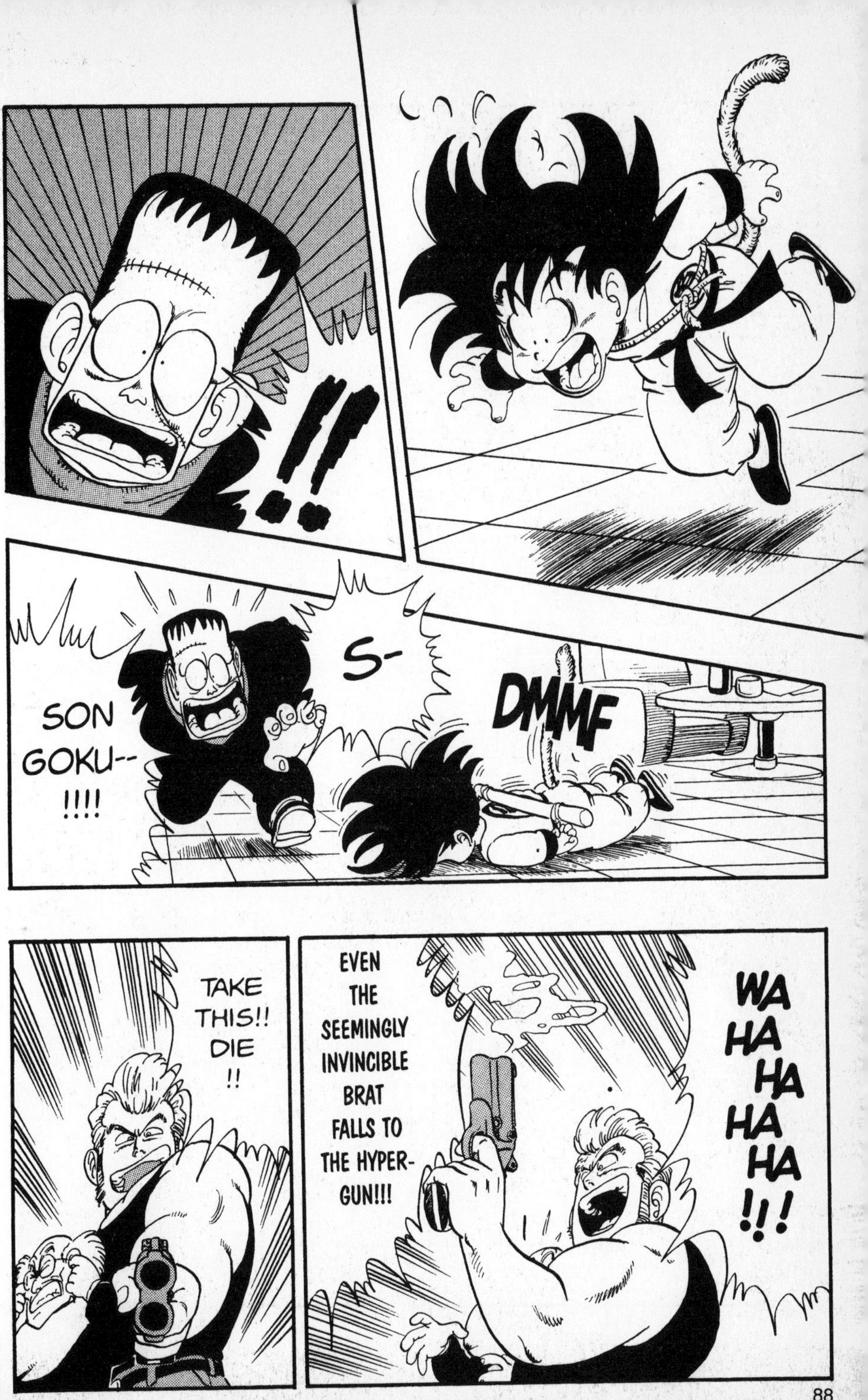
!!
DMMF
S-
SON GOKU--!!!!
WA HA HA HA HA!!!
EVEN THE SEEMINGLY INVINCIBLE BRAT FALLS TO THE HYPER-GUN!!!
TAKE THIS!! DIE !!

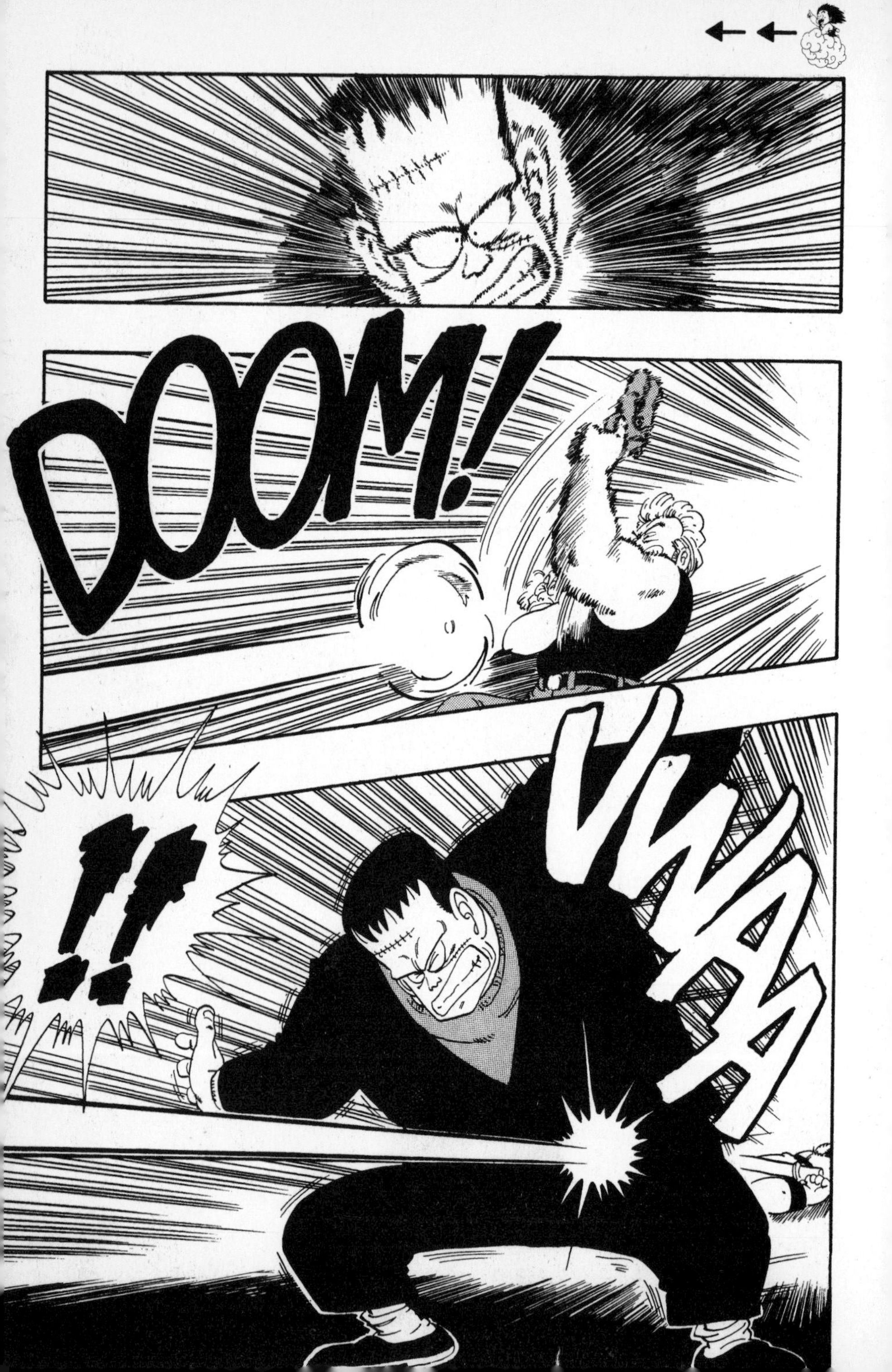

DOOM!
VWAAA
!!

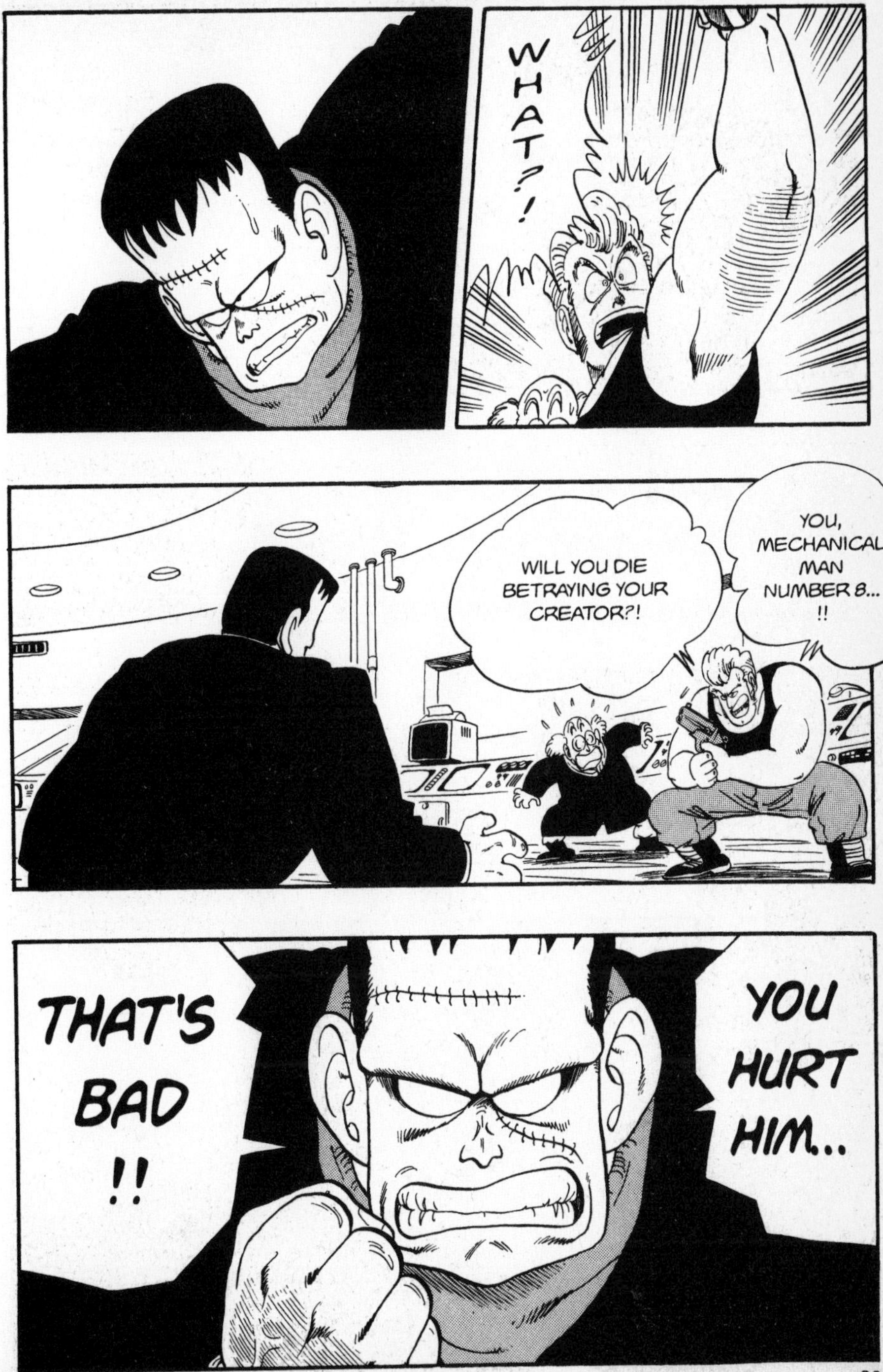
WHAT?!
YOU, MECHANICAL MAN NUMBER 8... !!
WILL YOU DIE BETRAYING YOUR CREATOR?!
YOU HURT HIM...
THAT'S BAD !!

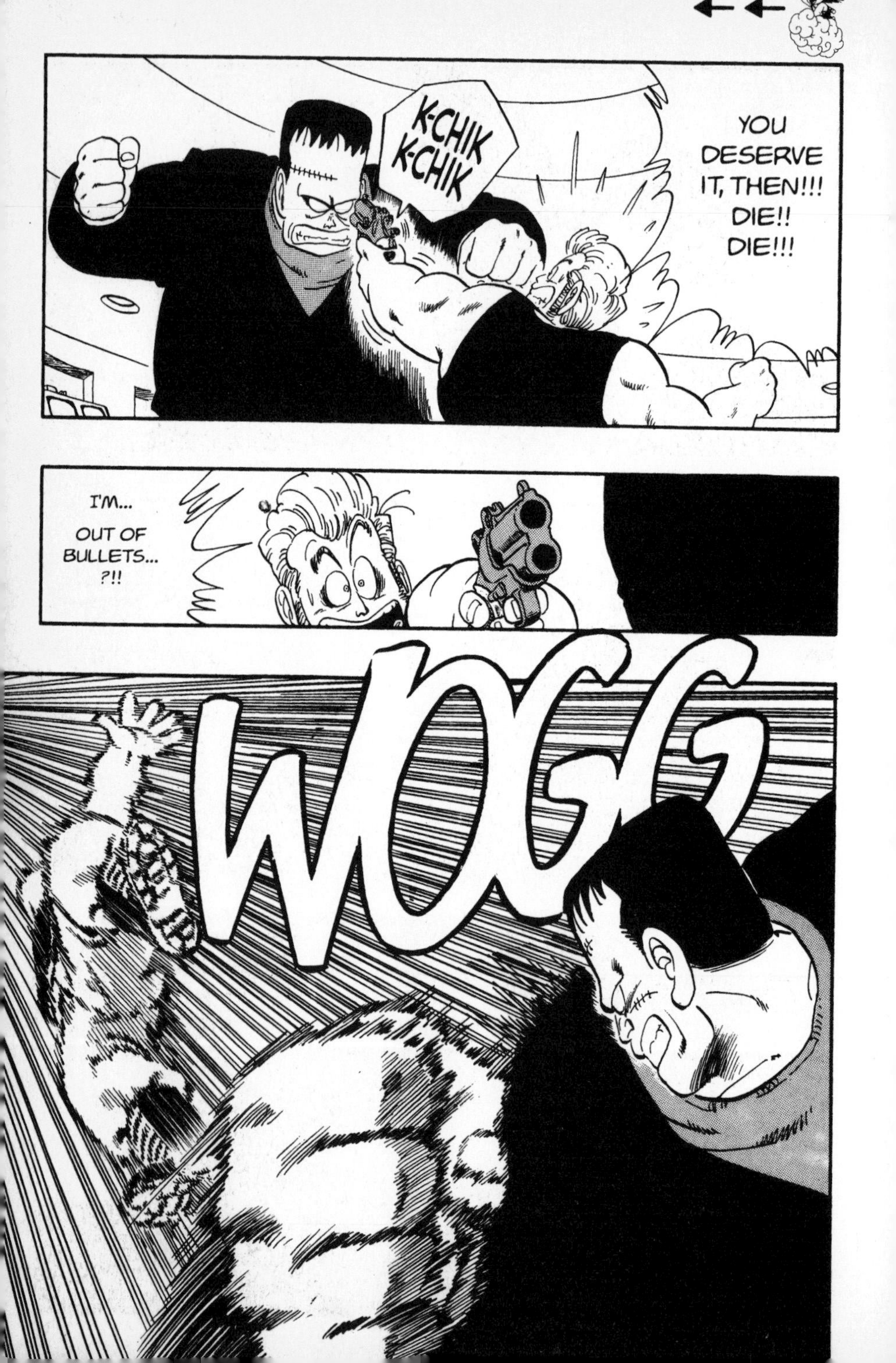
YOU DESERVE IT, THEN!!! DIE!! DIE!!!
K-CHIK K-CHIK
I'M...
OUT OF BULLETS... ?!!
WOGG

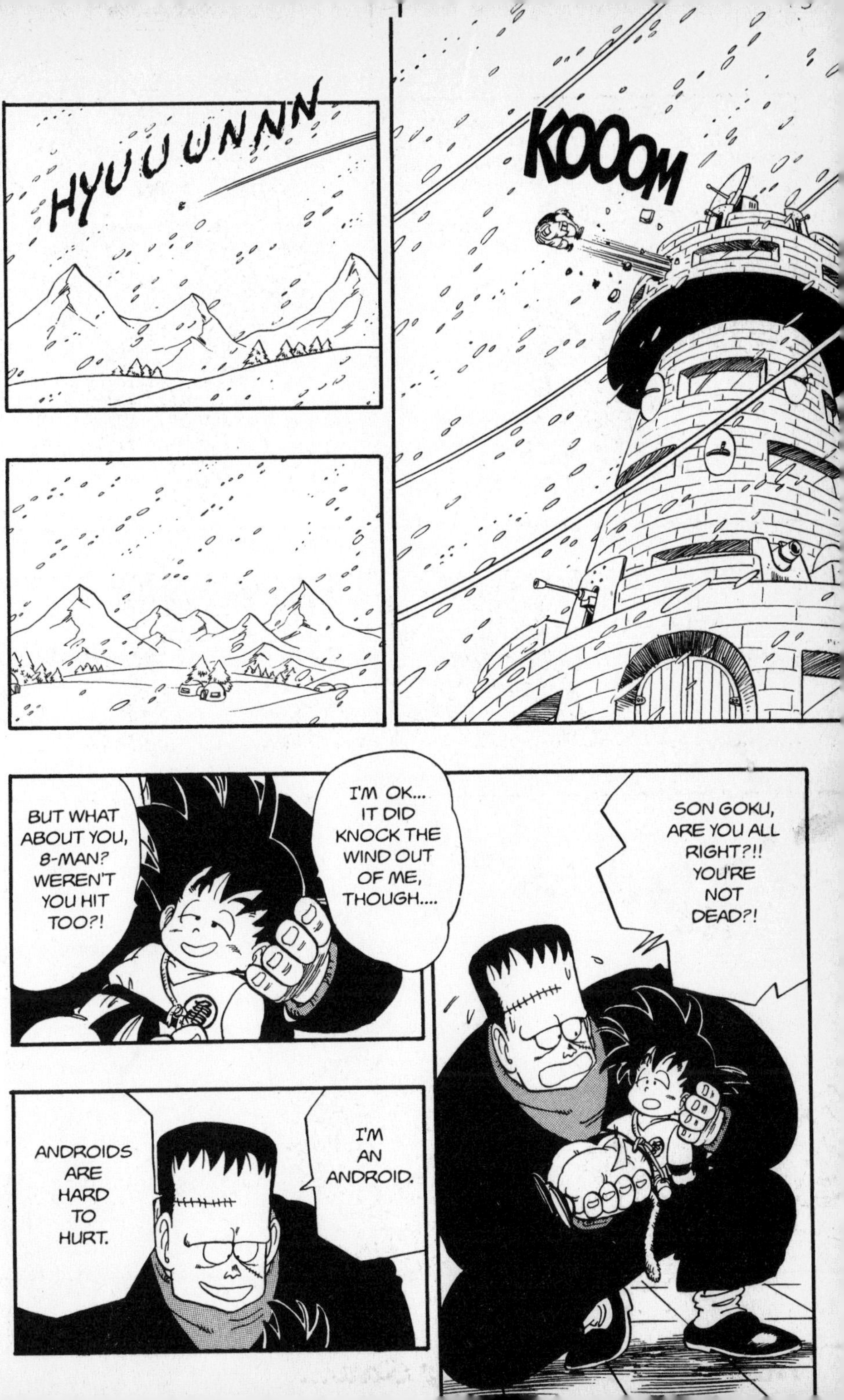
KOOOM
HYUUUNNN
SON GOKU, ARE YOU ALL RIGHT?!! YOU'RE NOT DEAD?!
I'M OK... IT DID KNOCK THE WIND OUT OF ME, THOUGH....
BUT WHAT ABOUT YOU, 8-MAN? WEREN'T YOU HIT TOO?!
I'M AN ANDROID.
ANDROIDS ARE HARD TO HURT.

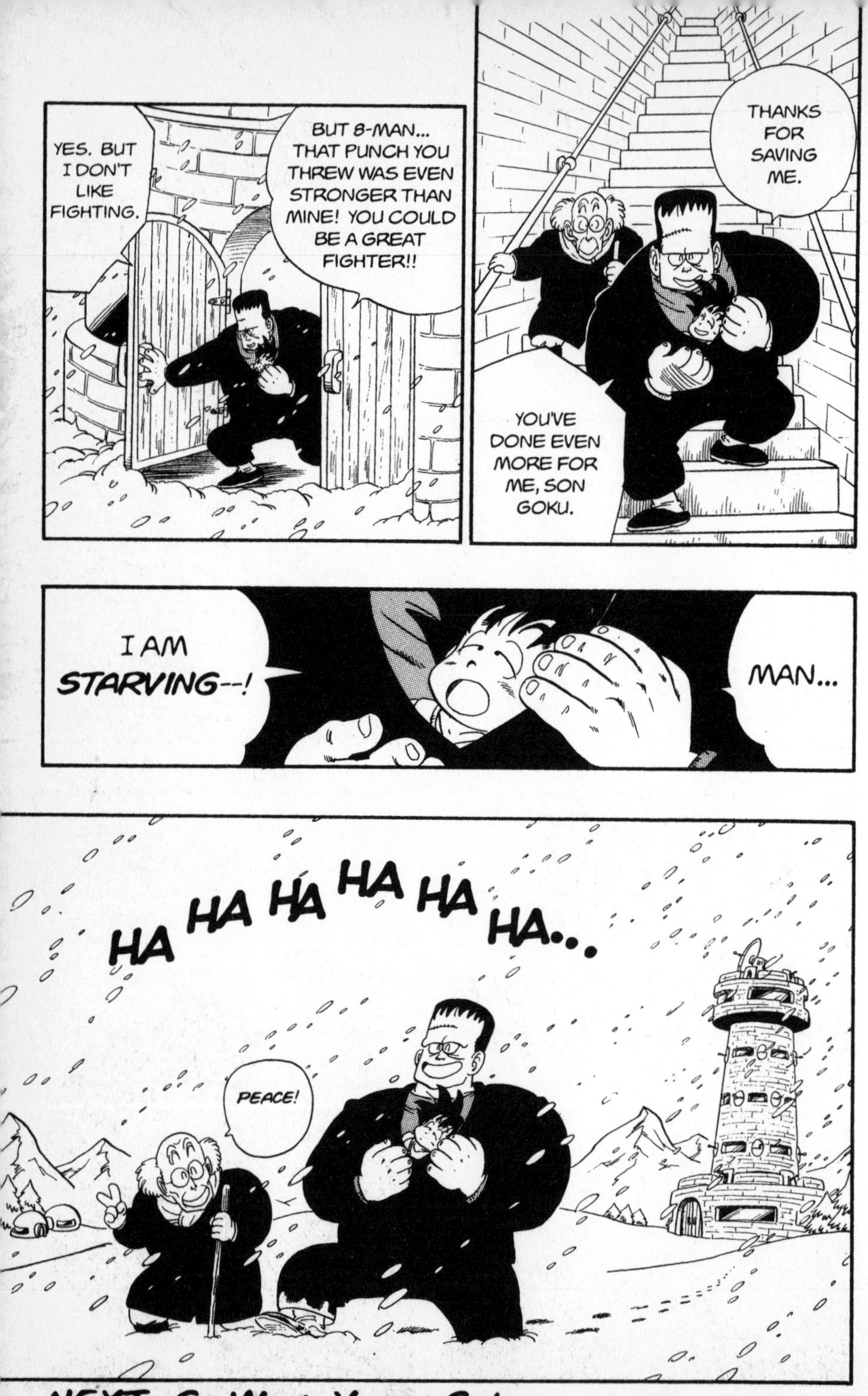
THANKS FOR SAVING ME.
YOU'VE DONE EVEN MORE FOR ME, SON GOKU.
BUT 8-MAN... THAT PUNCH YOU THREW WAS EVEN STRONGER THAN MINE! YOU COULD BE A GREAT FIGHTER!!
YES. BUT I DON'T LIKE FIGHTING.
MAN...
I AM STARVING--!
HA HA HA HA HA HA...
PEACE!

NEXT: Go West, Young Goku...

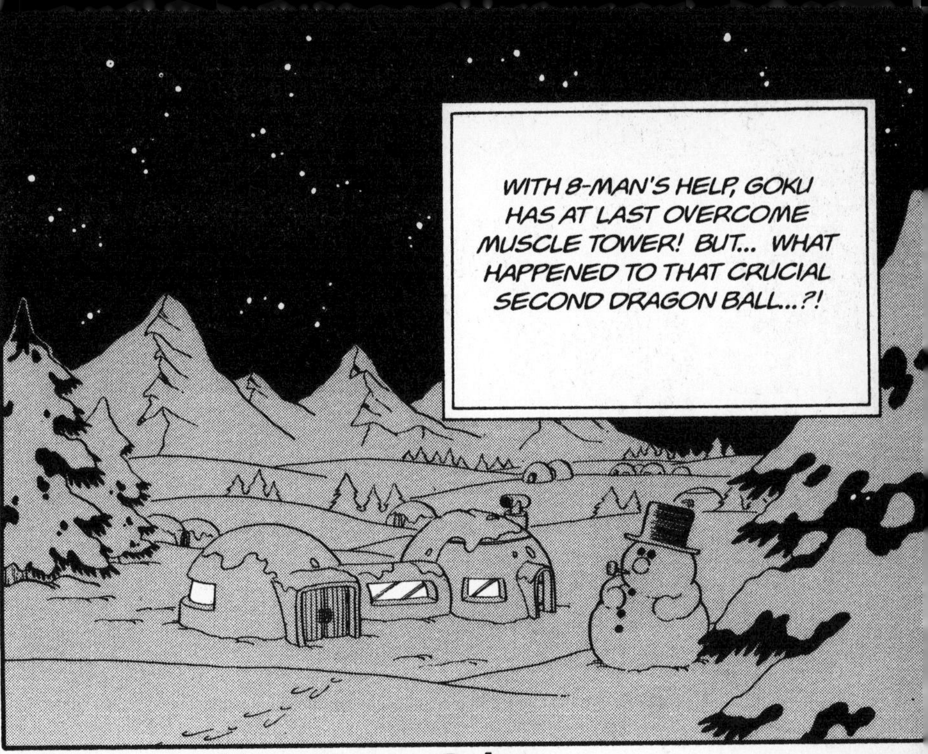
WITH 8-MAN'S HELP, GOKU HAS AT LAST OVERCOME MUSCLE TOWER! BUT... WHAT HAPPENED TO THAT CRUCIAL SECOND DRAGON BALL...?!

Tale 67 • Go West, Young Goku...

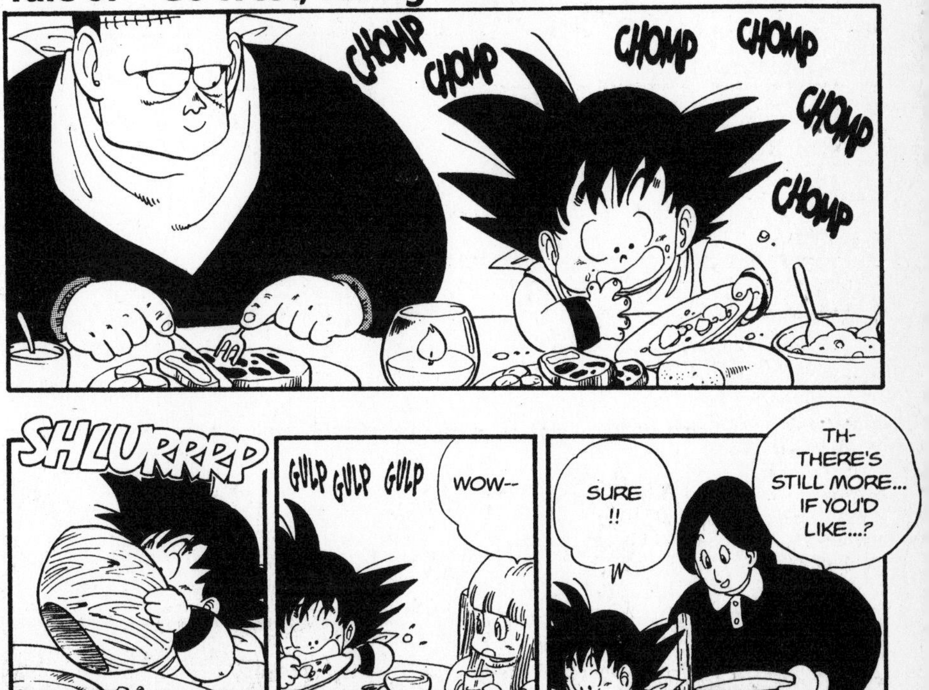
CHOMP
CHOMP
CHOMP
CHOMP
CHOMP
CHOMP
TH- THERE'S STILL MORE... IF YOU'D LIKE...?
SURE !!
WOW--
GULP GULP GULP
SHLURRRP

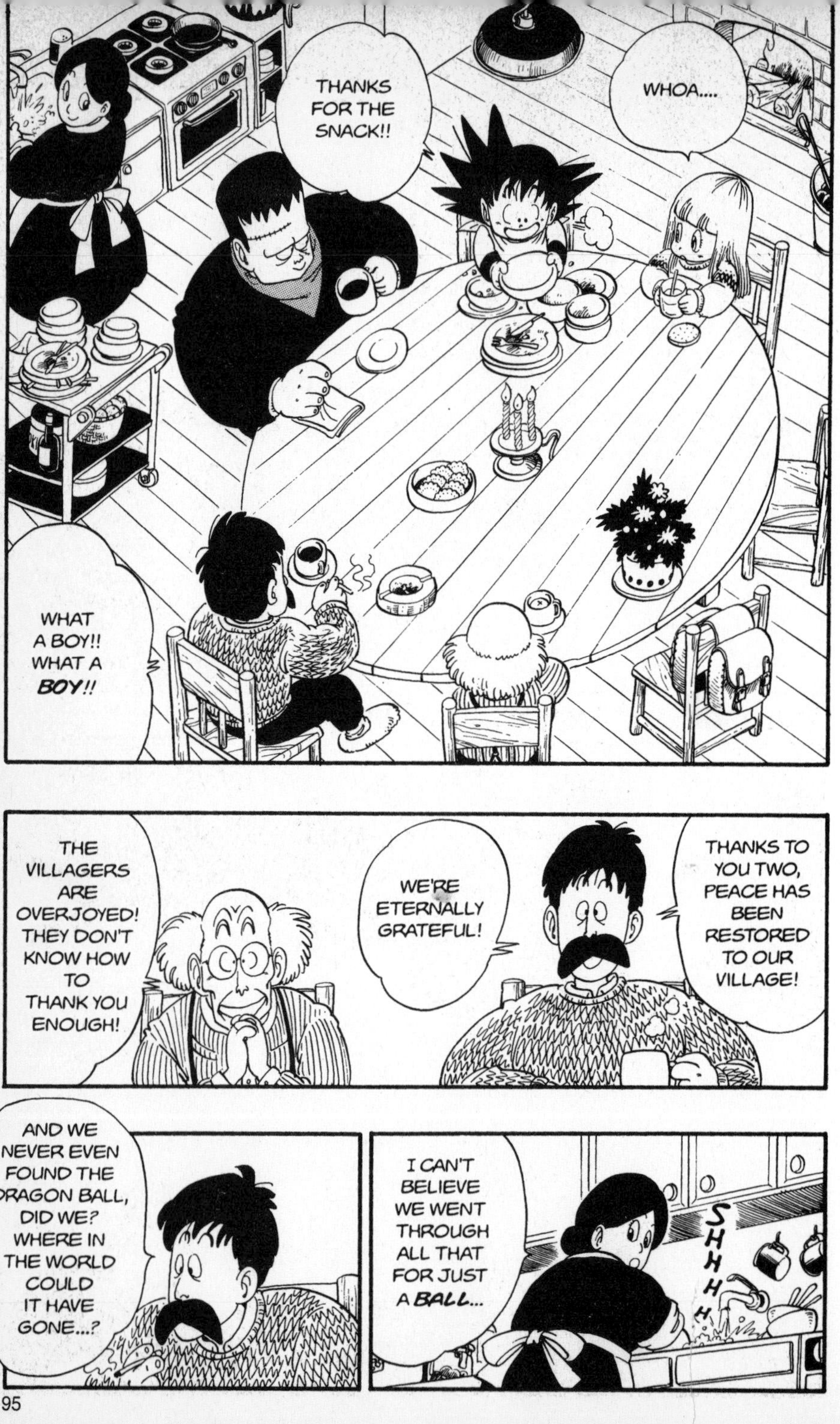
WHOA....
THANKS FOR THE SNACK!!
WHAT A BOY!! WHAT A *BOY*!!
THANKS TO YOU TWO, PEACE HAS BEEN RESTORED TO OUR VILLAGE!
WE'RE ETERNALLY GRATEFUL!
THE VILLAGERS ARE OVERJOYED! THEY DON'T KNOW HOW TO THANK YOU ENOUGH!
SHHHH
I CAN'T BELIEVE WE WENT THROUGH ALL THAT FOR JUST A *BALL*...
AND WE NEVER EVEN FOUND THE DRAGON BALL, DID WE? WHERE IN THE WORLD COULD IT HAVE GONE...?

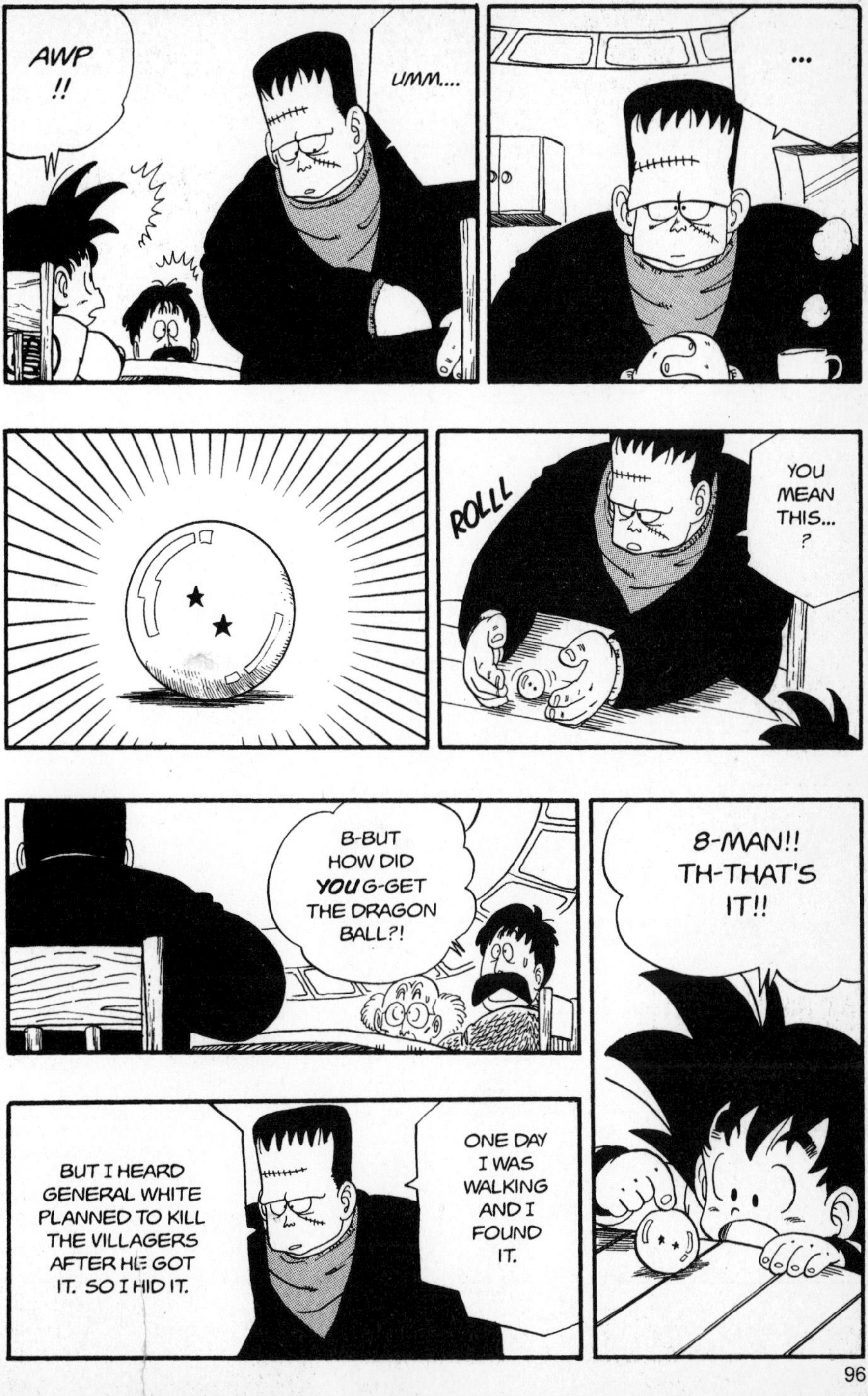
...
UMM....
AWP !!
YOU MEAN THIS... ?
ROLLL
8-MAN!! TH-THAT'S IT!!
B-BUT HOW DID YOU G-GET THE DRAGON BALL?!
ONE DAY I WAS WALKING AND I FOUND IT.
BUT I HEARD GENERAL WHITE PLANNED TO KILL THE VILLAGERS AFTER HE GOT IT. SO I HID IT.

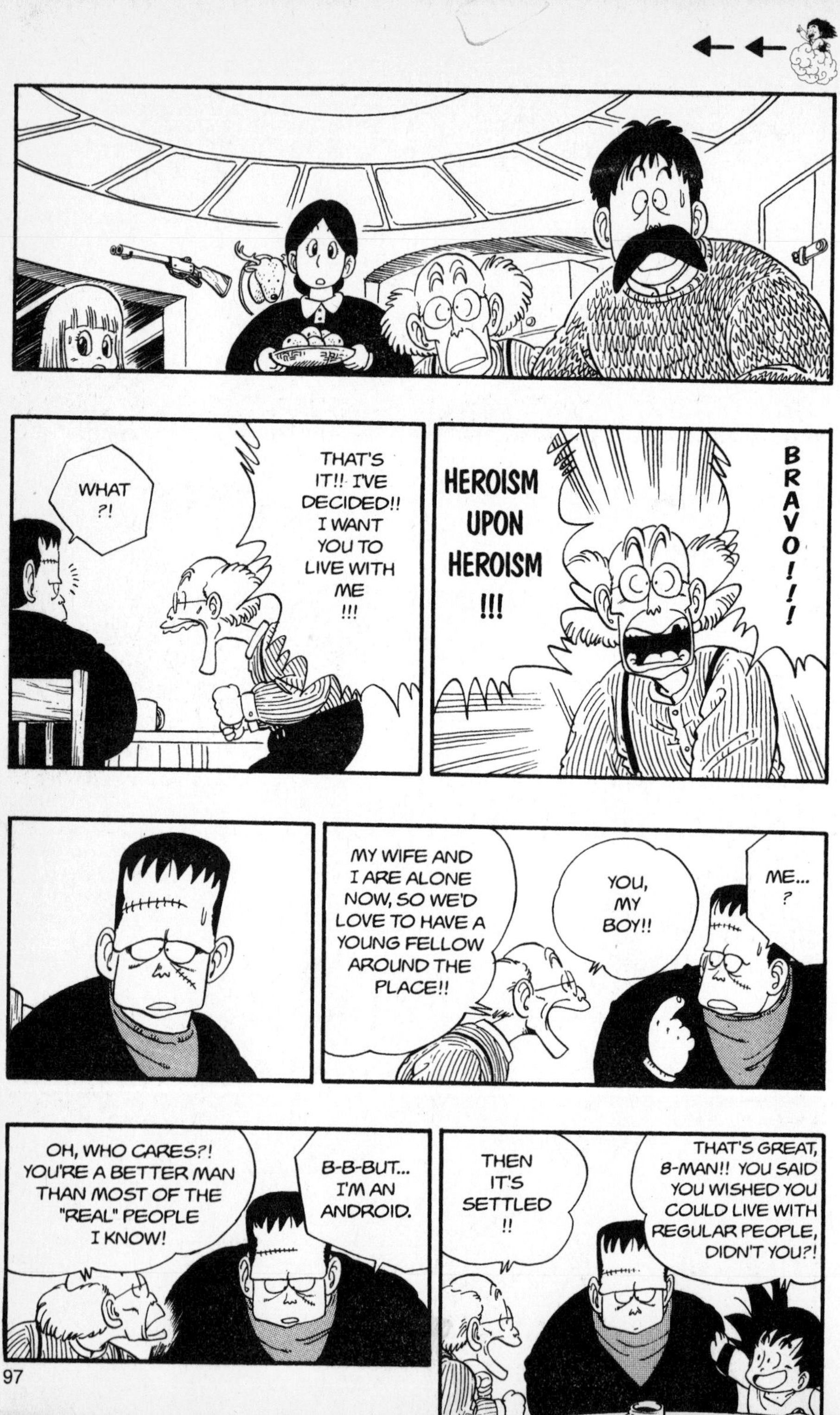
BRAVO!!!
HEROISM UPON HEROISM!!!
THAT'S IT!! I'VE DECIDED!! I WANT YOU TO LIVE WITH ME!!!
WHAT?!
ME...?
YOU, MY BOY!!
MY WIFE AND I ARE ALONE NOW, SO WE'D LOVE TO HAVE A YOUNG FELLOW AROUND THE PLACE!!
THAT'S GREAT, 8-MAN!! YOU SAID YOU WISHED YOU COULD LIVE WITH REGULAR PEOPLE, DIDN'T YOU?!
THEN IT'S SETTLED!!
B-B-BUT... I'M AN ANDROID.
OH, WHO CARES?! YOU'RE A BETTER MAN THAN MOST OF THE "REAL" PEOPLE I KNOW!

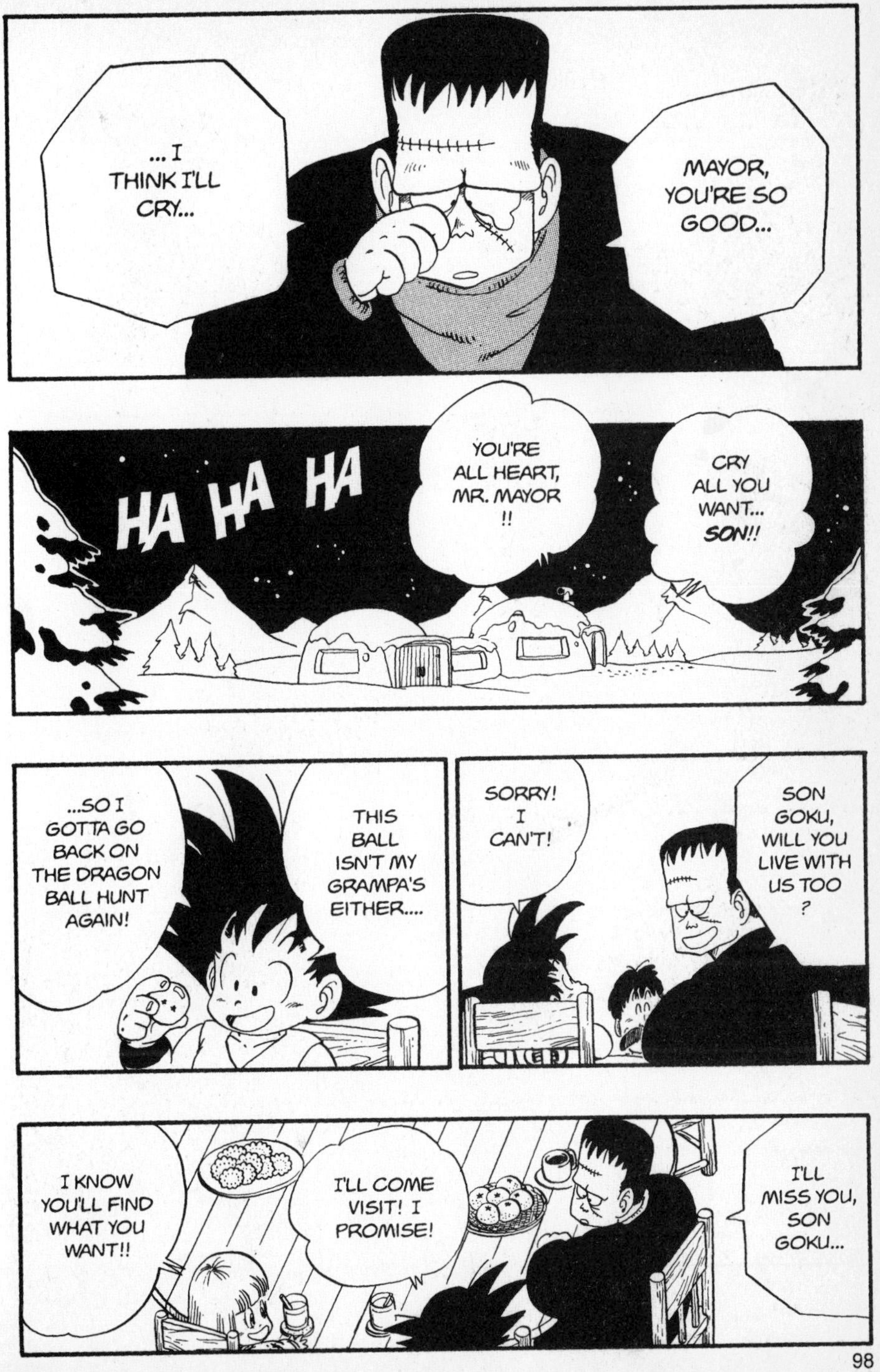
MAYOR, YOU'RE SO GOOD...
... I THINK I'LL CRY...
CRY ALL YOU WANT... SON!!
YOU'RE ALL HEART, MR. MAYOR !!
HA HA HA
SON GOKU, WILL YOU LIVE WITH US TOO ?
SORRY! I CAN'T!
THIS BALL ISN'T MY GRAMPA'S EITHER....
...SO I GOTTA GO BACK ON THE DRAGON BALL HUNT AGAIN!
I'LL MISS YOU, SON GOKU...
I'LL COME VISIT! I PROMISE!
I KNOW YOU'LL FIND WHAT YOU WANT!!

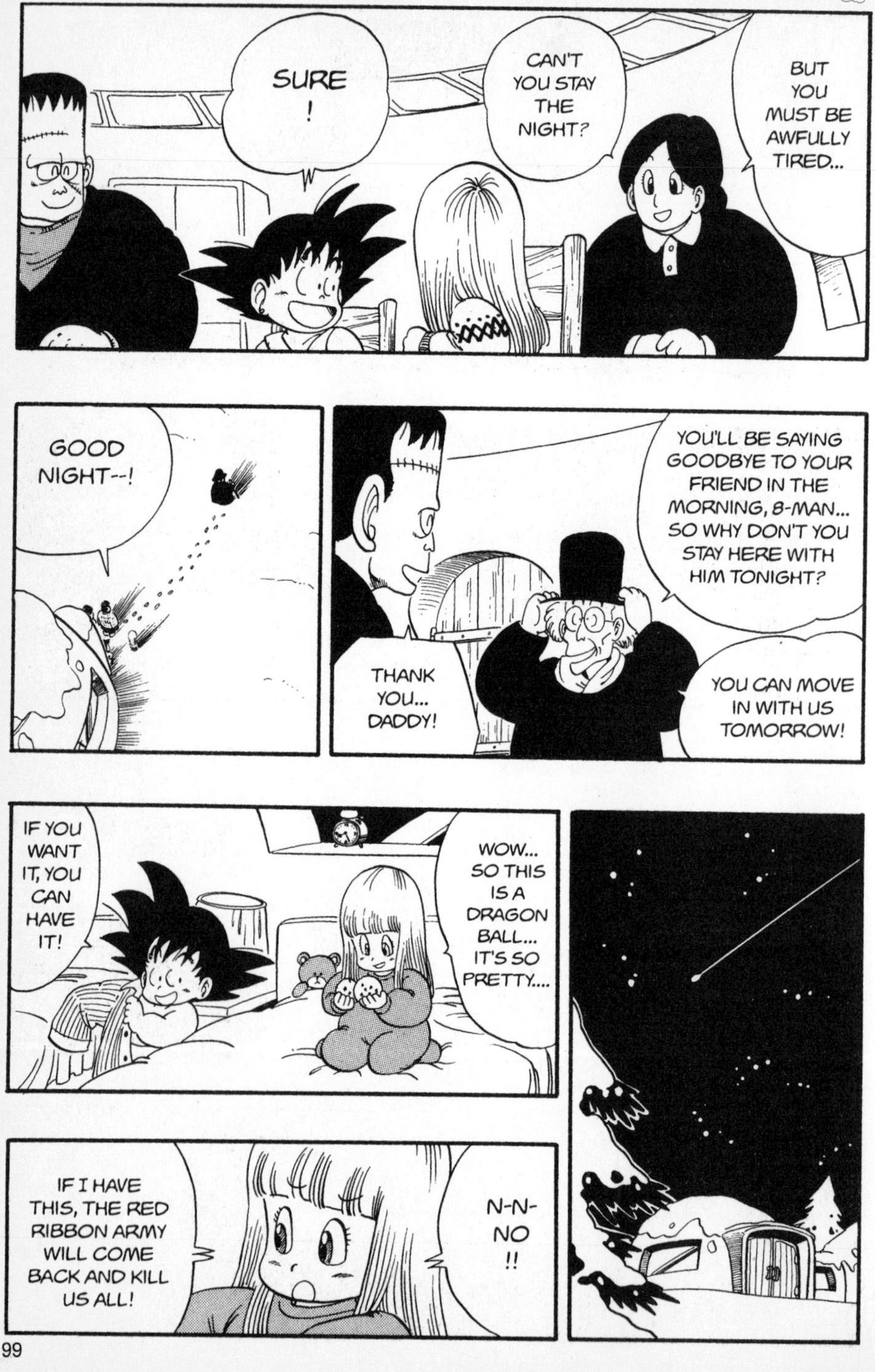
BUT YOU MUST BE AWFULLY TIRED...
CAN'T YOU STAY THE NIGHT?
SURE!
YOU'LL BE SAYING GOODBYE TO YOUR FRIEND IN THE MORNING, 8-MAN... SO WHY DON'T YOU STAY HERE WITH HIM TONIGHT?
YOU CAN MOVE IN WITH US TOMORROW!
THANK YOU... DADDY!
GOOD NIGHT--!
WOW... SO THIS IS A DRAGON BALL... IT'S SO PRETTY....
IF YOU WANT IT, YOU CAN HAVE IT!
N-N-NO!!
IF I HAVE THIS, THE RED RIBBON ARMY WILL COME BACK AND KILL US ALL!

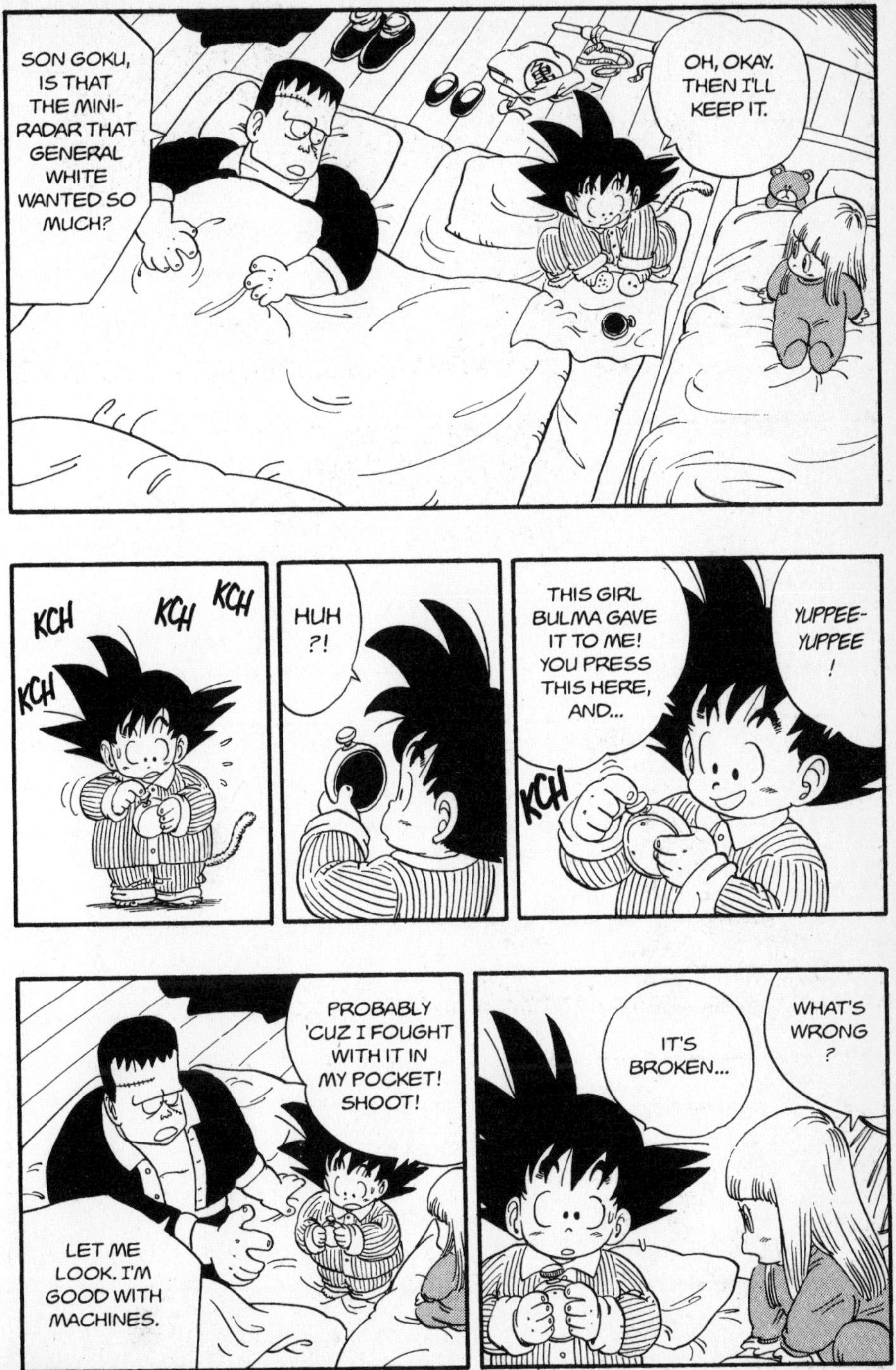
OH, OKAY. THEN I'LL KEEP IT.
SON GOKU, IS THAT THE MINI-RADAR THAT GENERAL WHITE WANTED SO MUCH?
YUPPEE-YUPPEE!
THIS GIRL BULMA GAVE IT TO ME! YOU PRESS THIS HERE, AND...
KCH
HUH ?!
KCH
KCH
KCH
KCH
WHAT'S WRONG ?
IT'S BROKEN...
PROBABLY 'CUZ I FOUGHT WITH IT IN MY POCKET! SHOOT!
LET ME LOOK. I'M GOOD WITH MACHINES.

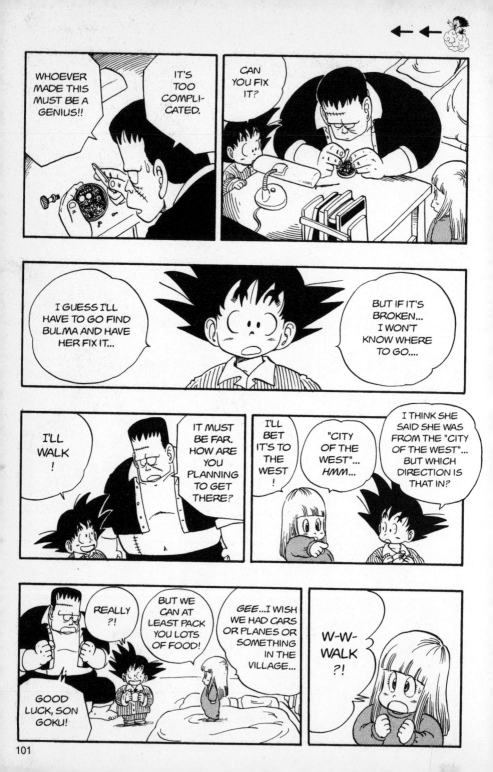

101

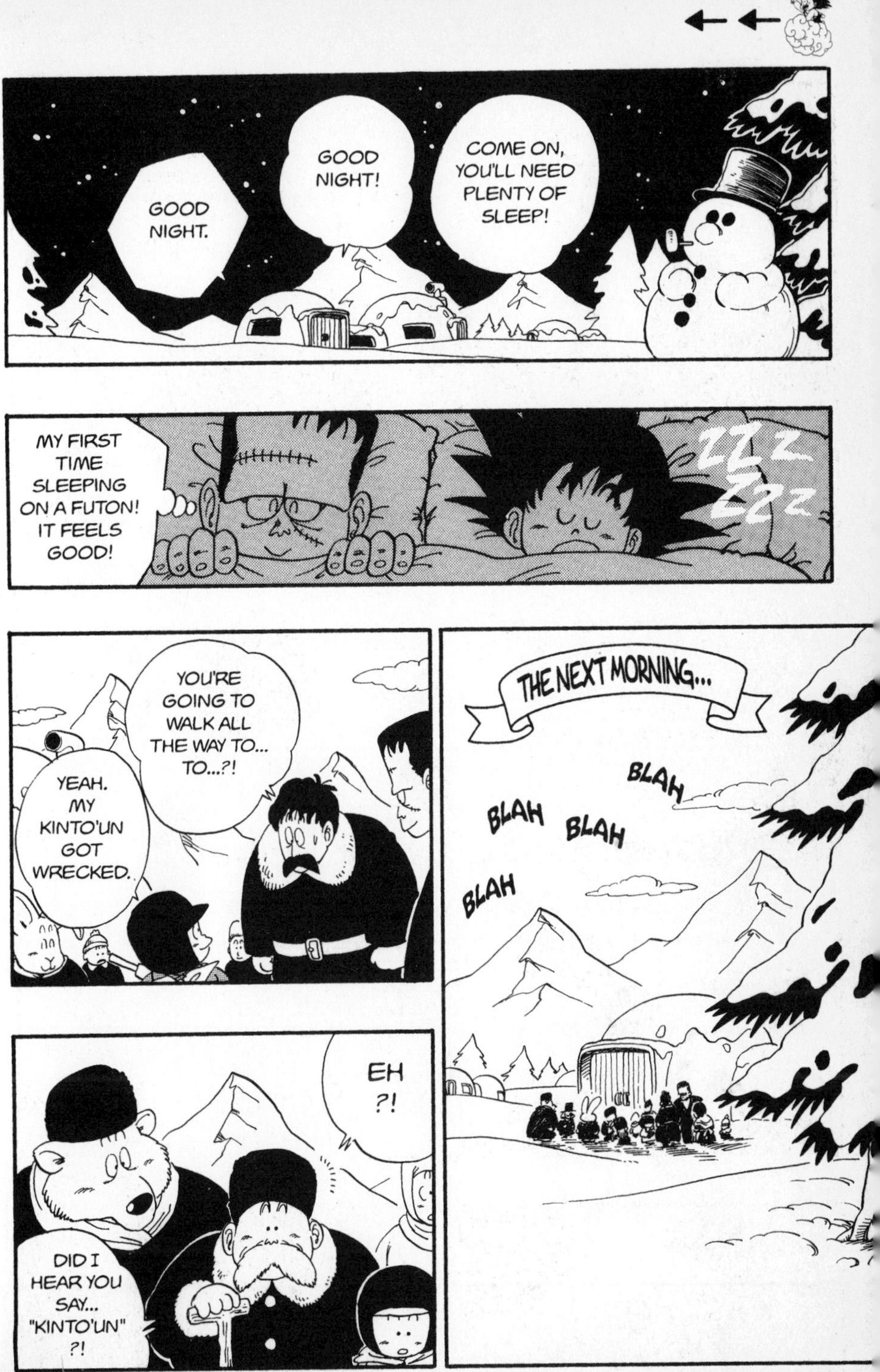
COME ON, YOU'LL NEED PLENTY OF SLEEP!
GOOD NIGHT!
GOOD NIGHT.
ZZZ ZZZ
MY FIRST TIME SLEEPING ON A FUTON! IT FEELS GOOD!
THE NEXT MORNING...
BLAH
BLAH
BLAH
BLAH
YOU'RE GOING TO WALK ALL THE WAY TO... TO...?!
YEAH. MY KINTO'UN GOT WRECKED.
EH ?!
DID I HEAR YOU SAY... "KINTO'UN" ?!

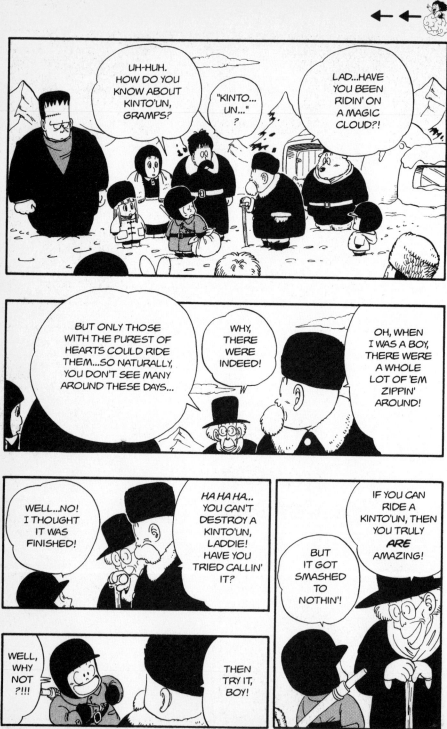

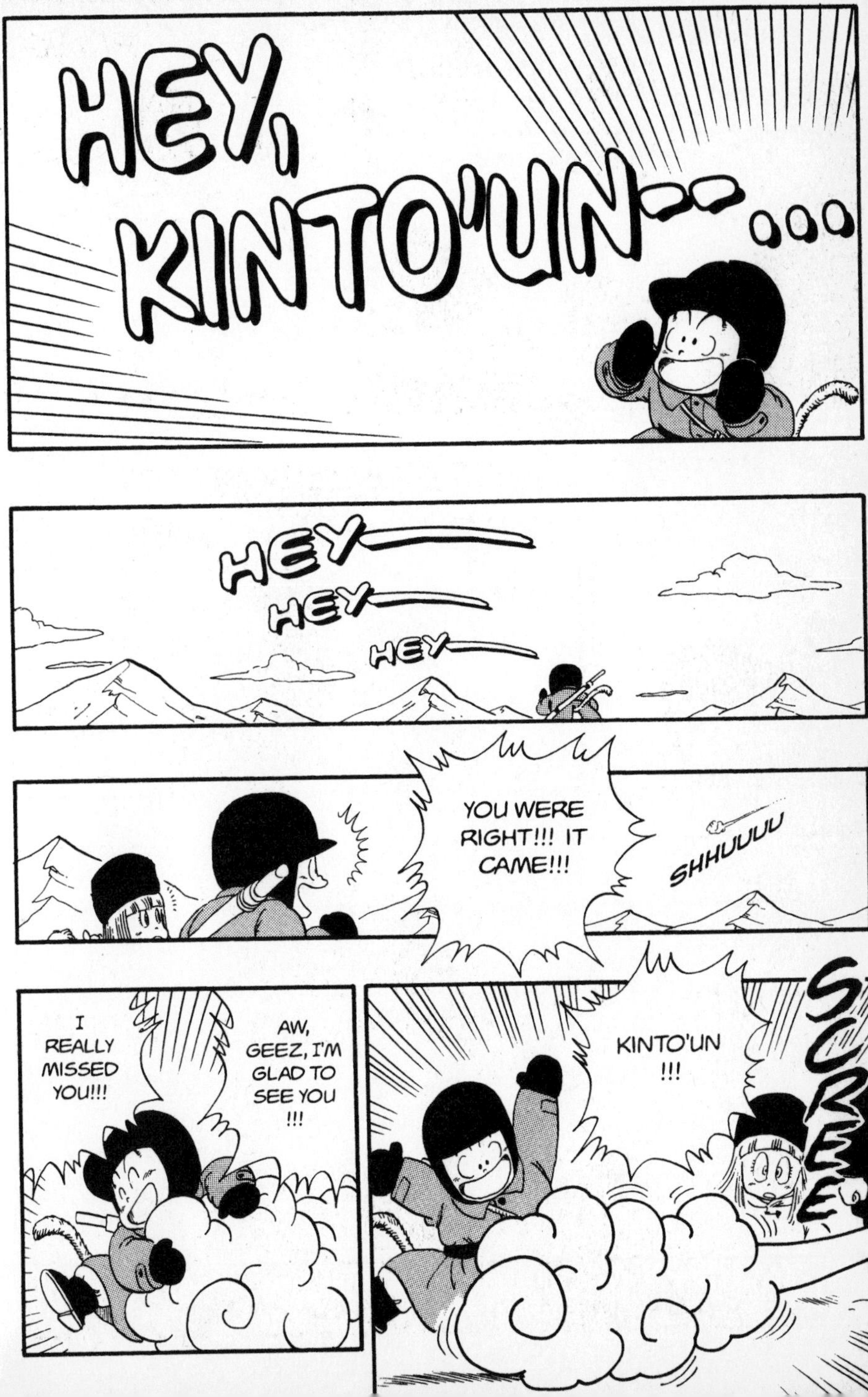
HEY, KINTO'UN-- ...
HEY— HEY— HEY—
SHHUUUU
YOU WERE RIGHT!!! IT CAME!!!
KINTO'UN !!!
AW, GEEZ, I'M GLAD TO SEE YOU !!!
I REALLY MISSED YOU!!!

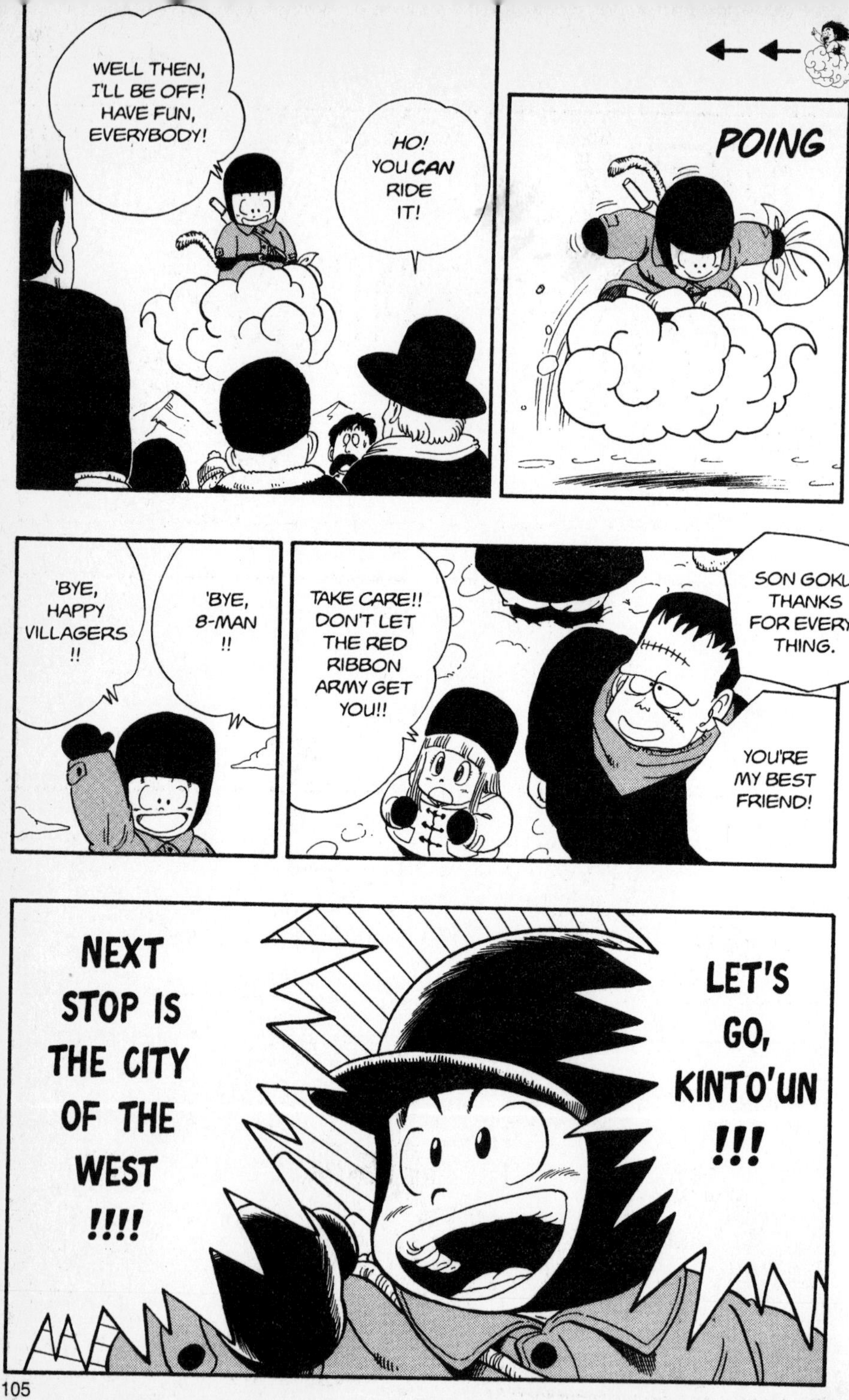
POING
WELL THEN, I'LL BE OFF! HAVE FUN, EVERYBODY!
HO! YOU CAN RIDE IT!
SON GOKU, THANKS FOR EVERY-THING.
YOU'RE MY BEST FRIEND!
TAKE CARE!! DON'T LET THE RED RIBBON ARMY GET YOU!!
'BYE, 8-MAN !!
'BYE, HAPPY VILLAGERS !!
LET'S GO, KINTO'UN !!!
NEXT STOP IS THE CITY OF THE WEST !!!!

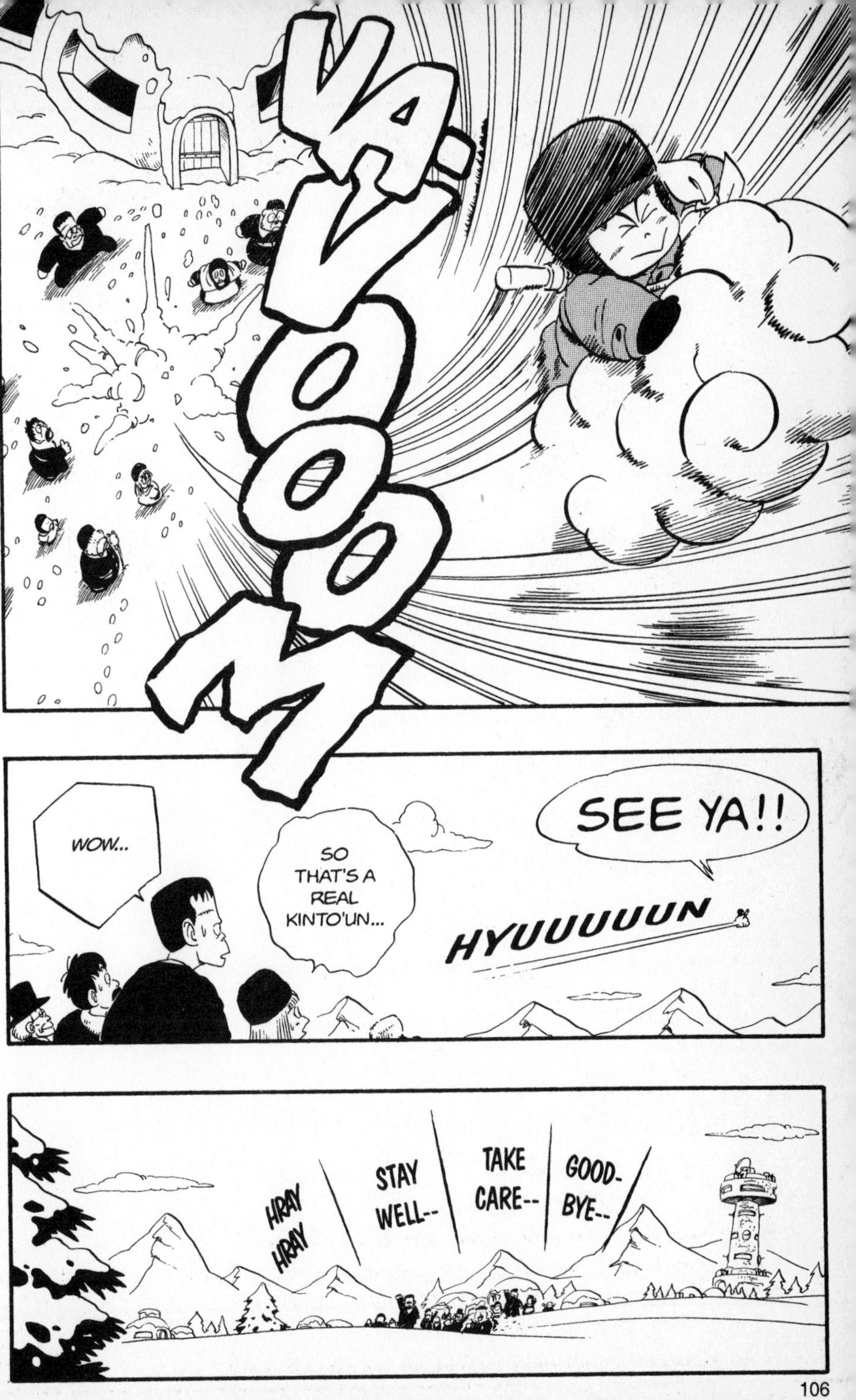
VAVOOOM
SEE YA!!
HYUUUUUN
SO THAT'S A REAL KINTO'UN...
WOW...
GOOD-BYE--
TAKE CARE--
STAY WELL--
HRAY HRAY

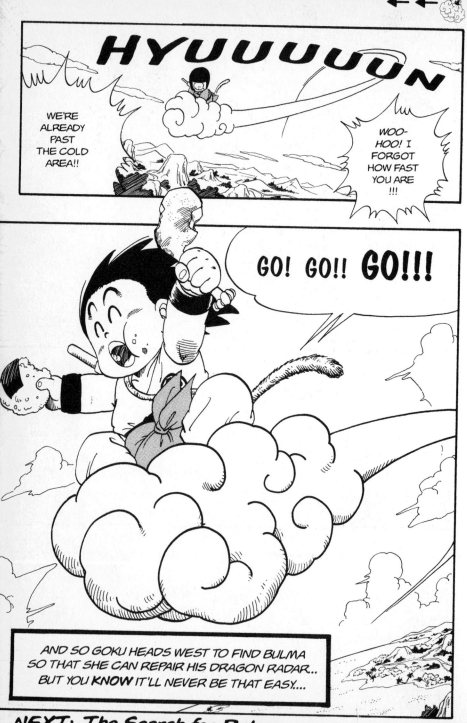

NEXT: The Search for Bulma

Tale 68 • Monkey in the City

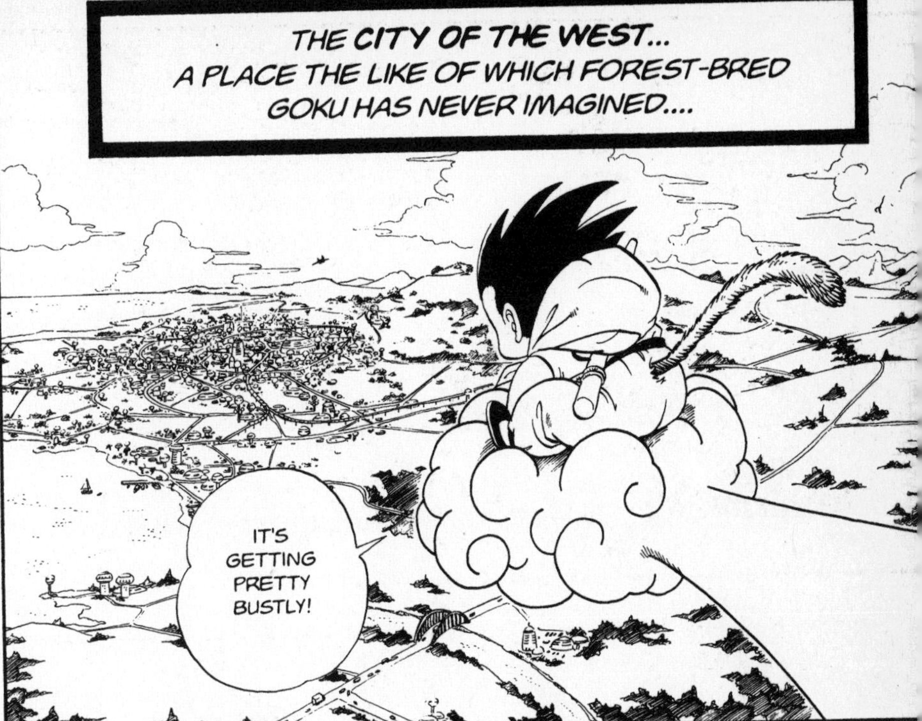
THE CITY OF THE WEST... A PLACE THE LIKE OF WHICH FOREST-BRED GOKU HAS NEVER IMAGINED....
IT'S GETTING PRETTY BUSTLY!

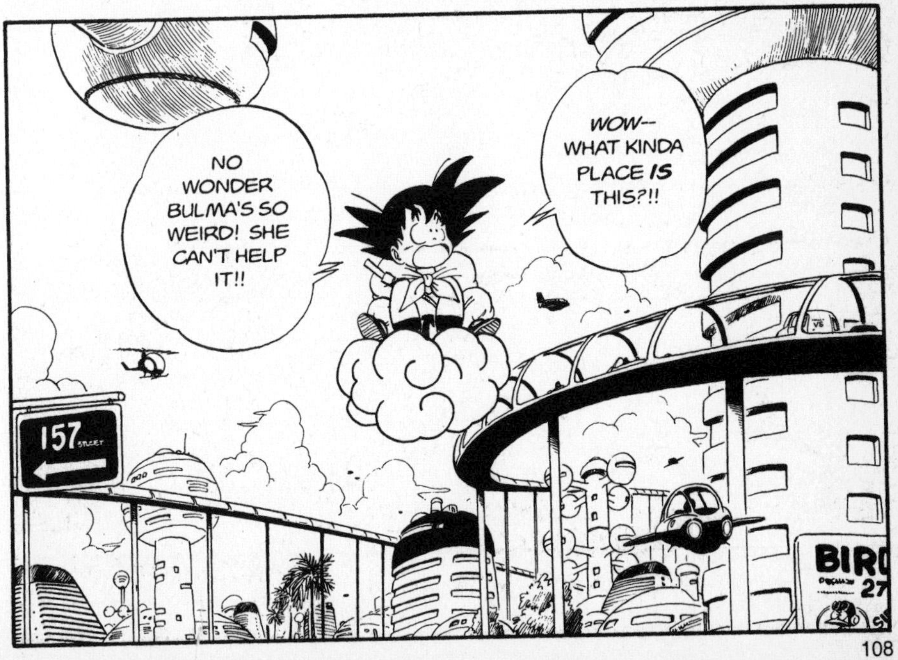
WOW-- WHAT KINDA PLACE *IS* THIS?!!
NO WONDER BULMA'S SO WEIRD! SHE CAN'T HELP IT!!
157

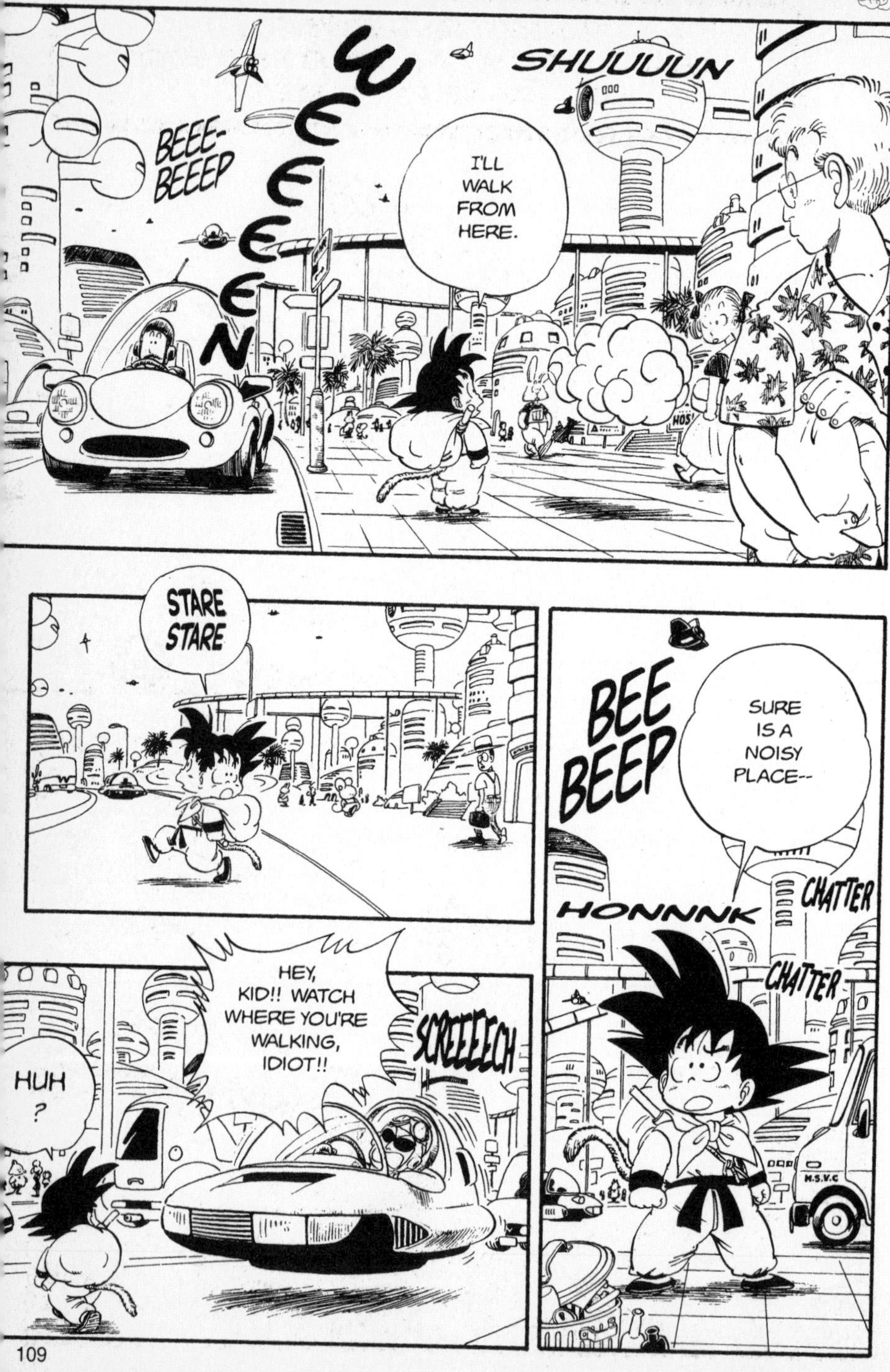
SHUUUUN
WEEEEEEN
I'LL WALK FROM HERE.
BEEE-BEEEP
SURE IS A NOISY PLACE--
BEE BEEP
CHATTER
CHATTER
HONNNK
STARE STARE
SCREEEEECH
HEY, KID!! WATCH WHERE YOU'RE WALKING, IDIOT!!
HUH ?

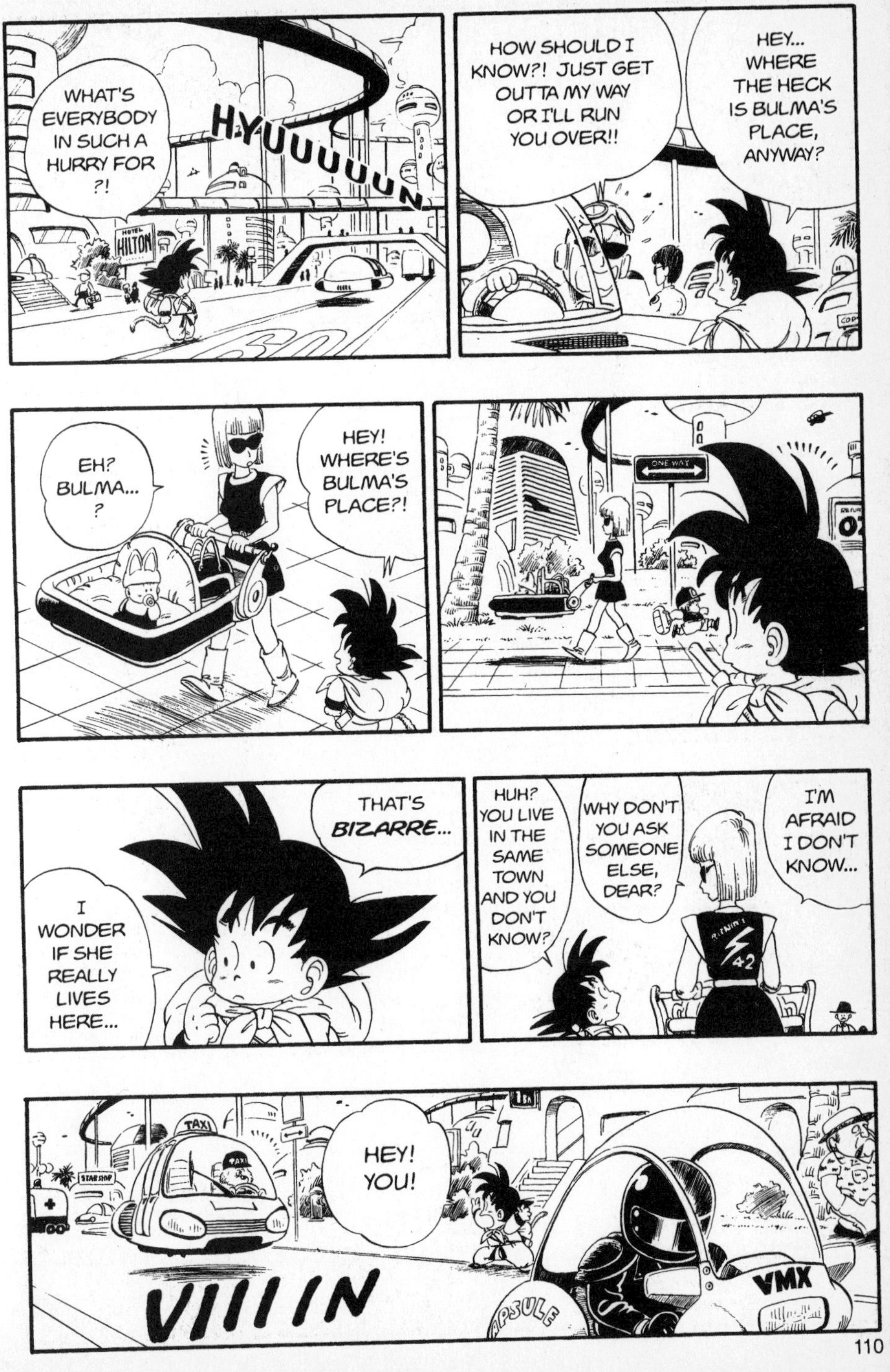
HEY... WHERE THE HECK IS BULMA'S PLACE, ANYWAY?
HOW SHOULD I KNOW?! JUST GET OUTTA MY WAY OR I'LL RUN YOU OVER!!
WHAT'S EVERYBODY IN SUCH A HURRY FOR ?!
HYUUUUUUN
HOTEL HILTON
ONE WAY
HEY! WHERE'S BULMA'S PLACE?!
EH? BULMA... ?
I'M AFRAID I DON'T KNOW...
WHY DON'T YOU ASK SOMEONE ELSE, DEAR?
HUH? YOU LIVE IN THE SAME TOWN AND YOU DON'T KNOW?
THAT'S *BIZARRE*...
I WONDER IF SHE REALLY LIVES HERE...
TAXI
HEY! YOU!
VIIIIN
VMX
APSULE

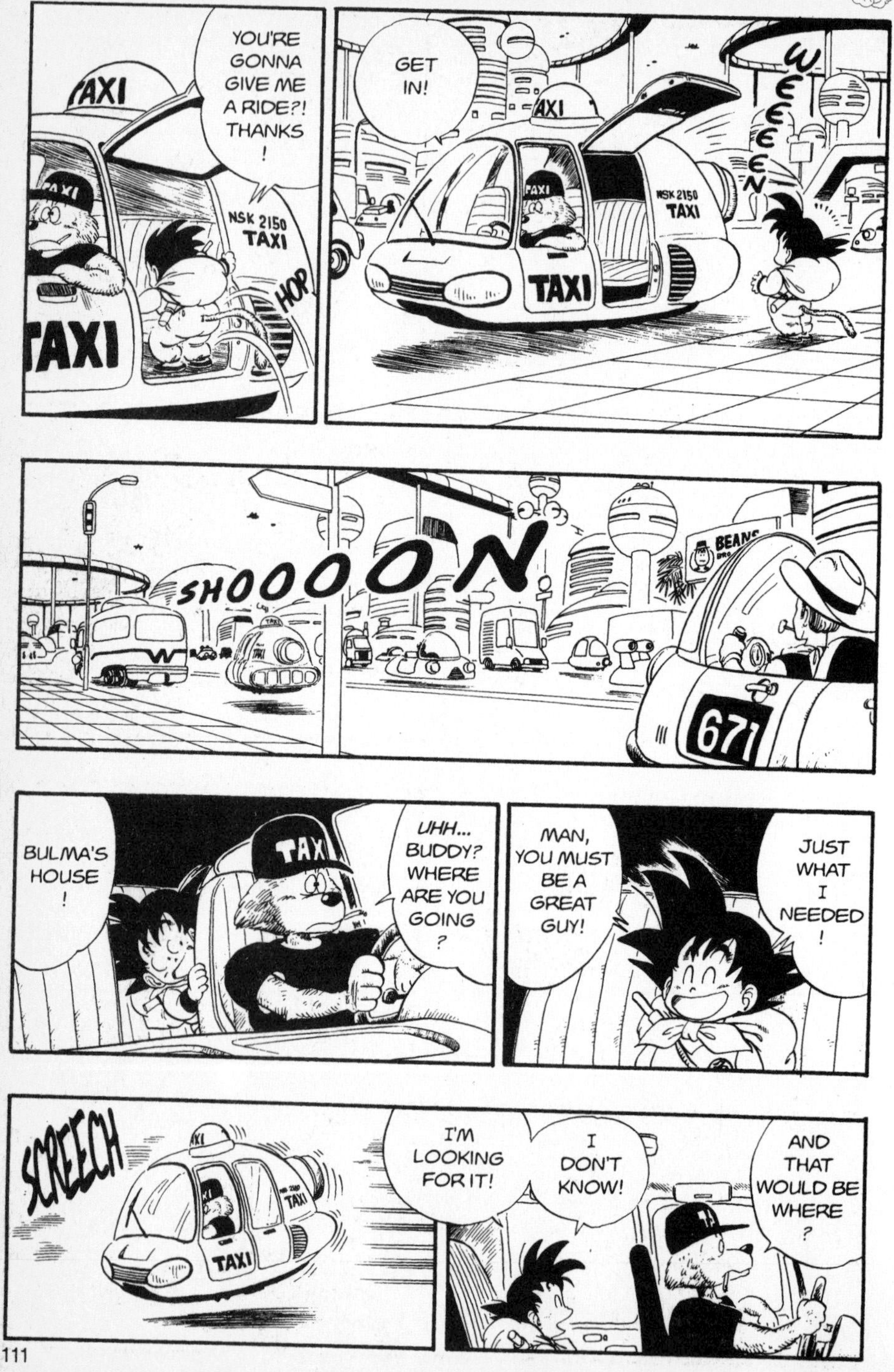
GET IN!
WEEEEEN
YOU'RE GONNA GIVE ME A RIDE?! THANKS!
NSK 2150 TAXI
TAXI
HOP
SHOOOOON
BEANS
671
JUST WHAT I NEEDED!
MAN, YOU MUST BE A GREAT GUY!
UHH... BUDDY? WHERE ARE YOU GOING?
BULMA'S HOUSE!
AND THAT WOULD BE WHERE?
I DON'T KNOW!
I'M LOOKING FOR IT!
SCREECH

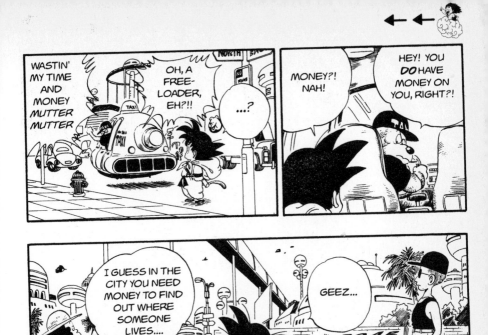

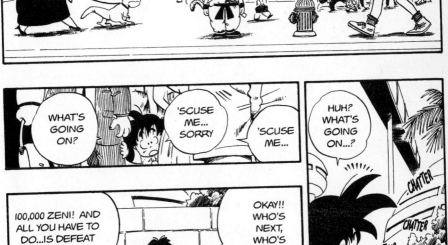

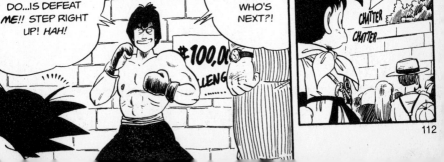

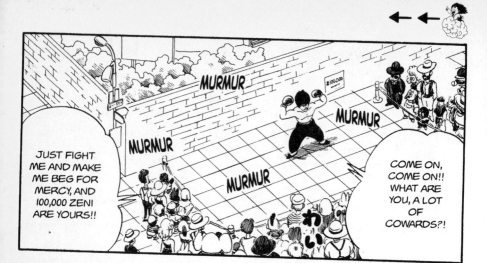

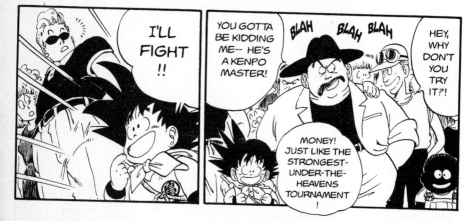

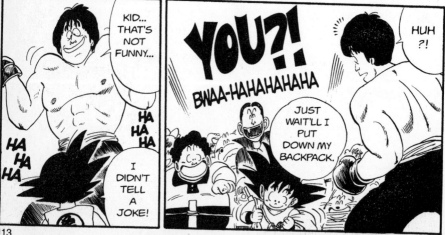

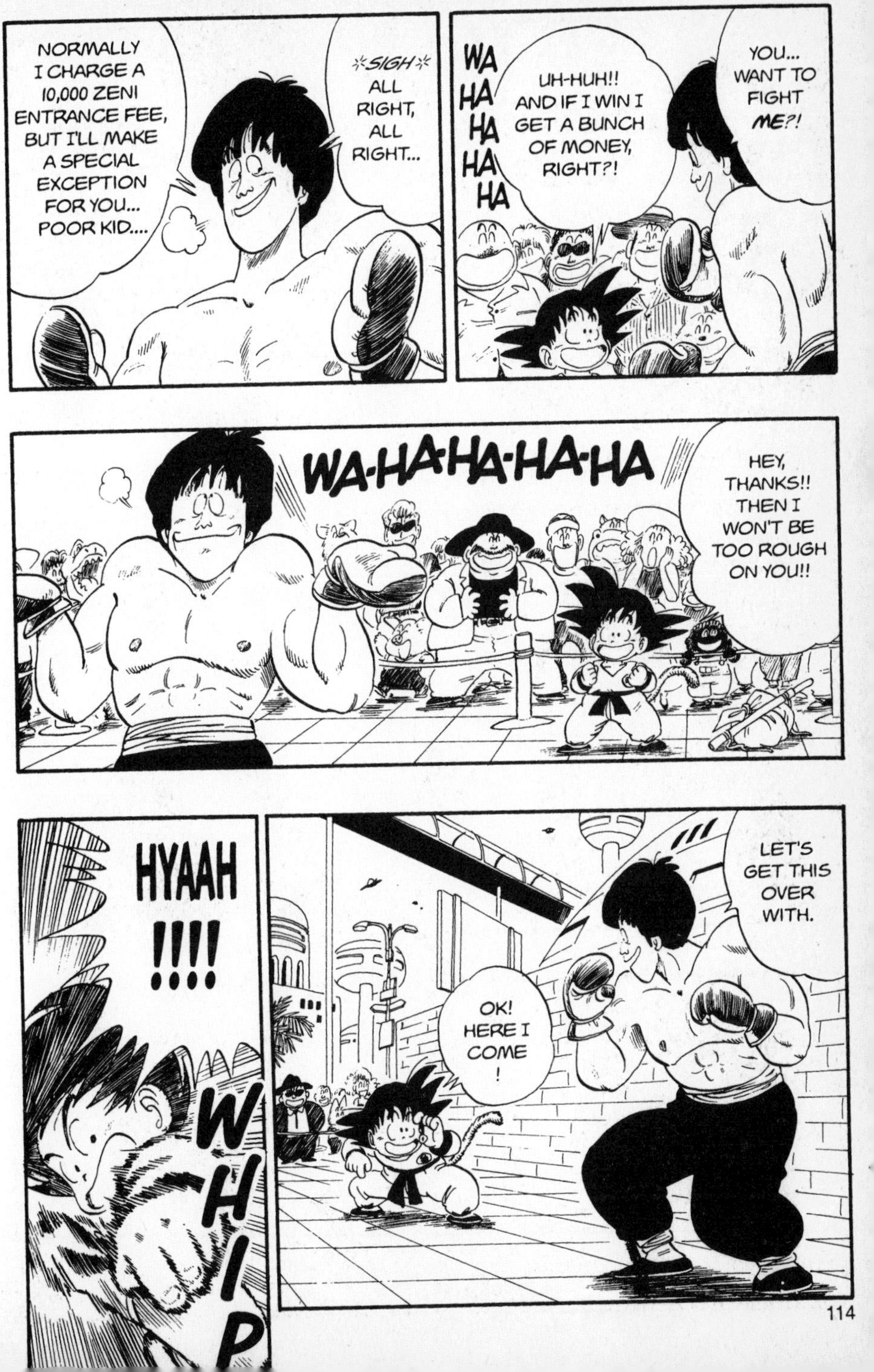
YOU... WANT TO FIGHT ME?!
UH-HUH!! AND IF I WIN I GET A BUNCH OF MONEY, RIGHT?!
WA HA HA HA HA
SIGH ALL RIGHT, ALL RIGHT...
NORMALLY I CHARGE A 10,000 ZENI ENTRANCE FEE, BUT I'LL MAKE A SPECIAL EXCEPTION FOR YOU... POOR KID....
HEY, THANKS!! THEN I WON'T BE TOO ROUGH ON YOU!!
WA-HA-HA-HA-HA
LET'S GET THIS OVER WITH.
OK! HERE I COME!
HYAAH!!!!
WHIP

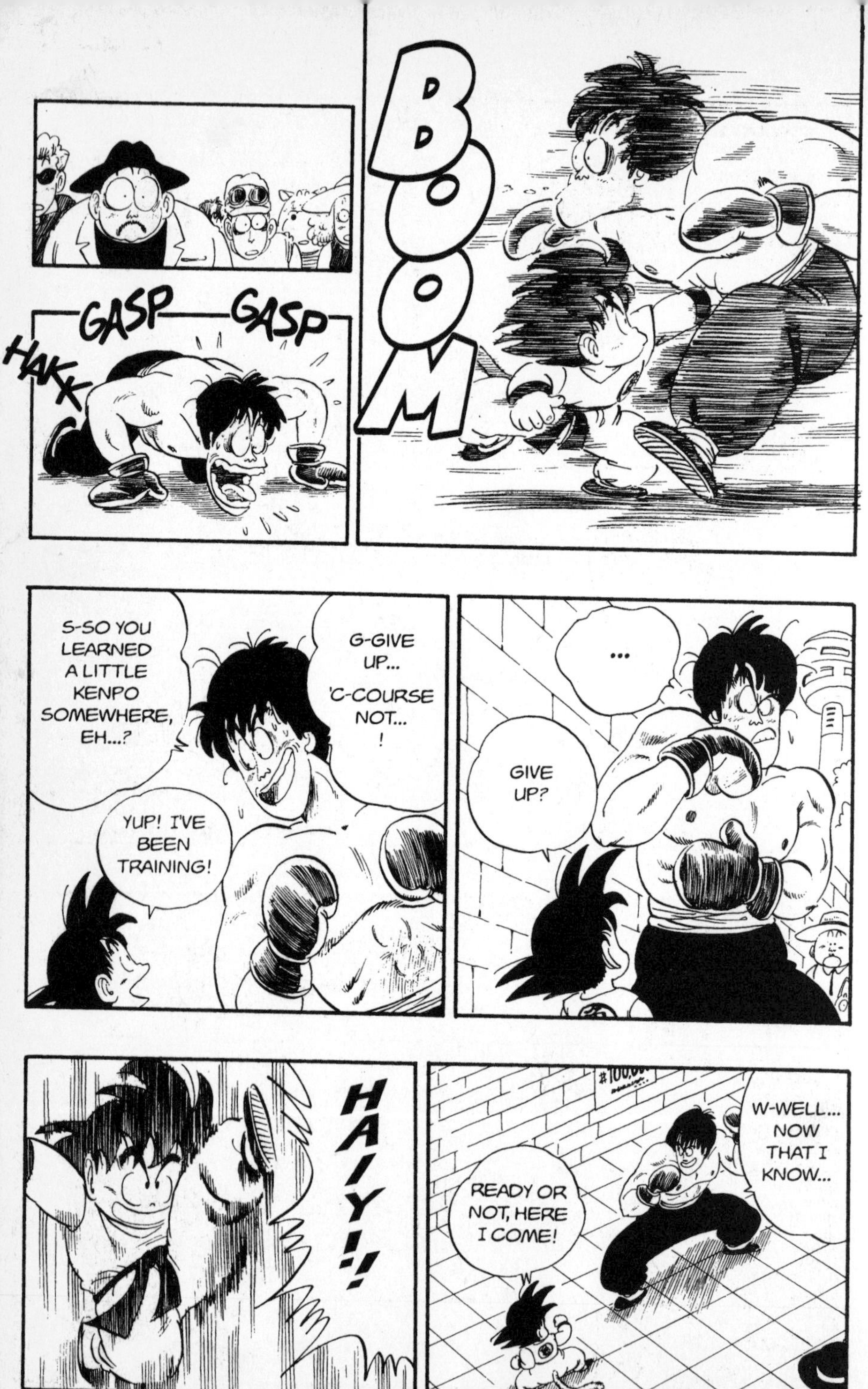
BOOOM
GASP
GASP
HAKK
...
GIVE UP?
G-GIVE UP...
'C-COURSE NOT... !
S-SO YOU LEARNED A LITTLE KENPO SOMEWHERE, EH...?
YUP! I'VE BEEN TRAINING!
W-WELL... NOW THAT I KNOW...
READY OR NOT, HERE I COME!
HAIYY!!!

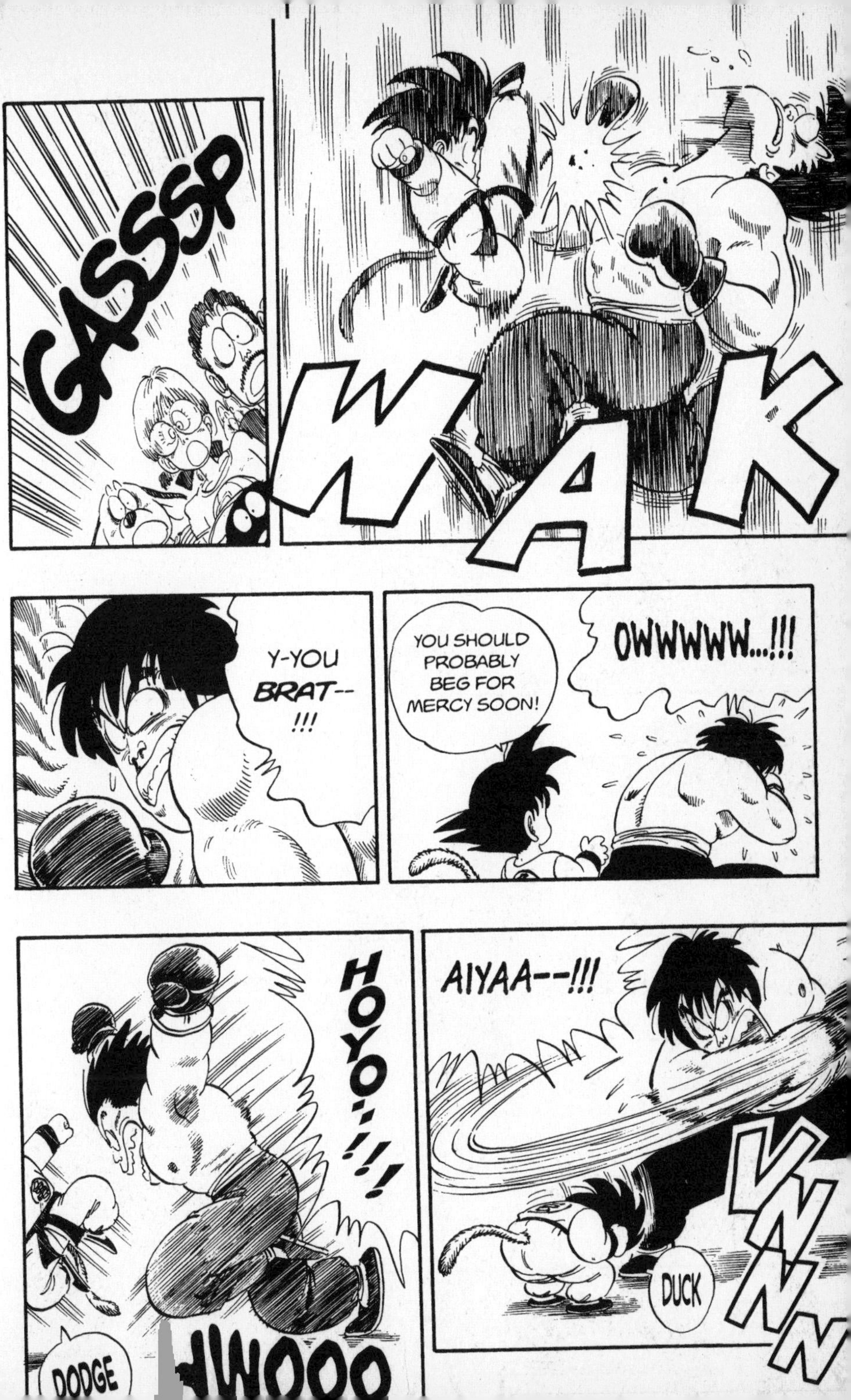
WAK
GASSSP
YOU SHOULD PROBABLY BEG FOR MERCY SOON!
OWWWWW...!!!
Y-YOU BRAT--!!!
AIYAA--!!!
VNNN
DUCK
HOYO..!!!
DODGE

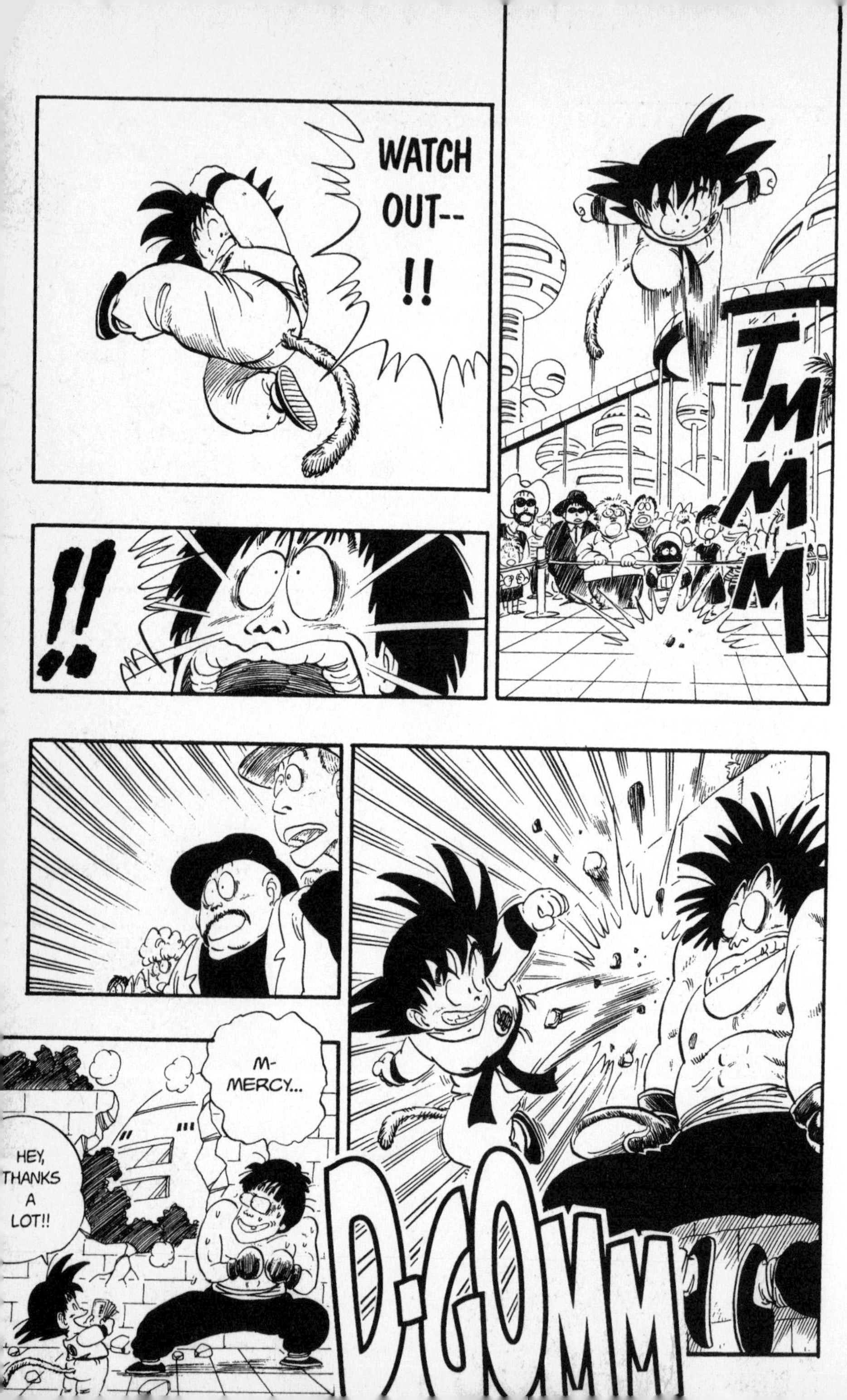
TMMMM
WATCH OUT-- !!
!!
D-GOMM
M-MERCY...
HEY, THANKS A LOT!!

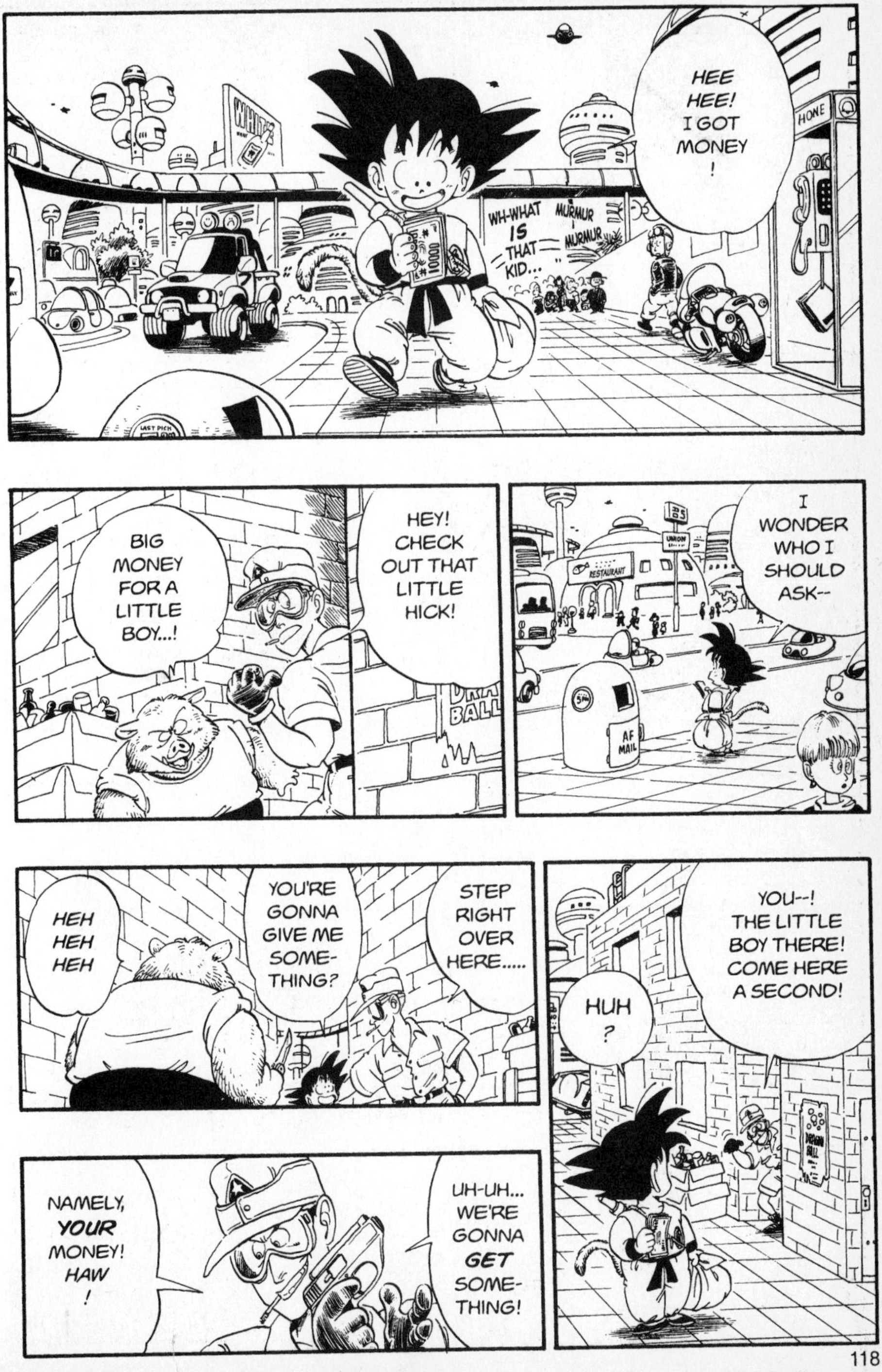
HEE HEE! I GOT MONEY!
WH-WHAT IS THAT KID...
MURMUR MURMUR
I WONDER WHO I SHOULD ASK--
HEY! CHECK OUT THAT LITTLE HICK!
BIG MONEY FOR A LITTLE BOY...!
YOU--! THE LITTLE BOY THERE! COME HERE A SECOND!
HUH?
STEP RIGHT OVER HERE.....
YOU'RE GONNA GIVE ME SOMETHING?
HEH HEH HEH
UH-UH... WE'RE GONNA GET SOMETHING!
NAMELY, YOUR MONEY! HAW!

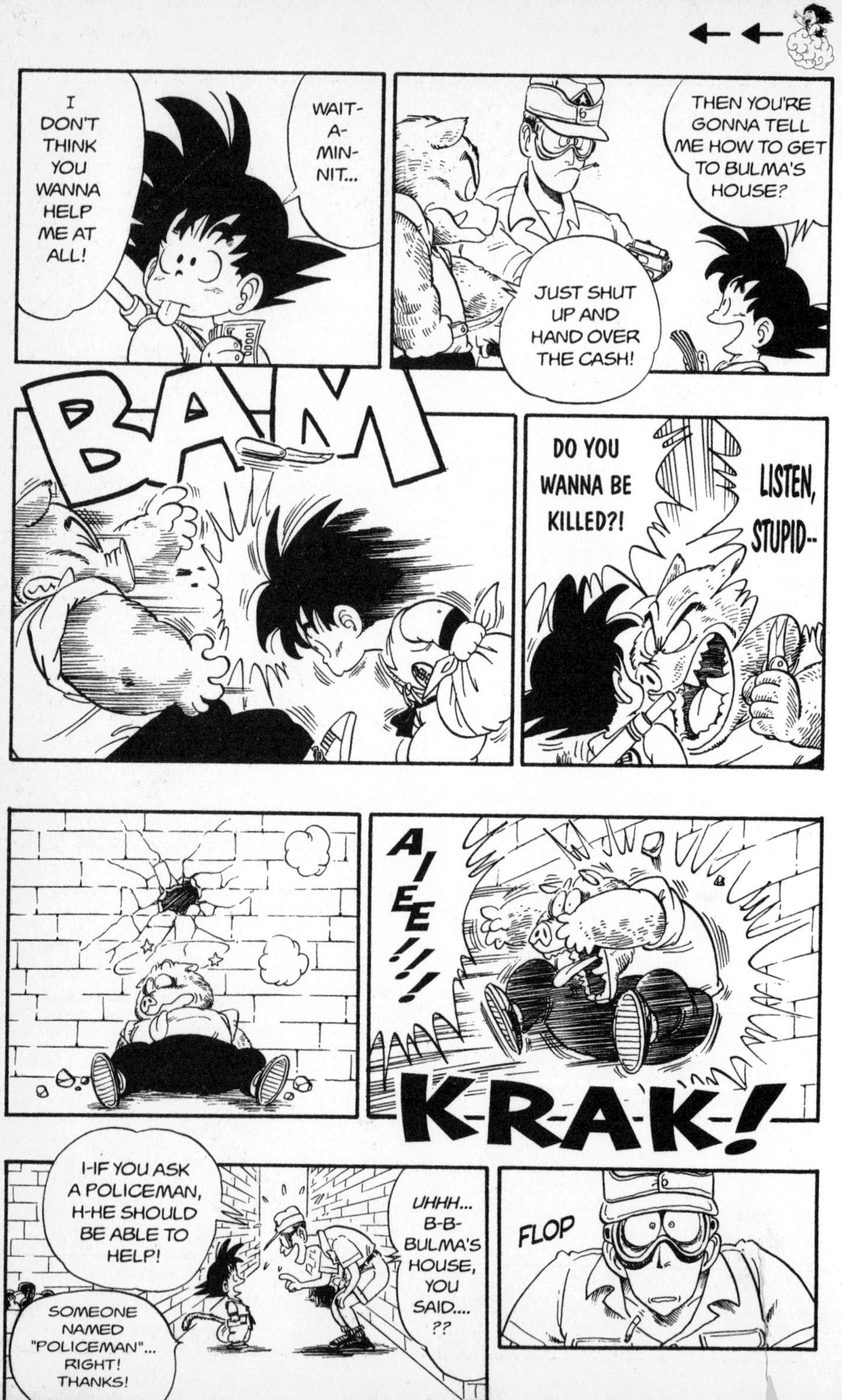
THEN YOU'RE GONNA TELL ME HOW TO GET TO BULMA'S HOUSE?
JUST SHUT UP AND HAND OVER THE CASH!
WAIT-A-MIN-NIT...
I DON'T THINK YOU WANNA HELP ME AT ALL!
LISTEN, STUPID--
DO YOU WANNA BE KILLED?!
BAM
AIEE!!!
KRAK!
FLOP
UHHH... B-B-BULMA'S HOUSE, YOU SAID....??
I-IF YOU ASK A POLICEMAN, H-HE SHOULD BE ABLE TO HELP!
SOMEONE NAMED "POLICEMAN"... RIGHT! THANKS!

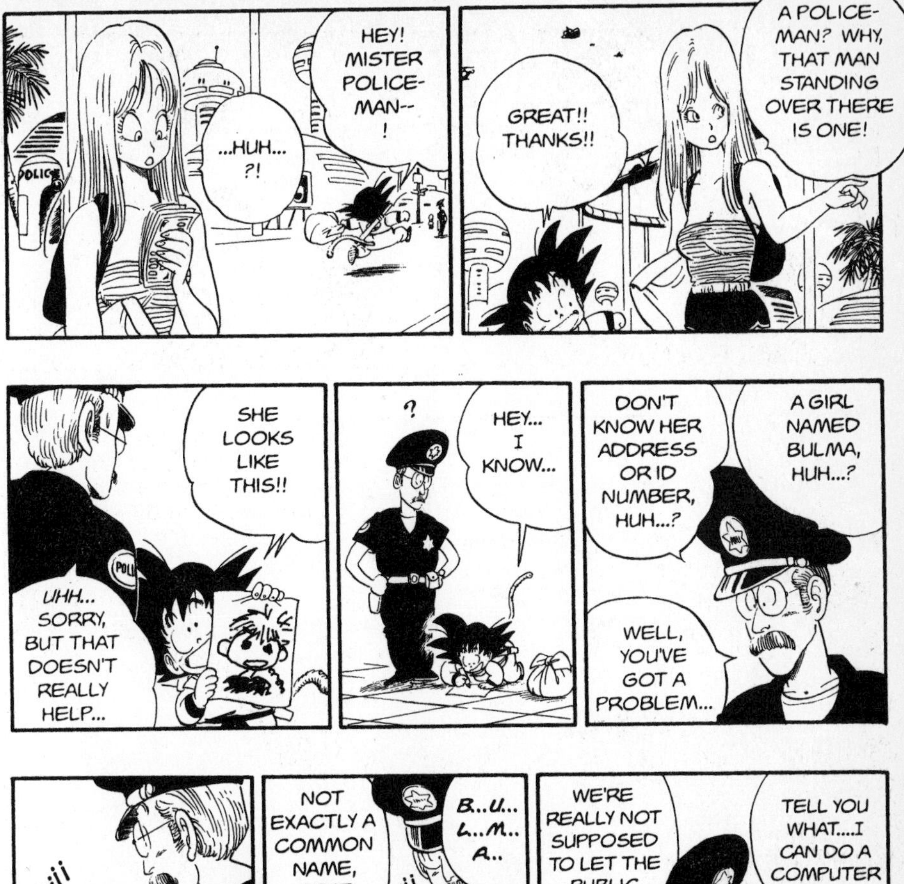
A POLICE-MAN? WHY, THAT MAN STANDING OVER THERE IS ONE!
GREAT!! THANKS!!
HEY! MISTER POLICE-MAN-- !
...HUH... ?!
POLICE
A GIRL NAMED BULMA, HUH...?
DON'T KNOW HER ADDRESS OR ID NUMBER, HUH...?
WELL, YOU'VE GOT A PROBLEM...
?
HEY... I KNOW...
SHE LOOKS LIKE THIS!!
UHH... SORRY, BUT THAT DOESN'T REALLY HELP...
TELL YOU WHAT....I CAN DO A COMPUTER INQUIRY.
WE'RE REALLY NOT SUPPOSED TO LET THE PUBLIC KNOW ABOUT THIS, BUT...
B..U.. L..M.. A..
NOT EXACTLY A COMMON NAME, SO IT SHOULDN'T TAKE TOO...
piii piii
POLICE
piii
WHOA! THERE ARE THREE OF 'EM! LET'S SEE...
IS THIS HER ?
NOPE
KM 118755 BULMA
ICE
THEN WHAT ABOUT THIS ONE?
piii
SSC 41453 BULMA
THAT'S HER!!

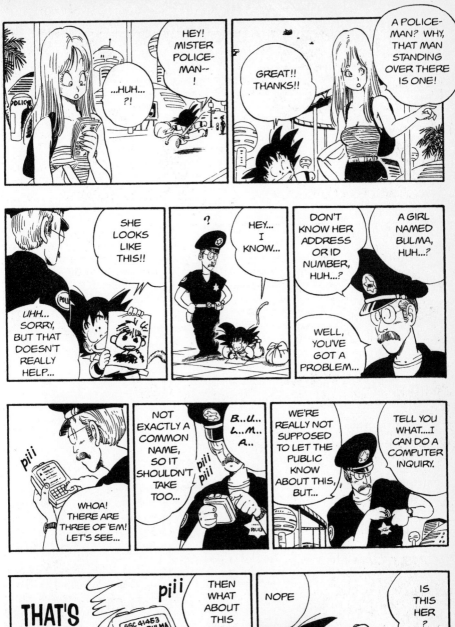

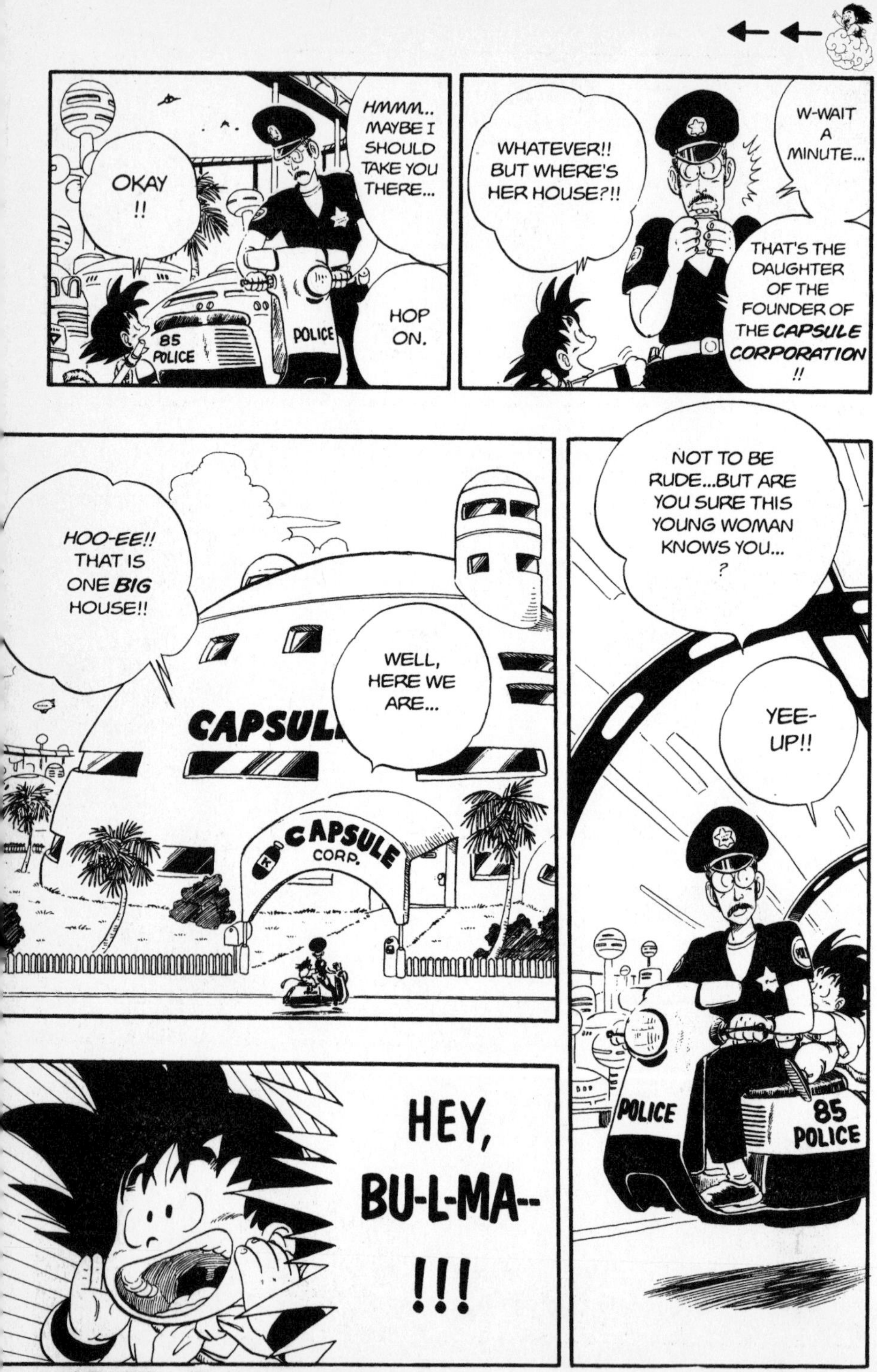
W-WAIT A MINUTE...
THAT'S THE DAUGHTER OF THE FOUNDER OF THE CAPSULE CORPORATION !!
WHATEVER!! BUT WHERE'S HER HOUSE?!!
HMMM... MAYBE I SHOULD TAKE YOU THERE...
HOP ON.
OKAY !!
POLICE
85 POLICE
NOT TO BE RUDE...BUT ARE YOU SURE THIS YOUNG WOMAN KNOWS YOU... ?
YEE-UP!!
POLICE
85 POLICE
WELL, HERE WE ARE...
HOO-EE!! THAT IS ONE BIG HOUSE!!
CAPSUL
CAPSULE CORP.
HEY, BU-L-MA-- !!!

NEXT: Bulma at Home

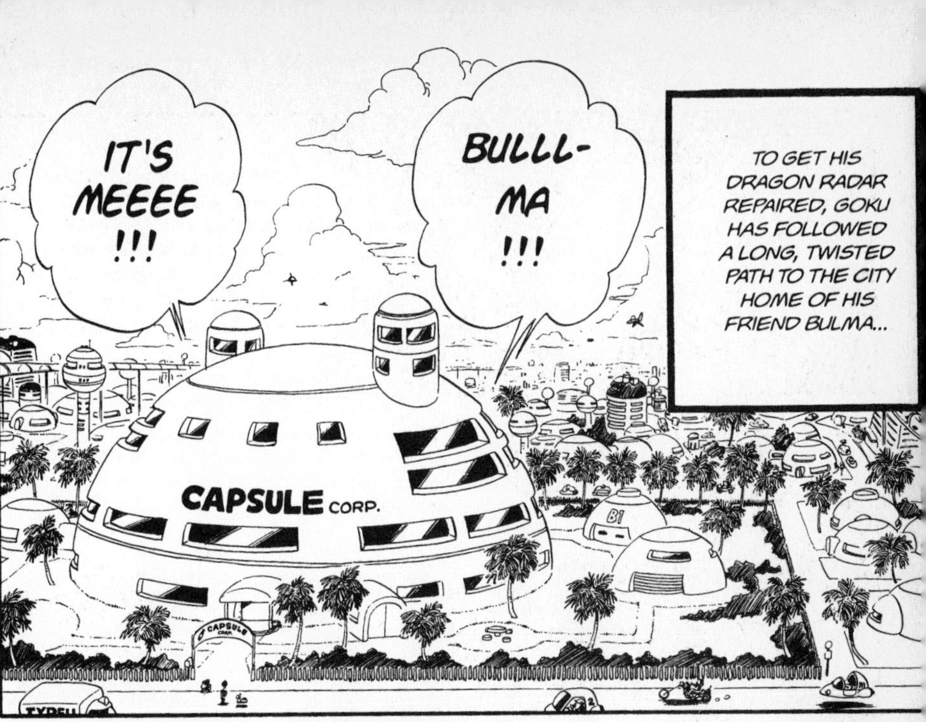
TO GET HIS DRAGON RADAR REPAIRED, GOKU HAS FOLLOWED A LONG, TWISTED PATH TO THE CITY HOME OF HIS FRIEND BULMA...
BULLL-MA !!!
IT'S MEEEE !!!
CAPSULE CORP.

Tale 69 • Bulma and Goku

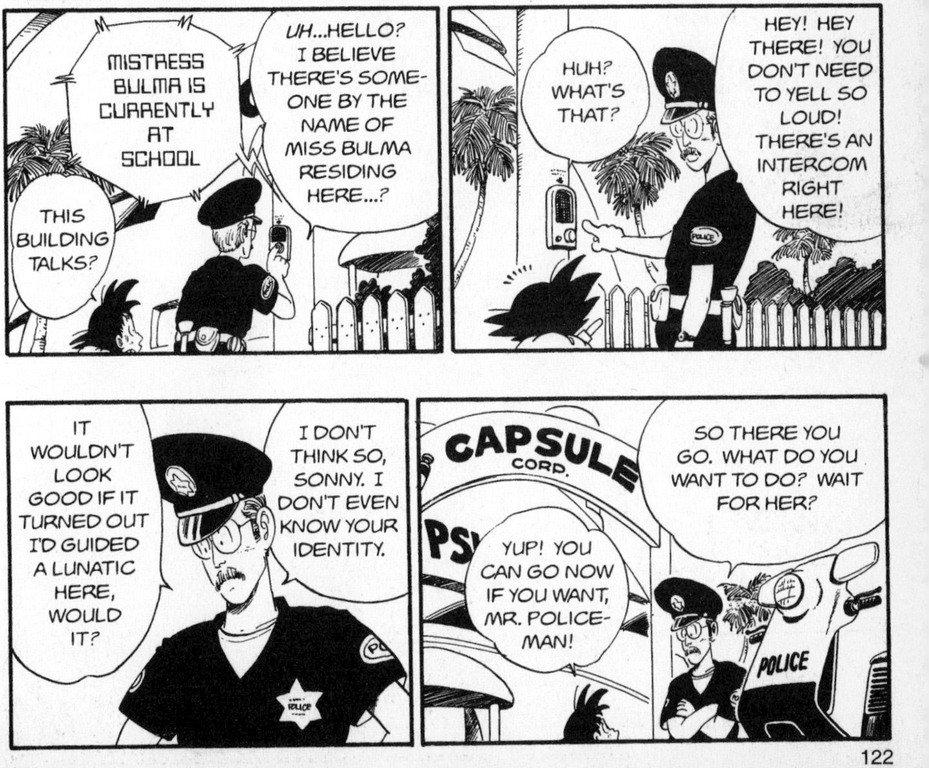
HEY! HEY THERE! YOU DON'T NEED TO YELL SO LOUD! THERE'S AN INTERCOM RIGHT HERE!
HUH? WHAT'S THAT?
UH...HELLO? I BELIEVE THERE'S SOME-ONE BY THE NAME OF MISS BULMA RESIDING HERE...?
MISTRESS BULMA IS CURRENTLY AT SCHOOL
THIS BUILDING TALKS?
SO THERE YOU GO. WHAT DO YOU WANT TO DO? WAIT FOR HER?
YUP! YOU CAN GO NOW IF YOU WANT, MR. POLICE-MAN!
CAPSULE CORP.
POLICE
I DON'T THINK SO, SONNY. I DON'T EVEN KNOW YOUR IDENTITY.
IT WOULDN'T LOOK GOOD IF IT TURNED OUT I'D GUIDED A LUNATIC HERE, WOULD IT?

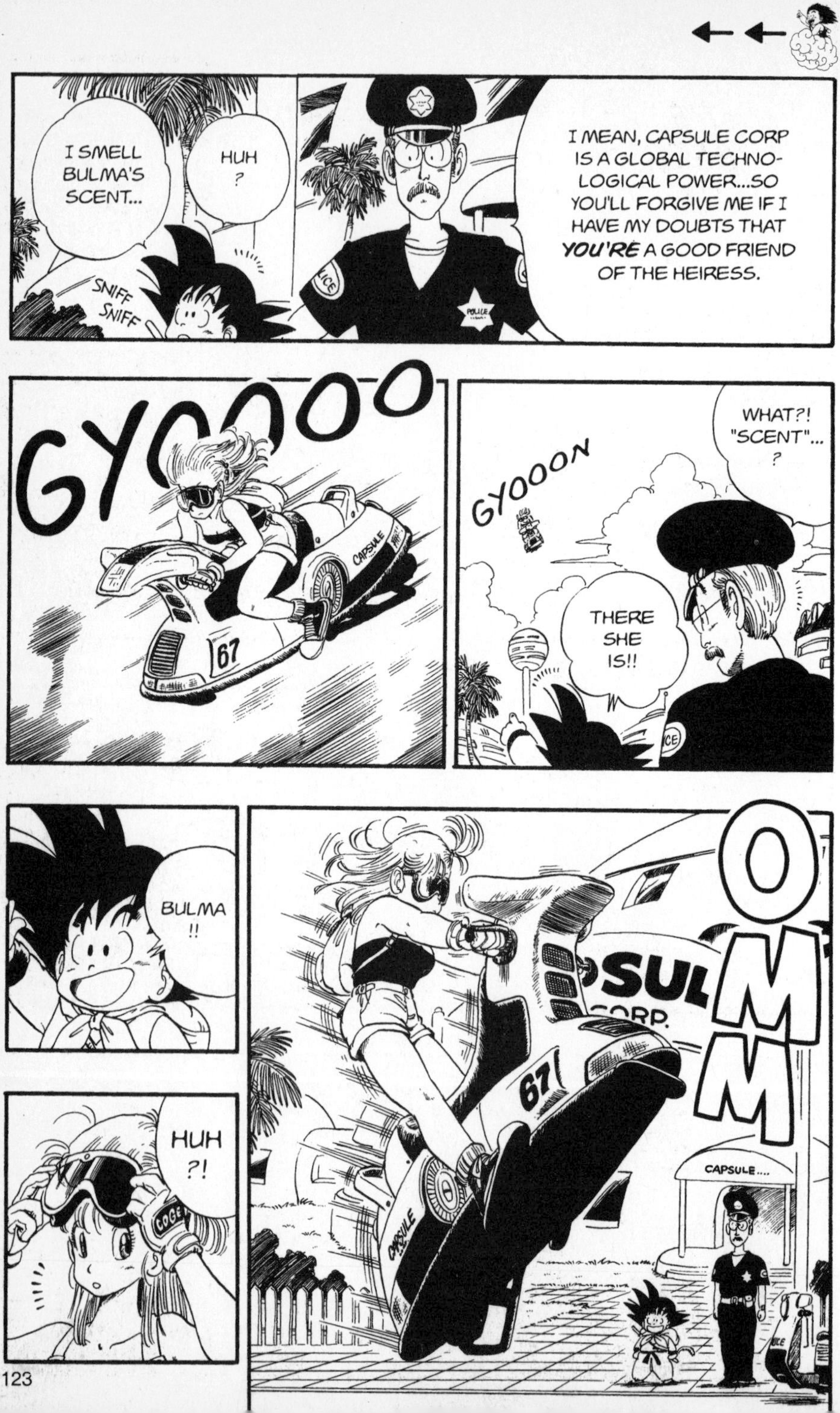
I MEAN, CAPSULE CORP IS A GLOBAL TECHNOLOGICAL POWER...SO YOU'LL FORGIVE ME IF I HAVE MY DOUBTS THAT ***YOU'RE*** A GOOD FRIEND OF THE HEIRESS.
POLICE
I SMELL BULMA'S SCENT...
HUH ?
SNIFF SNIFF
WHAT?! "SCENT"... ?
GYOOON
THERE SHE IS!!
GYOOOO
CAPSULE
67
OMMM
SUL CORP.
67
CAPSULE
CAPSULE....
BULMA !!
HUH ?!

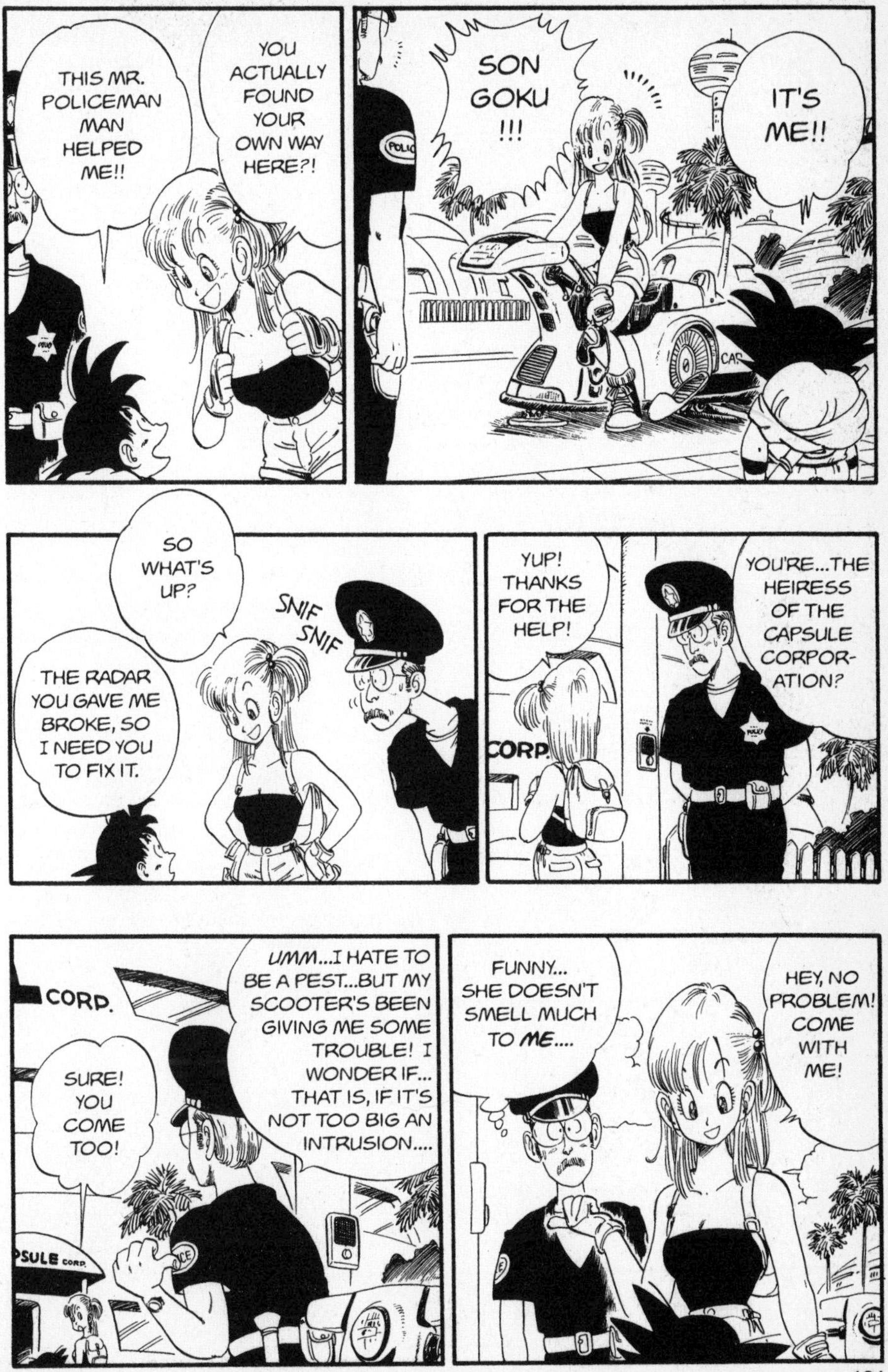
IT'S ME!!
SON GOKU !!!
YOU ACTUALLY FOUND YOUR OWN WAY HERE?!
THIS MR. POLICEMAN MAN HELPED ME!!
YOU'RE...THE HEIRESS OF THE CAPSULE CORPOR-ATION?
YUP! THANKS FOR THE HELP!
SO WHAT'S UP?
SNIF SNIF
THE RADAR YOU GAVE ME BROKE, SO I NEED YOU TO FIX IT.
HEY, NO PROBLEM! COME WITH ME!
FUNNY... SHE DOESN'T SMELL MUCH TO *ME*....
UMM...I HATE TO BE A PEST...BUT MY SCOOTER'S BEEN GIVING ME SOME TROUBLE! I WONDER IF... THAT IS, IF IT'S NOT TOO BIG AN INTRUSION....
SURE! YOU COME TOO!

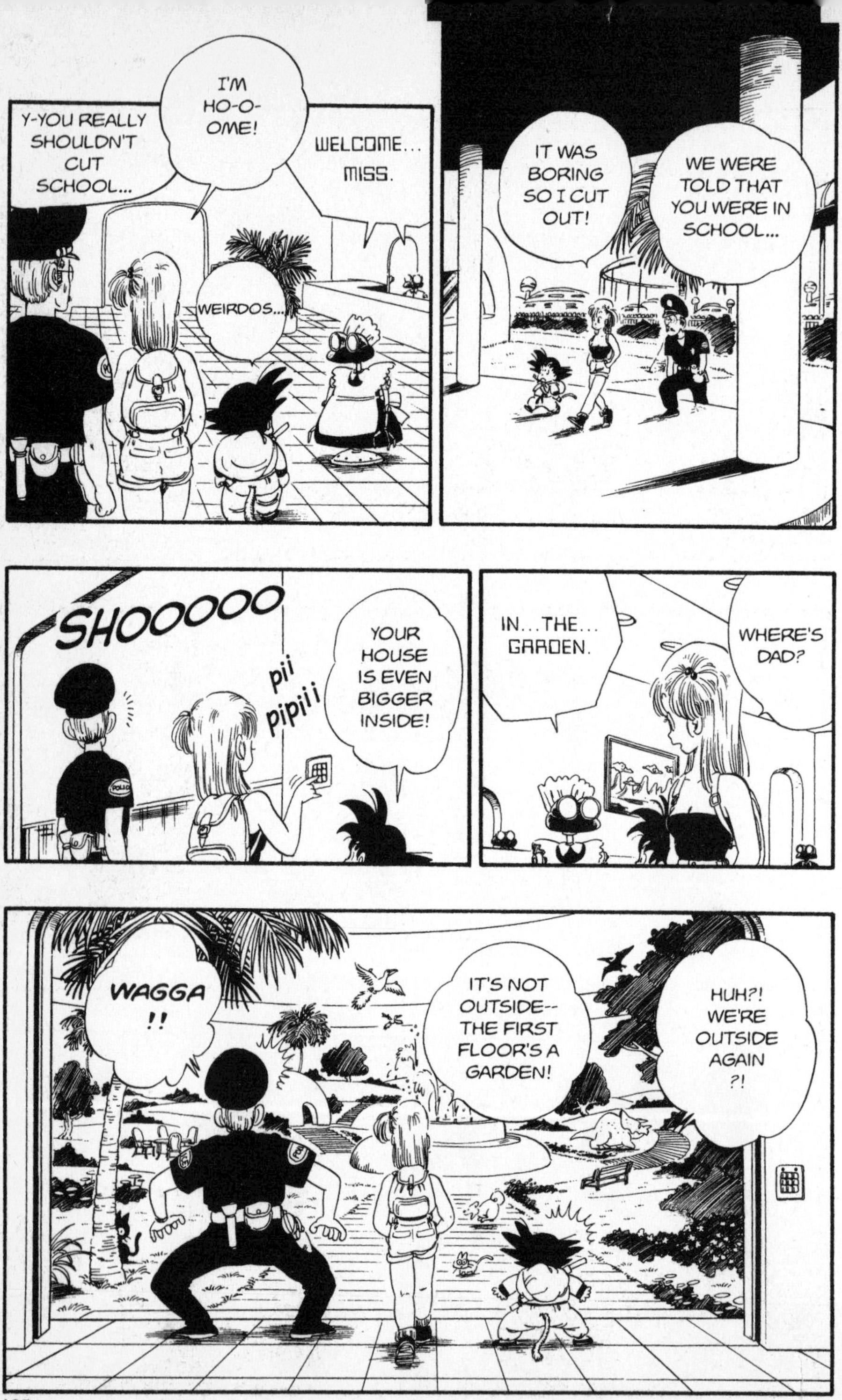
WE WERE TOLD THAT YOU WERE IN SCHOOL...
IT WAS BORING SO I CUT OUT!
WELCOME... MISS.
I'M HO-O-OME!
Y-YOU REALLY SHOULDN'T CUT SCHOOL...
WEIRDOS...
WHERE'S DAD?
IN... THE... GARDEN.
YOUR HOUSE IS EVEN BIGGER INSIDE!
pii pipiii
SHOOOOO
HUH?! WE'RE OUTSIDE AGAIN ?!
IT'S NOT OUTSIDE-- THE FIRST FLOOR'S A GARDEN!
WAGGA !!

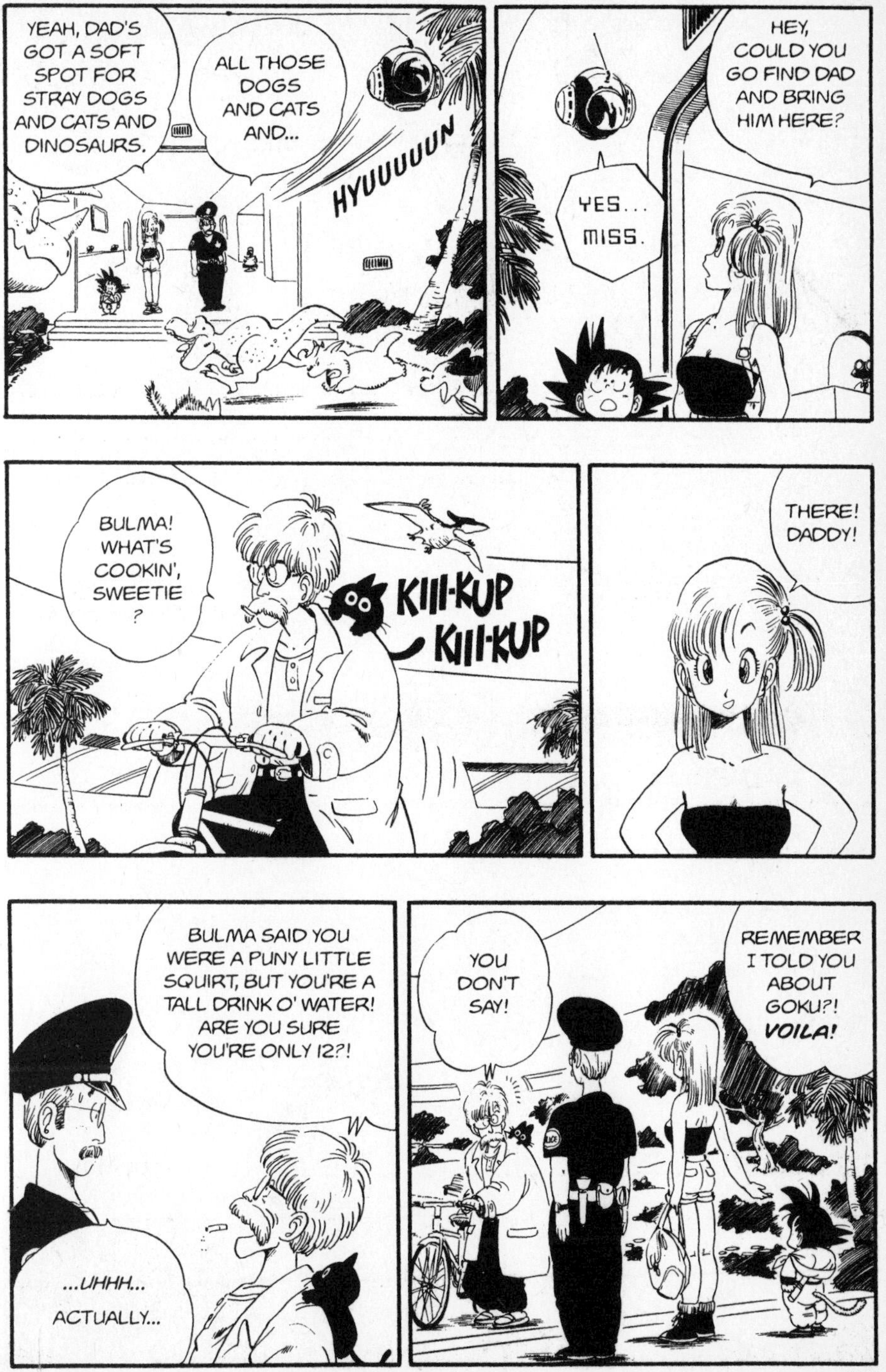
HEY, COULD YOU GO FIND DAD AND BRING HIM HERE?
YES... MISS.
ALL THOSE DOGS AND CATS AND...
YEAH, DAD'S GOT A SOFT SPOT FOR STRAY DOGS AND CATS AND DINOSAURS.
HYUUUUUN
THERE! DADDY!
BULMA! WHAT'S COOKIN', SWEETIE?
KIII-KUP
KIII-KUP
REMEMBER I TOLD YOU ABOUT GOKU?! ***VOILA!***
YOU DON'T SAY!
BULMA SAID YOU WERE A PUNY LITTLE SQUIRT, BUT YOU'RE A TALL DRINK O' WATER! ARE YOU SURE YOU'RE ONLY 12?!
...UHHH... ACTUALLY...

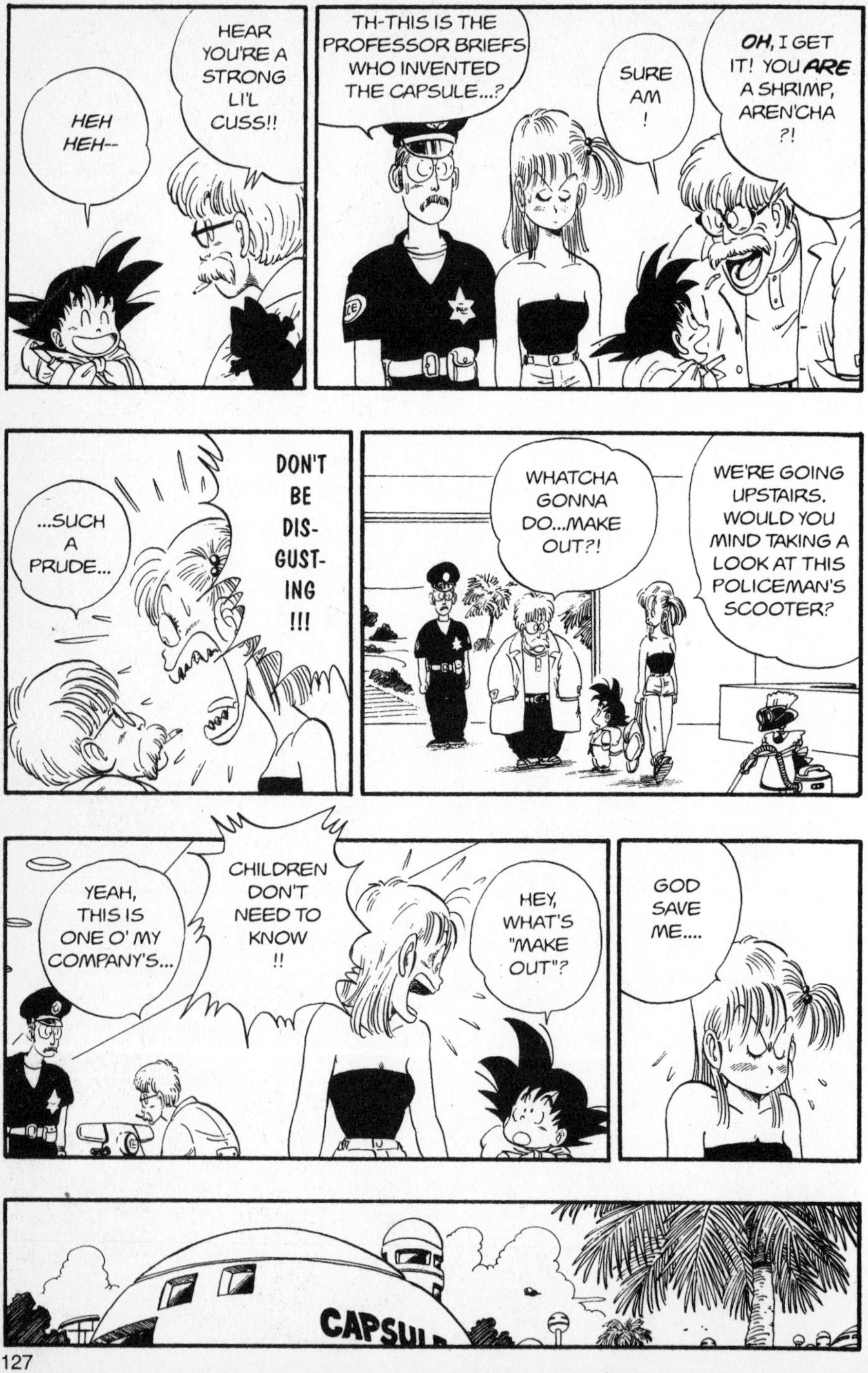
OH, I GET IT! YOU ARE A SHRIMP, AREN'CHA ?!
SURE AM !
TH-THIS IS THE PROFESSOR BRIEFS WHO INVENTED THE CAPSULE...?
HEAR YOU'RE A STRONG LI'L CUSS!!
HEH HEH--
WE'RE GOING UPSTAIRS. WOULD YOU MIND TAKING A LOOK AT THIS POLICEMAN'S SCOOTER?
WHATCHA GONNA DO...MAKE OUT?!
DON'T BE DIS-GUST-ING !!!
...SUCH A PRUDE...
GOD SAVE ME....
HEY, WHAT'S "MAKE OUT"?
CHILDREN DON'T NEED TO KNOW !!
YEAH, THIS IS ONE O' MY COMPANY'S...
CAPSUL

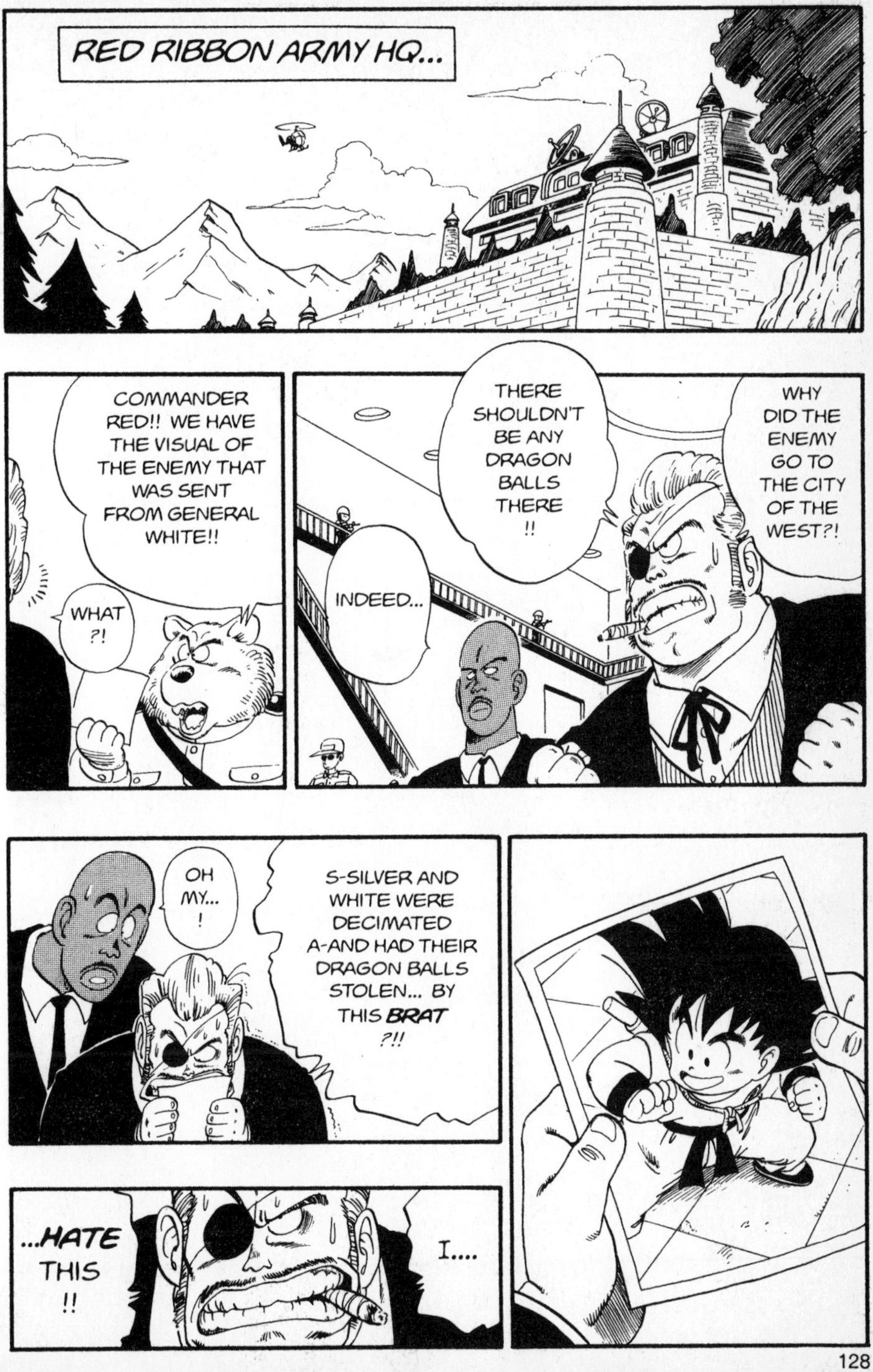
RED RIBBON ARMY HQ...
WHY DID THE ENEMY GO TO THE CITY OF THE WEST?!
THERE SHOULDN'T BE ANY DRAGON BALLS THERE!!
INDEED...
COMMANDER RED!! WE HAVE THE VISUAL OF THE ENEMY THAT WAS SENT FROM GENERAL WHITE!!
WHAT?!
S-SILVER AND WHITE WERE DECIMATED A-AND HAD THEIR DRAGON BALLS STOLEN... BY THIS ***BRAT***?!!
OH MY...!
I....
...HATE THIS!!

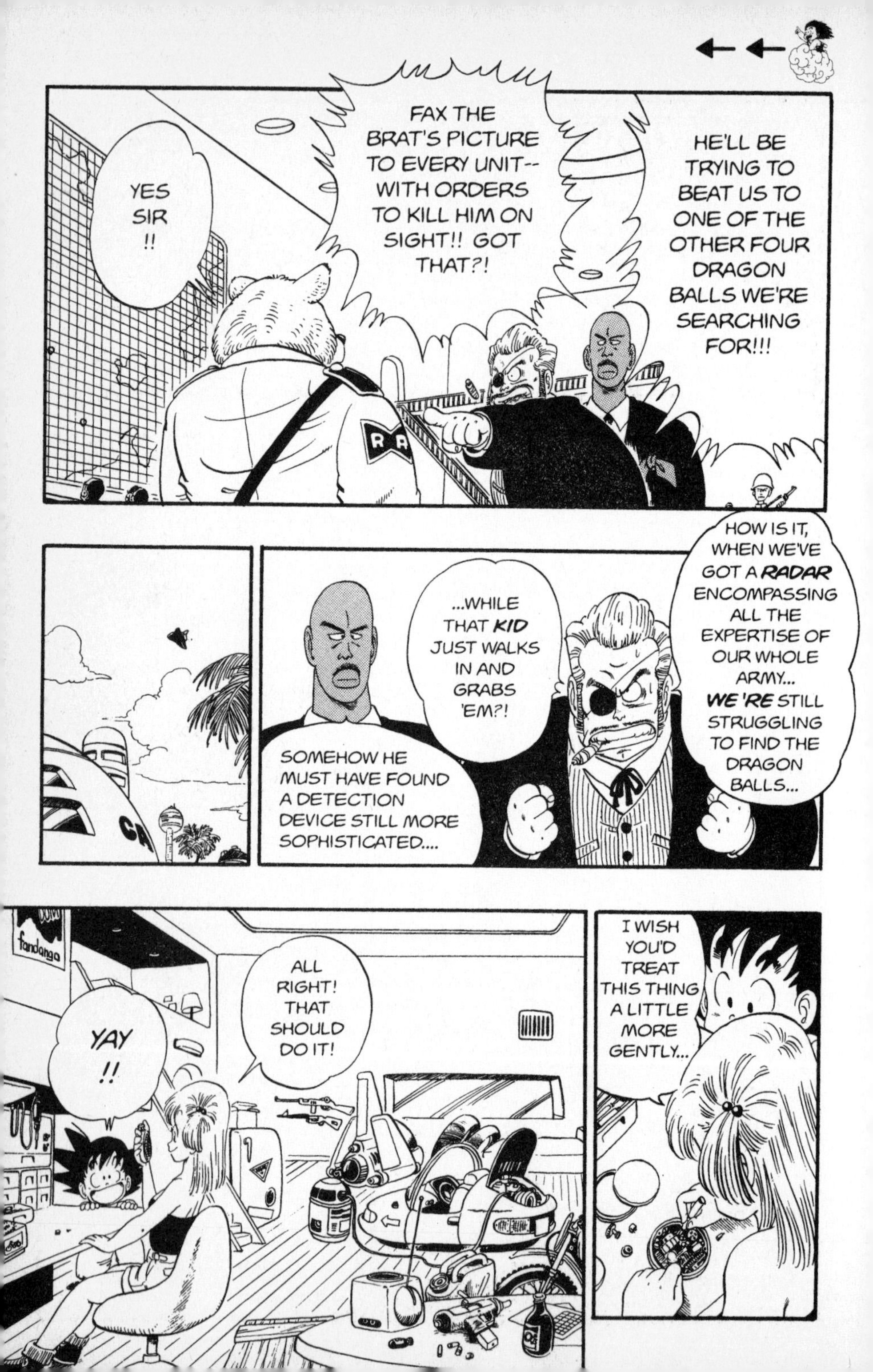
HE'LL BE TRYING TO BEAT US TO ONE OF THE OTHER FOUR DRAGON BALLS WE'RE SEARCHING FOR!!!
FAX THE BRAT'S PICTURE TO EVERY UNIT-- WITH ORDERS TO KILL HIM ON SIGHT!! GOT THAT?!
YES SIR !!
HOW IS IT, WHEN WE'VE GOT A **RADAR** ENCOMPASSING ALL THE EXPERTISE OF OUR WHOLE ARMY... **WE'RE** STILL STRUGGLING TO FIND THE DRAGON BALLS...
...WHILE THAT **KID** JUST WALKS IN AND GRABS 'EM?!
SOMEHOW HE MUST HAVE FOUND A DETECTION DEVICE STILL MORE SOPHISTICATED....
I WISH YOU'D TREAT THIS THING A LITTLE MORE GENTLY...
ALL RIGHT! THAT SHOULD DO IT!
fandanga
YAY !!

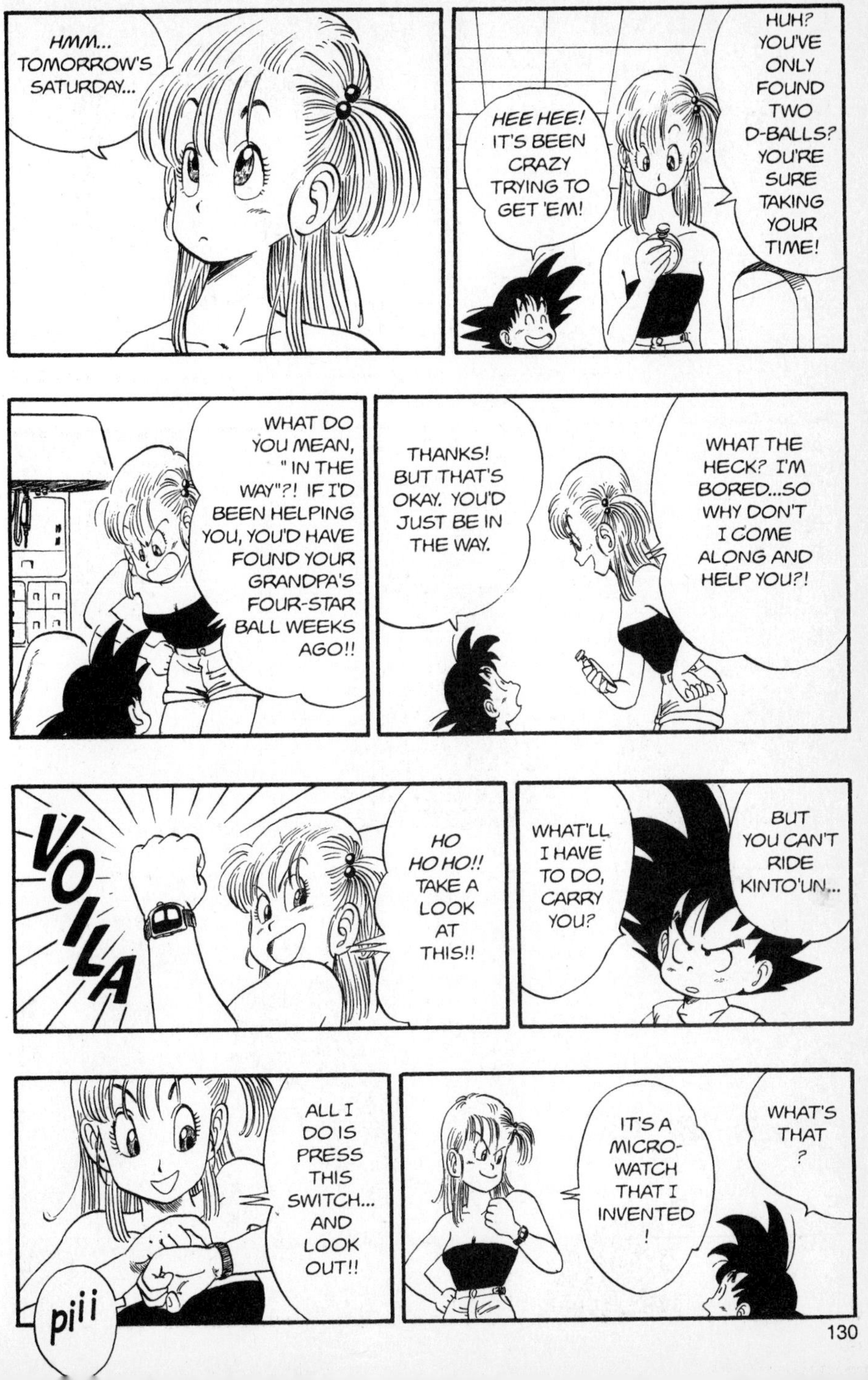
HUH? YOU'VE ONLY FOUND TWO D-BALLS? YOU'RE SURE TAKING YOUR TIME!
HEE HEE! IT'S BEEN CRAZY TRYING TO GET 'EM!
HMM... TOMORROW'S SATURDAY...
WHAT THE HECK? I'M BORED...SO WHY DON'T I COME ALONG AND HELP YOU?!
THANKS! BUT THAT'S OKAY. YOU'D JUST BE IN THE WAY.
WHAT DO YOU MEAN, " IN THE WAY"?! IF I'D BEEN HELPING YOU, YOU'D HAVE FOUND YOUR GRANDPA'S FOUR-STAR BALL WEEKS AGO!!
BUT YOU CAN'T RIDE KINTO'UN...
WHAT'LL I HAVE TO DO, CARRY YOU?
HO HO HO!! TAKE A LOOK AT THIS!!
VOILA
WHAT'S THAT ?
IT'S A MICRO-WATCH THAT I INVENTED !
ALL I DO IS PRESS THIS SWITCH... AND LOOK OUT!!
piii

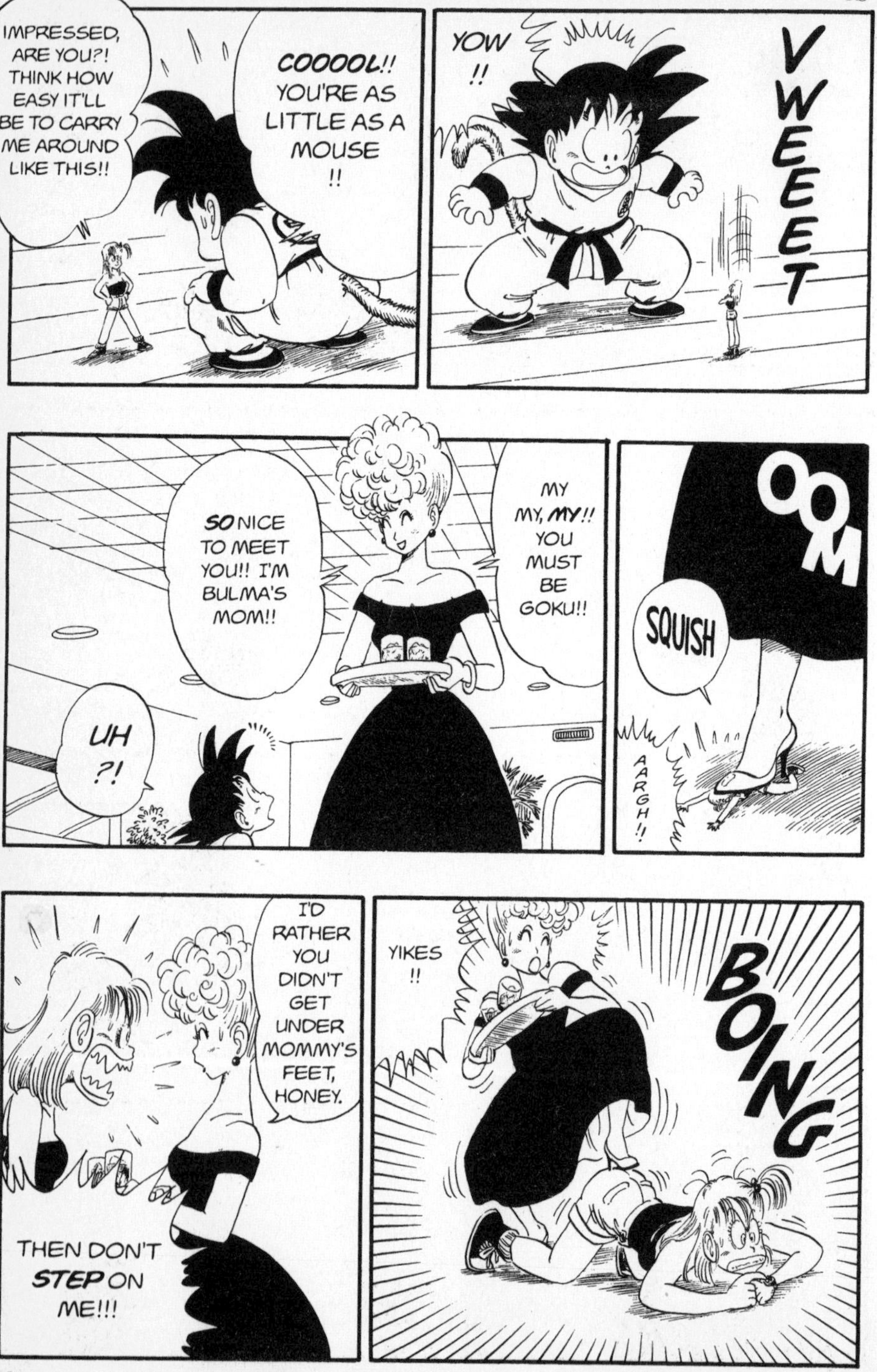
VWEEET
YOW !!
COOOOL!! YOU'RE AS LITTLE AS A MOUSE !!
IMPRESSED, ARE YOU?! THINK HOW EASY IT'LL BE TO CARRY ME AROUND LIKE THIS!!
OOM
SQUISH
AARGH!!
MY MY, MY!! YOU MUST BE GOKU!!
SO NICE TO MEET YOU!! I'M BULMA'S MOM!!
UH ?!
BOING
YIKES !!
I'D RATHER YOU DIDN'T GET UNDER MOMMY'S FEET, HONEY.
THEN DON'T STEP ON ME!!!

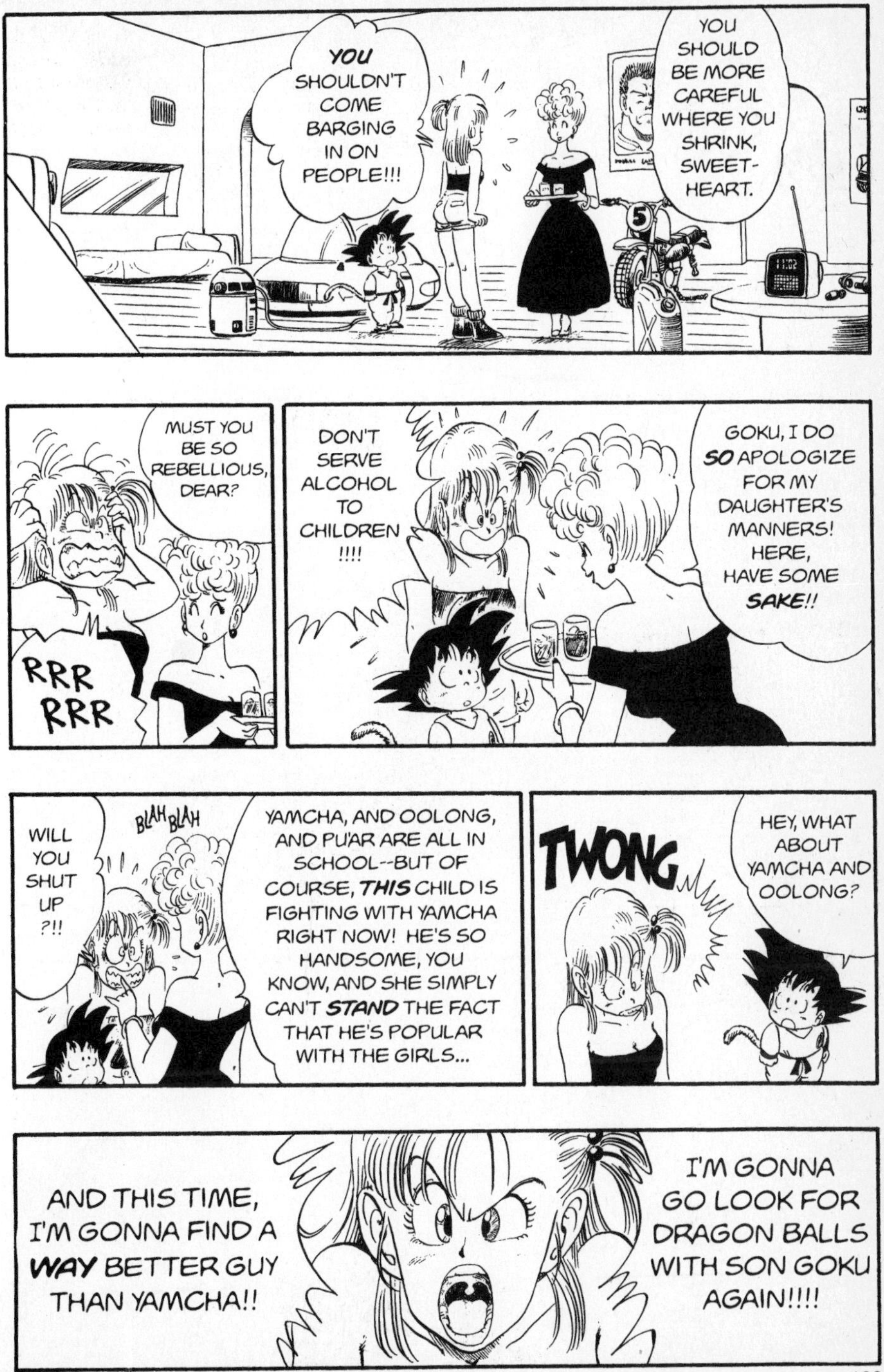
YOU SHOULD BE MORE CAREFUL WHERE YOU SHRINK, SWEET-HEART.
YOU SHOULDN'T COME BARGING IN ON PEOPLE!!!
GOKU, I DO SO APOLOGIZE FOR MY DAUGHTER'S MANNERS! HERE, HAVE SOME SAKE!!
DON'T SERVE ALCOHOL TO CHILDREN !!!!
MUST YOU BE SO REBELLIOUS, DEAR?
RRR RRR
HEY, WHAT ABOUT YAMCHA AND OOLONG?
TWONG
YAMCHA, AND OOLONG, AND PU'AR ARE ALL IN SCHOOL--BUT OF COURSE, THIS CHILD IS FIGHTING WITH YAMCHA RIGHT NOW! HE'S SO HANDSOME, YOU KNOW, AND SHE SIMPLY CAN'T STAND THE FACT THAT HE'S POPULAR WITH THE GIRLS...
BLAH BLAH
WILL YOU SHUT UP ?!!
I'M GONNA GO LOOK FOR DRAGON BALLS WITH SON GOKU AGAIN!!!!
AND THIS TIME, I'M GONNA FIND A WAY BETTER GUY THAN YAMCHA!!

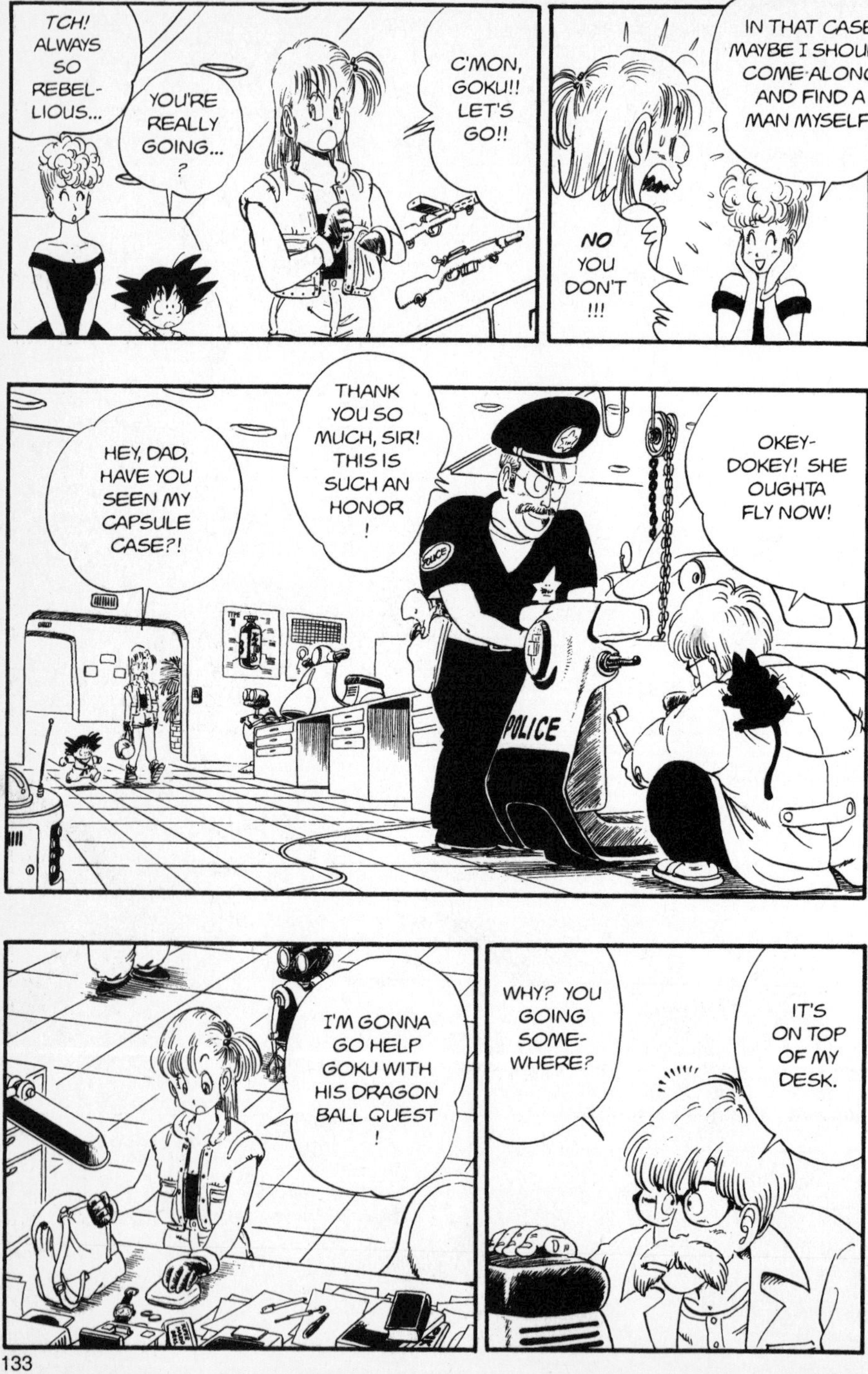
IN THAT CASE MAYBE I SHOULD COME ALONG AND FIND A MAN MYSELF!
NO YOU DON'T !!!
C'MON, GOKU!! LET'S GO!!
YOU'RE REALLY GOING...?
TCH! ALWAYS SO REBEL-LIOUS...
OKEY-DOKEY! SHE OUGHTA FLY NOW!
THANK YOU SO MUCH, SIR! THIS IS SUCH AN HONOR!
HEY, DAD, HAVE YOU SEEN MY CAPSULE CASE?!
POLICE
IT'S ON TOP OF MY DESK.
WHY? YOU GOING SOME-WHERE?
I'M GONNA GO HELP GOKU WITH HIS DRAGON BALL QUEST!

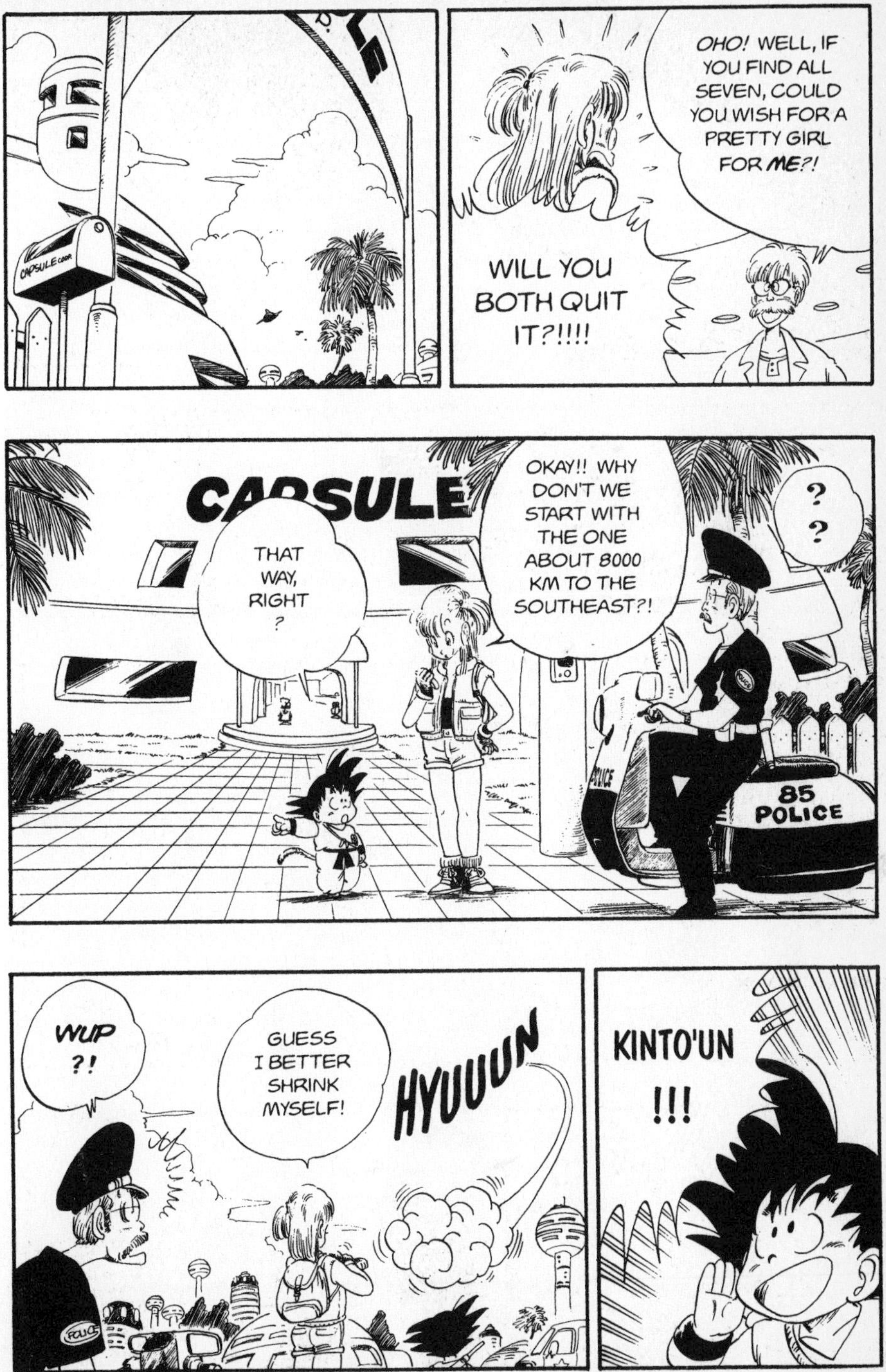
OHO! WELL, IF YOU FIND ALL SEVEN, COULD YOU WISH FOR A PRETTY GIRL FOR ME?!
WILL YOU BOTH QUIT IT?!!!!
??
OKAY!! WHY DON'T WE START WITH THE ONE ABOUT 8000 KM TO THE SOUTHEAST?!
CAPSULE
THAT WAY, RIGHT?
85 POLICE
KINTO'UN !!!
HYUUUN
GUESS I BETTER SHRINK MYSELF!
WUP ?!

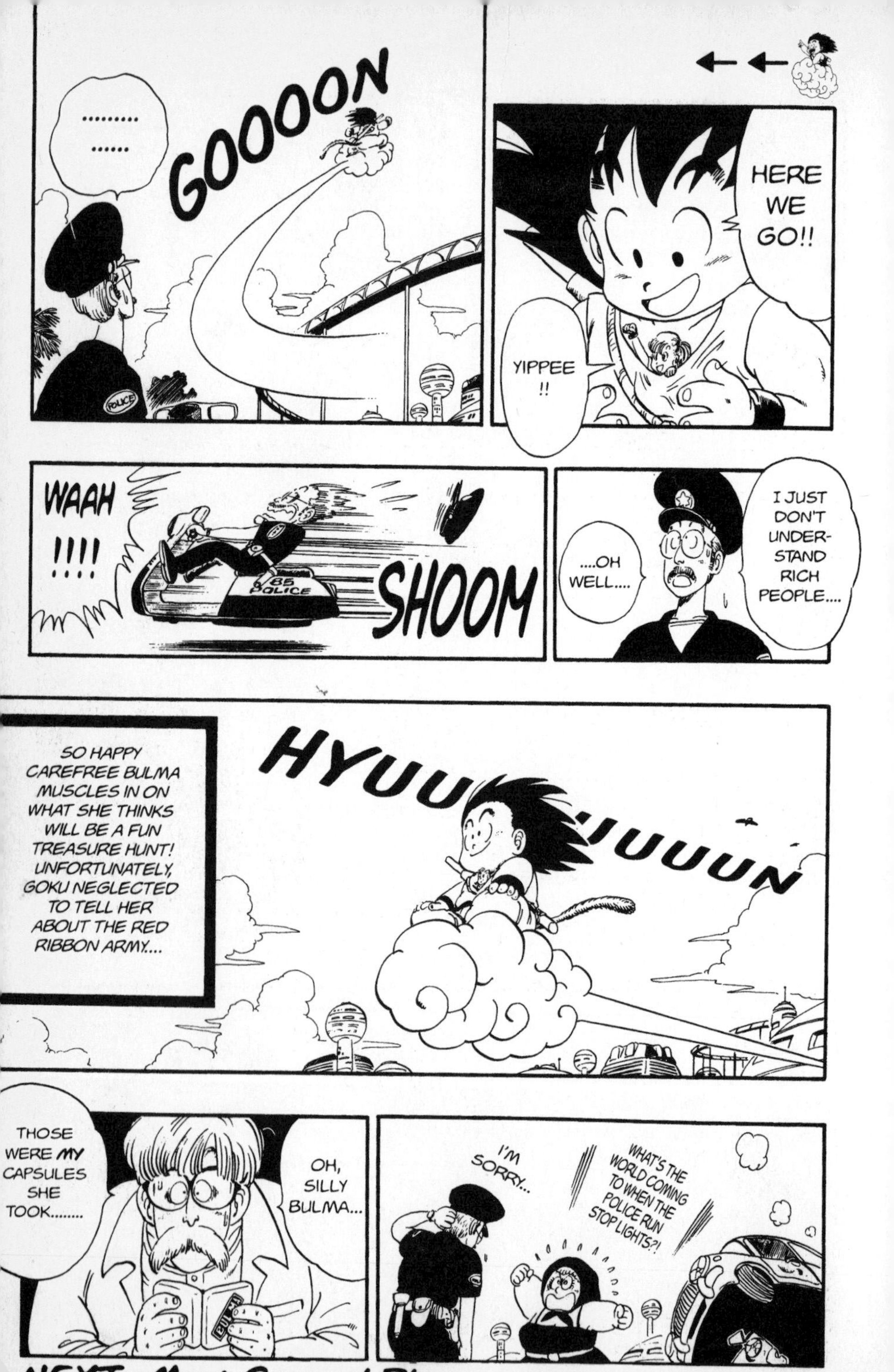
HERE WE GO!!
YIPPEE !!
....
......
GOOOON
I JUST DON'T UNDER-STAND RICH PEOPLE....
....OH WELL....
WAAH !!!!
SHOOM
HYUUUUUUUUN
SO HAPPY CAREFREE BULMA MUSCLES IN ON WHAT SHE THINKS WILL BE A FUN TREASURE HUNT! UNFORTUNATELY, GOKU NEGLECTED TO TELL HER ABOUT THE RED RIBBON ARMY....
WHAT'S THE WORLD COMING TO WHEN THE POLICE RUN STOP LIGHTS?!
I'M SORRY...
THOSE WERE *MY* CAPSULES SHE TOOK........
OH, SILLY BULMA...

NEXT: Meet General Blue

Tale 70
Bulma's Big Mistake!!

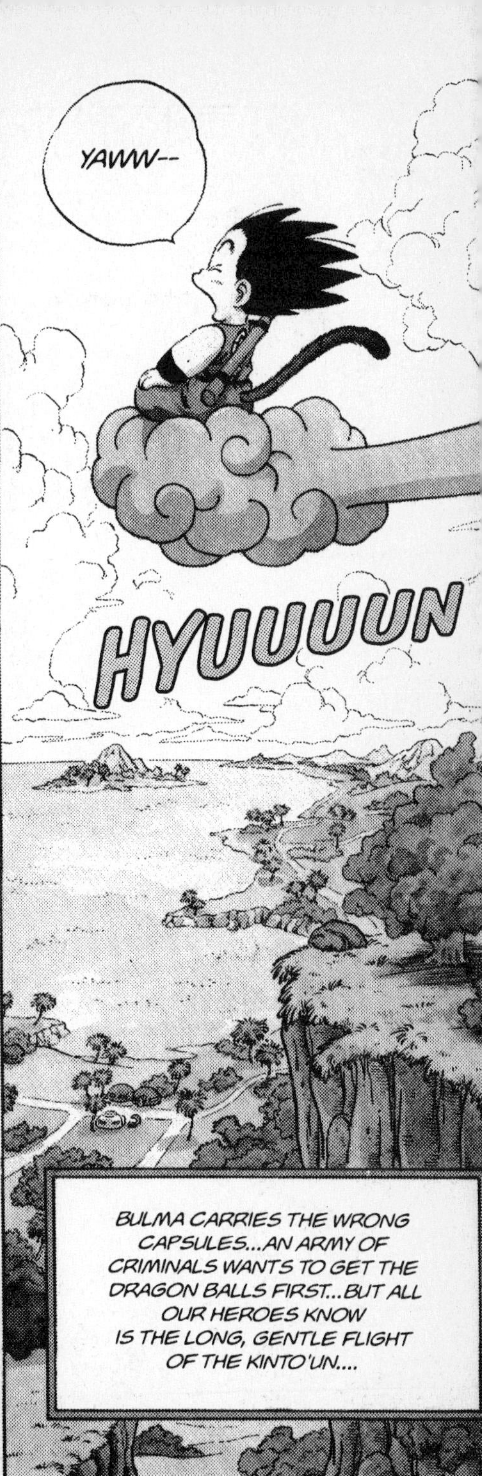

YAWW--
HYUUUUUN
BULMA CARRIES THE WRONG CAPSULES...AN ARMY OF CRIMINALS WANTS TO GET THE DRAGON BALLS FIRST...BUT ALL OUR HEROES KNOW IS THE LONG, GENTLE FLIGHT OF THE KINTO'UN....

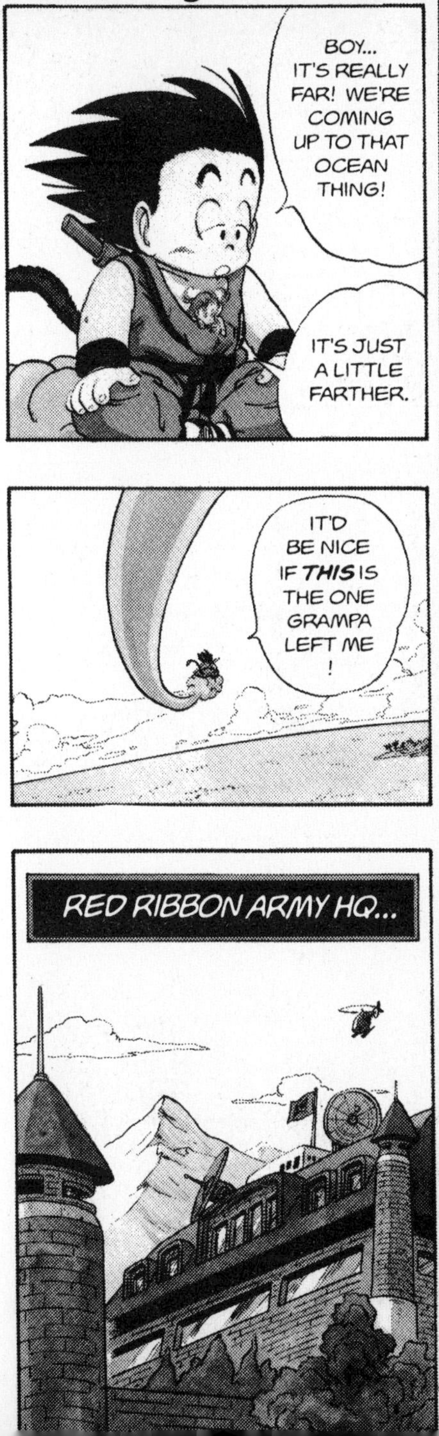

BOY... IT'S REALLY FAR! WE'RE COMING UP TO THAT OCEAN THING!
IT'S JUST A LITTLE FARTHER.
IT'D BE NICE IF THIS IS THE ONE GRAMPA LEFT ME!
RED RIBBON ARMY HQ...

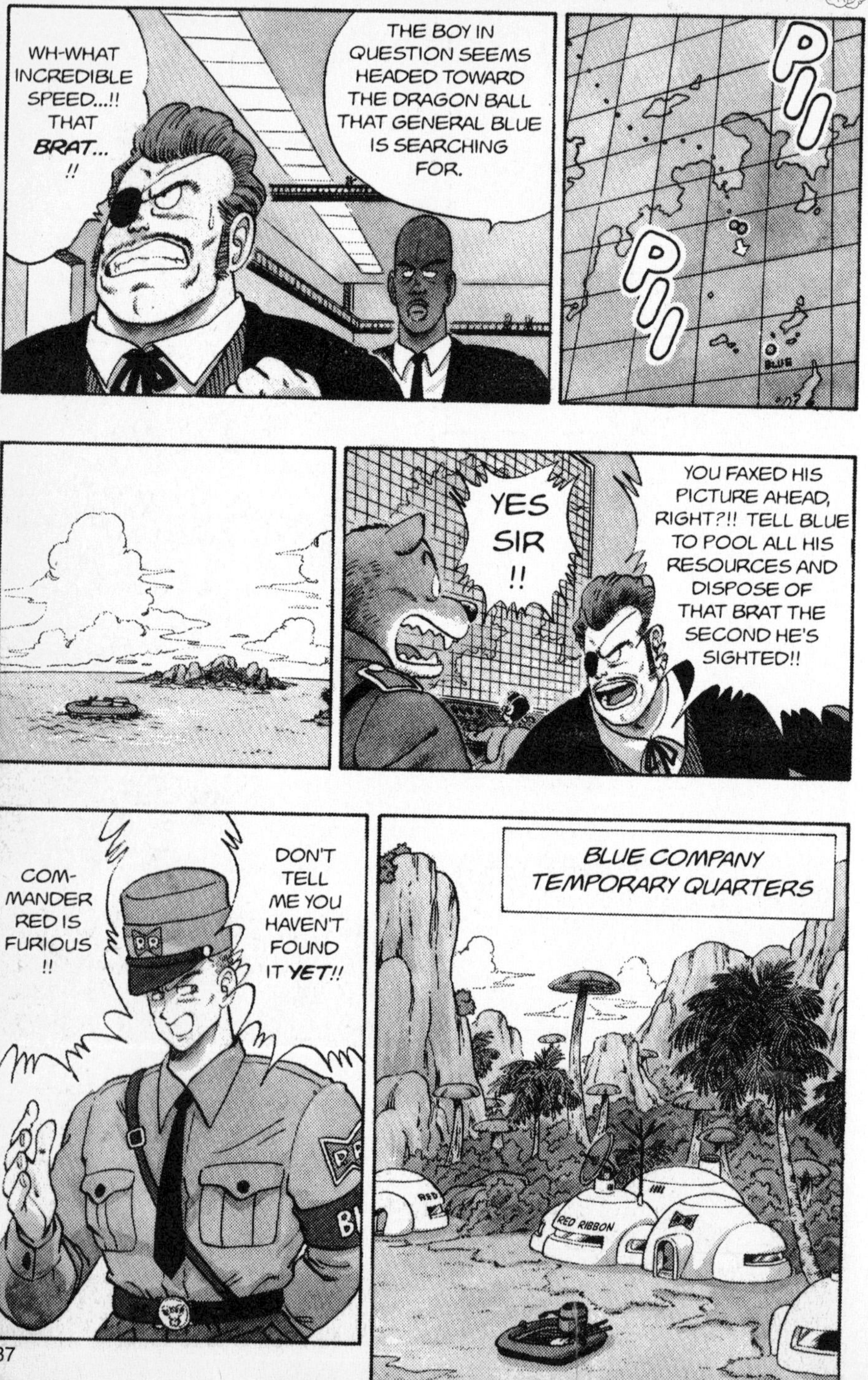
PII
PII
BLUE
THE BOY IN QUESTION SEEMS HEADED TOWARD THE DRAGON BALL THAT GENERAL BLUE IS SEARCHING FOR.
WH-WHAT INCREDIBLE SPEED...!! THAT BRAT... !!
YOU FAXED HIS PICTURE AHEAD, RIGHT?!! TELL BLUE TO POOL ALL HIS RESOURCES AND DISPOSE OF THAT BRAT THE SECOND HE'S SIGHTED!!
YES SIR !!
BLUE COMPANY TEMPORARY QUARTERS
RED
RED RIBBON
DON'T TELL ME YOU HAVEN'T FOUND IT YET!!
COM-MANDER RED IS FURIOUS !!

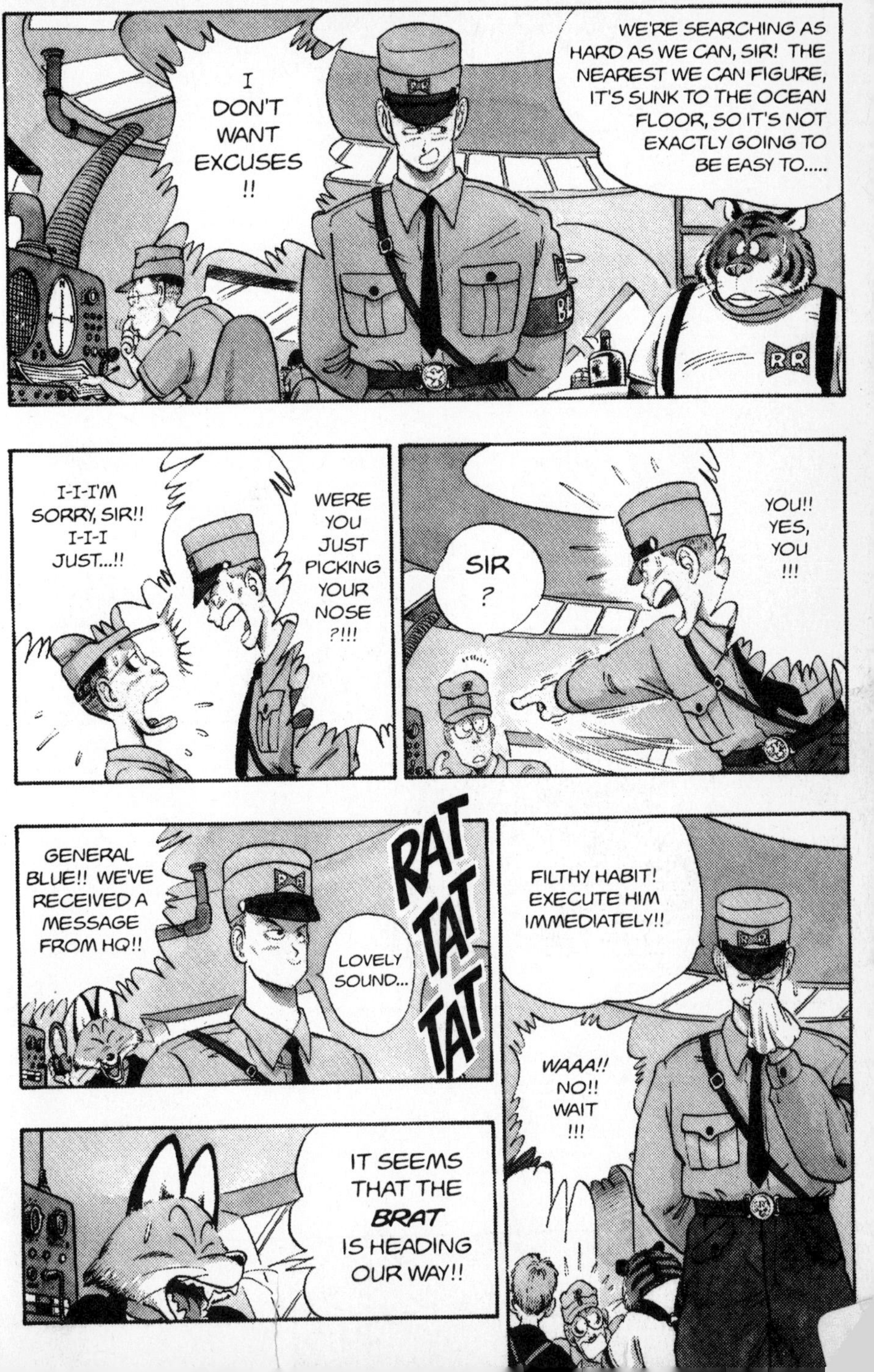
WE'RE SEARCHING AS HARD AS WE CAN, SIR! THE NEAREST WE CAN FIGURE, IT'S SUNK TO THE OCEAN FLOOR, SO IT'S NOT EXACTLY GOING TO BE EASY TO.....
I DON'T WANT EXCUSES !!
YOU!! YES, YOU !!!
SIR ?
WERE YOU JUST PICKING YOUR NOSE ?!!!
I-I-I'M SORRY, SIR!! I-I-I JUST...!!
FILTHY HABIT! EXECUTE HIM IMMEDIATELY!!
WAAA!! NO!! WAIT !!!
RAT TAT TAT
LOVELY SOUND...
GENERAL BLUE!! WE'VE RECEIVED A MESSAGE FROM HQ!!
IT SEEMS THAT THE *BRAT* IS HEADING OUR WAY!!

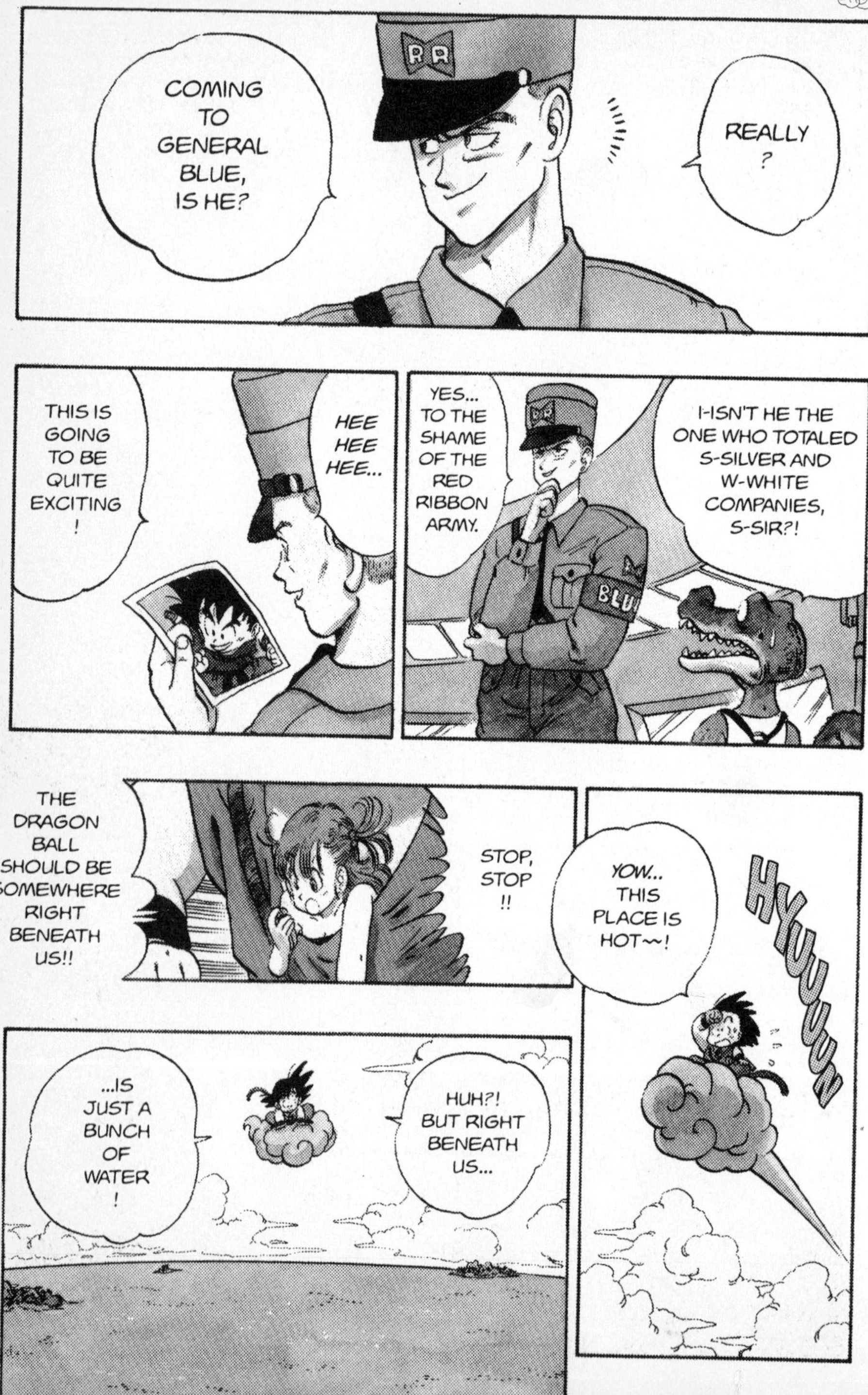
REALLY?
COMING TO GENERAL BLUE, IS HE?
I-ISN'T HE THE ONE WHO TOTALED S-SILVER AND W-WHITE COMPANIES, S-SIR?!
YES... TO THE SHAME OF THE RED RIBBON ARMY.
HEE HEE HEE...
THIS IS GOING TO BE QUITE EXCITING!
HYUUUUN
YOW... THIS PLACE IS HOT~!
STOP, STOP!!
THE DRAGON BALL SHOULD BE SOMEWHERE RIGHT BENEATH US!!
HUH?! BUT RIGHT BENEATH US...
...IS JUST A BUNCH OF WATER!

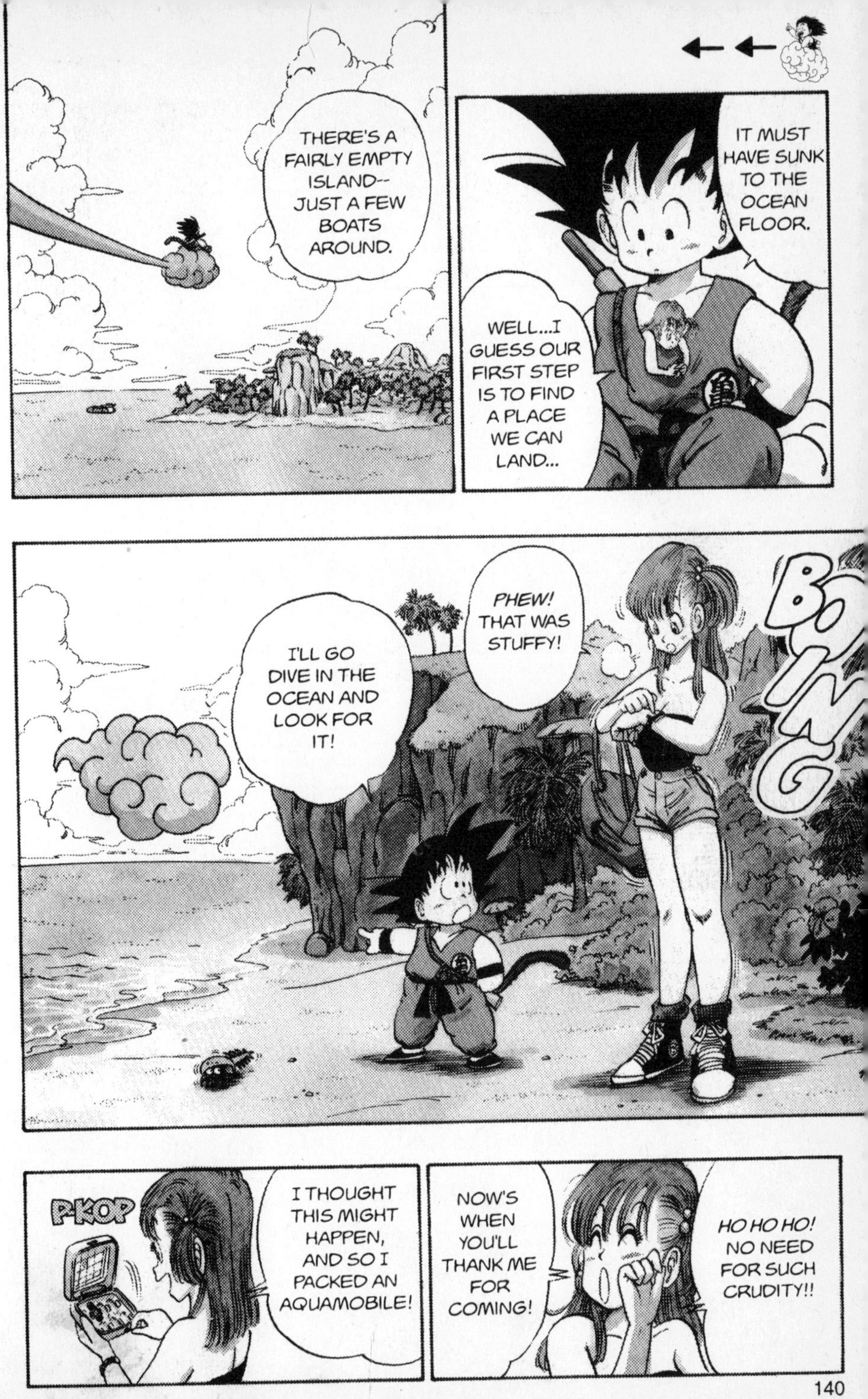
IT MUST HAVE SUNK TO THE OCEAN FLOOR.
WELL...I GUESS OUR FIRST STEP IS TO FIND A PLACE WE CAN LAND...
THERE'S A FAIRLY EMPTY ISLAND-- JUST A FEW BOATS AROUND.
BOING
PHEW! THAT WAS STUFFY!
I'LL GO DIVE IN THE OCEAN AND LOOK FOR IT!
HO HO HO! NO NEED FOR SUCH CRUDITY!!
NOW'S WHEN YOU'LL THANK ME FOR COMING!
I THOUGHT THIS MIGHT HAPPEN, AND SO I PACKED AN AQUAMOBILE!
P-KOP

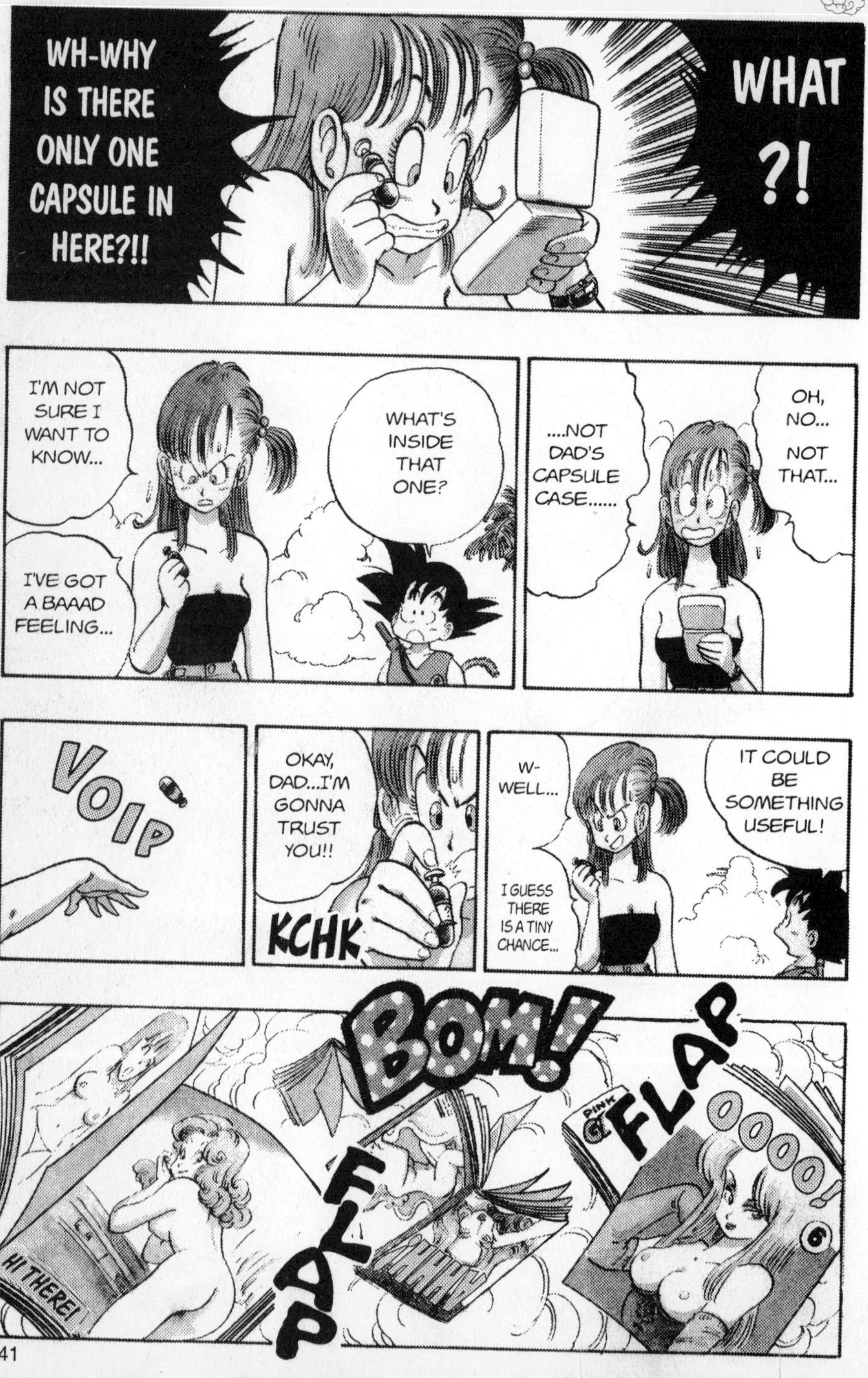
WHAT ?!
WH-WHY IS THERE ONLY ONE CAPSULE IN HERE?!!
OH, NO... NOT THAT...
....NOT DAD'S CAPSULE CASE......
WHAT'S INSIDE THAT ONE?
I'M NOT SURE I WANT TO KNOW...
I'VE GOT A BAAAD FEELING...
IT COULD BE SOMETHING USEFUL!
W-WELL...
I GUESS THERE IS A TINY CHANCE...
OKAY, DAD...I'M GONNA TRUST YOU!!
KCHK
VOIP
FLAP
BOM!
PINK
OOOOO!
FLAP
HI THERE!

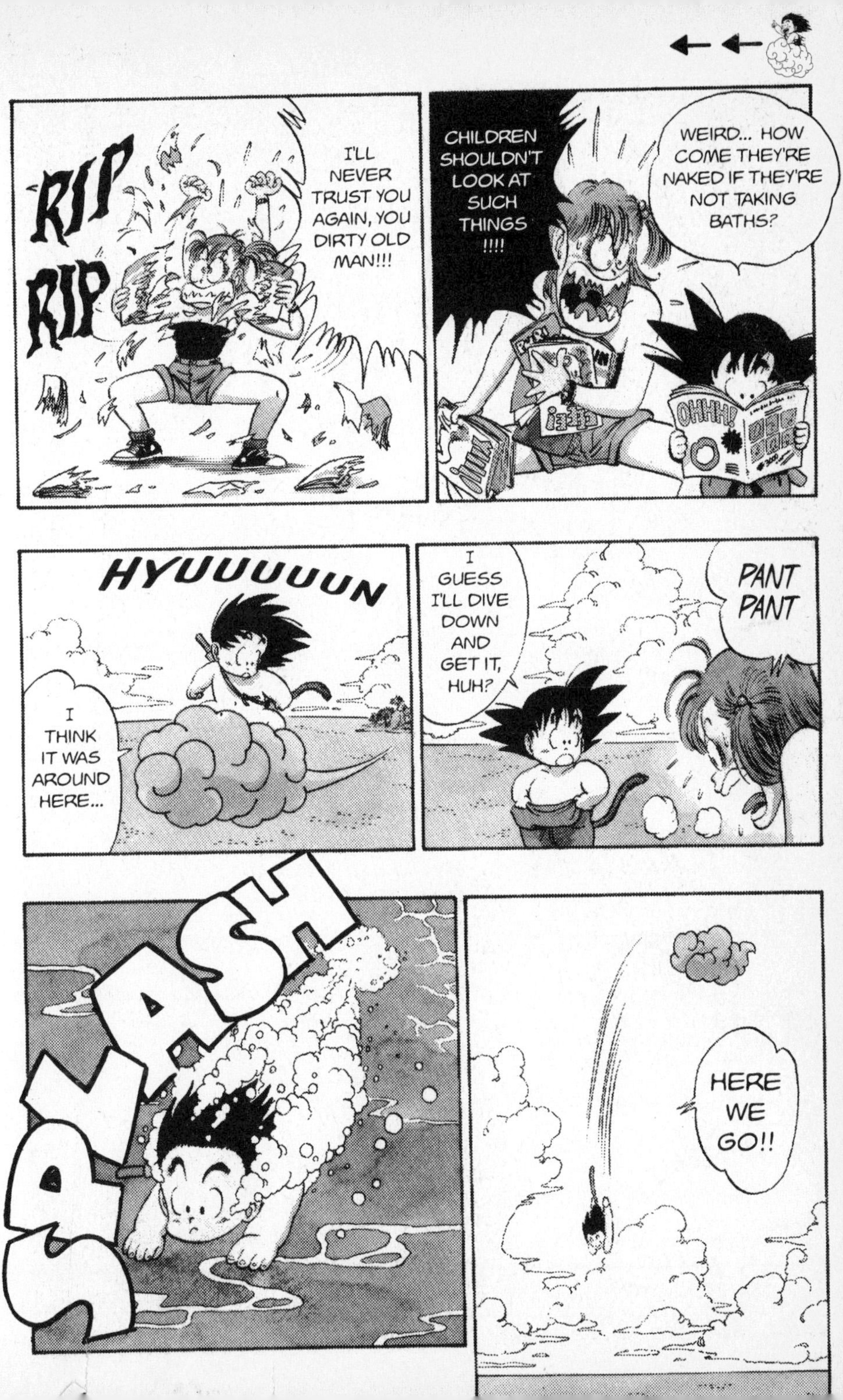
WEIRD... HOW COME THEY'RE NAKED IF THEY'RE NOT TAKING BATHS?
CHILDREN SHOULDN'T LOOK AT SUCH THINGS !!!!
OHHH!
I'LL NEVER TRUST YOU AGAIN, YOU DIRTY OLD MAN!!!
RIP RIP
PANT PANT
I GUESS I'LL DIVE DOWN AND GET IT, HUH?
HYUUUUUN
I THINK IT WAS AROUND HERE...
HERE WE GO!!
SPLASH

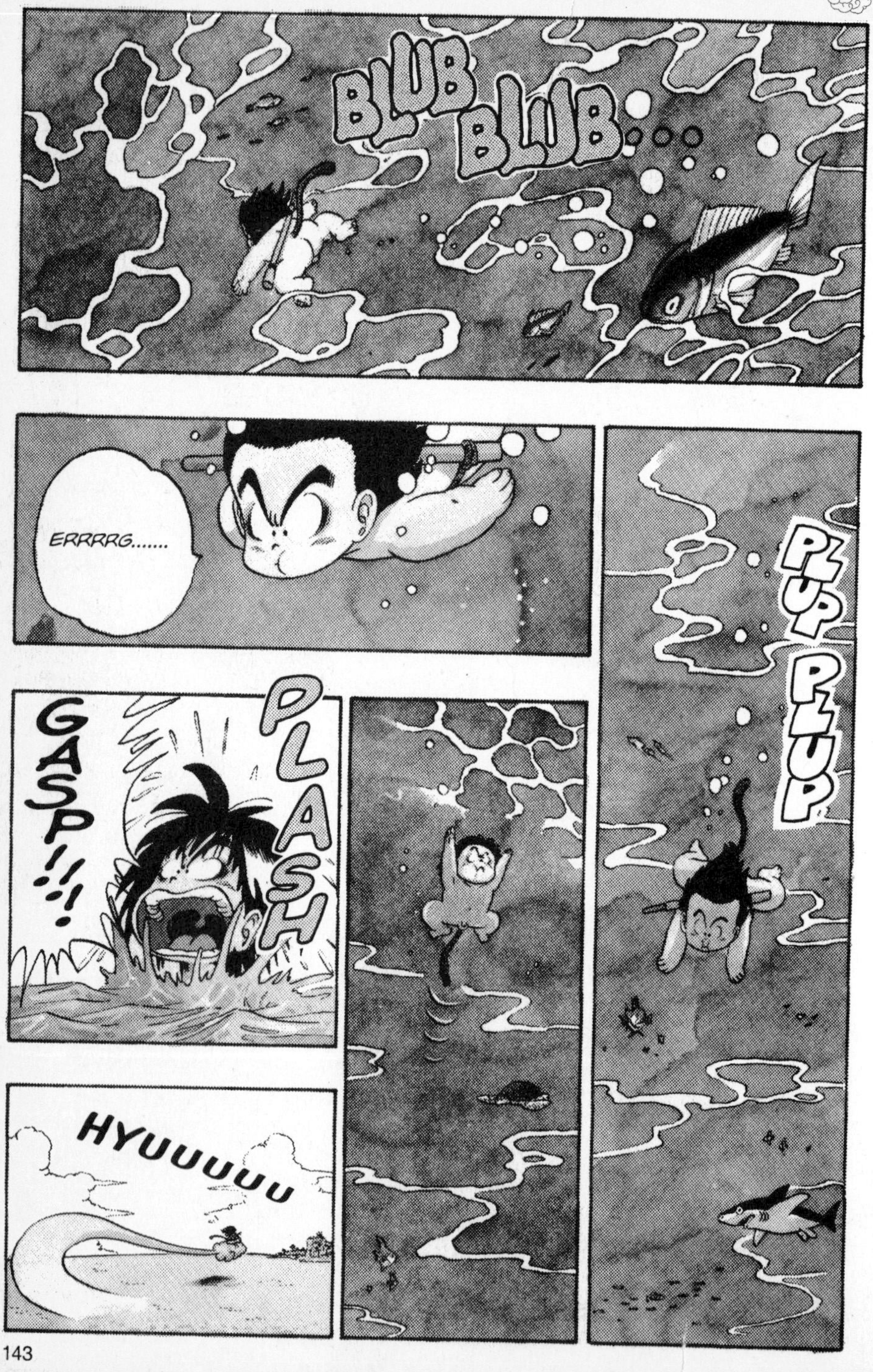
BLUB BLUB
PLUP PLUP PLUP
ERRRRG.......
PLASH
GASP!!!!
HYUUUUUU

WE INTERRUPT THIS DULL STORY
FOR A THRILLING ANNOUNCEMENT!

GENERAL BLUE IS APPROACHING!!

WHAT WILL HAPPEN?! READ THE
NEXT DRAGON BALL!!

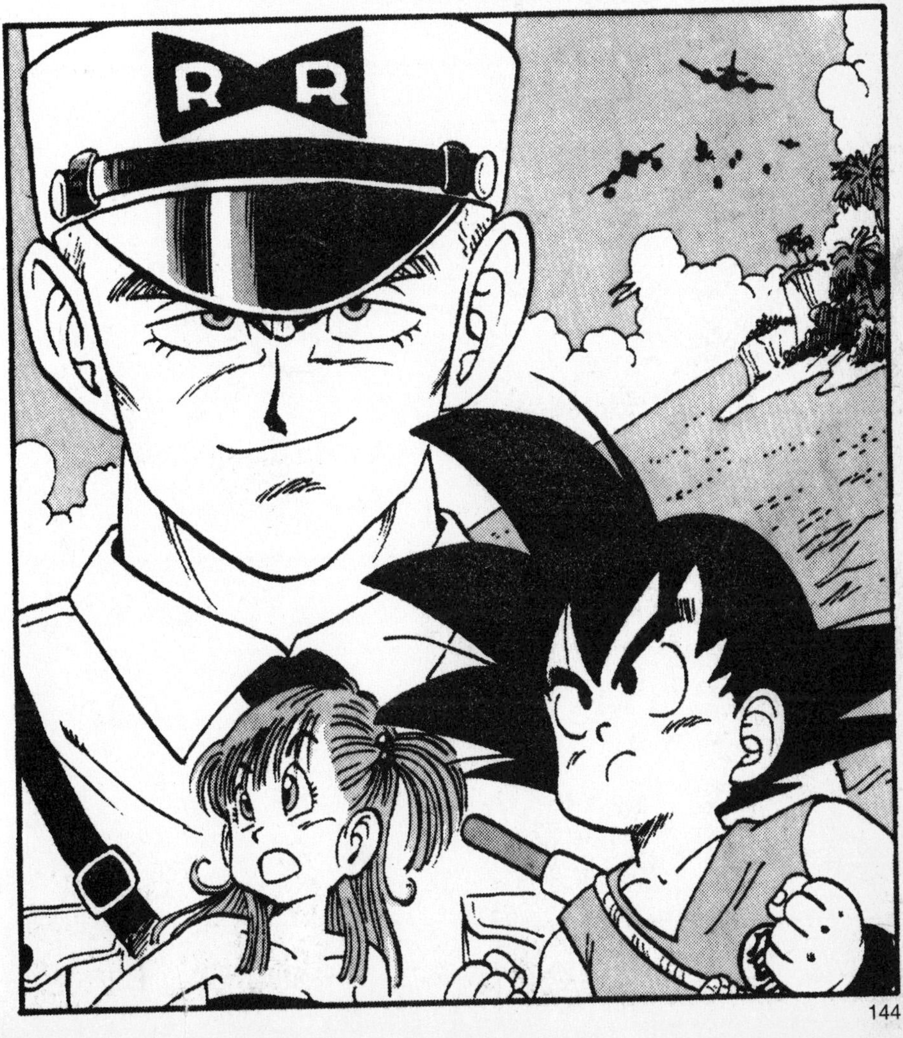

R R

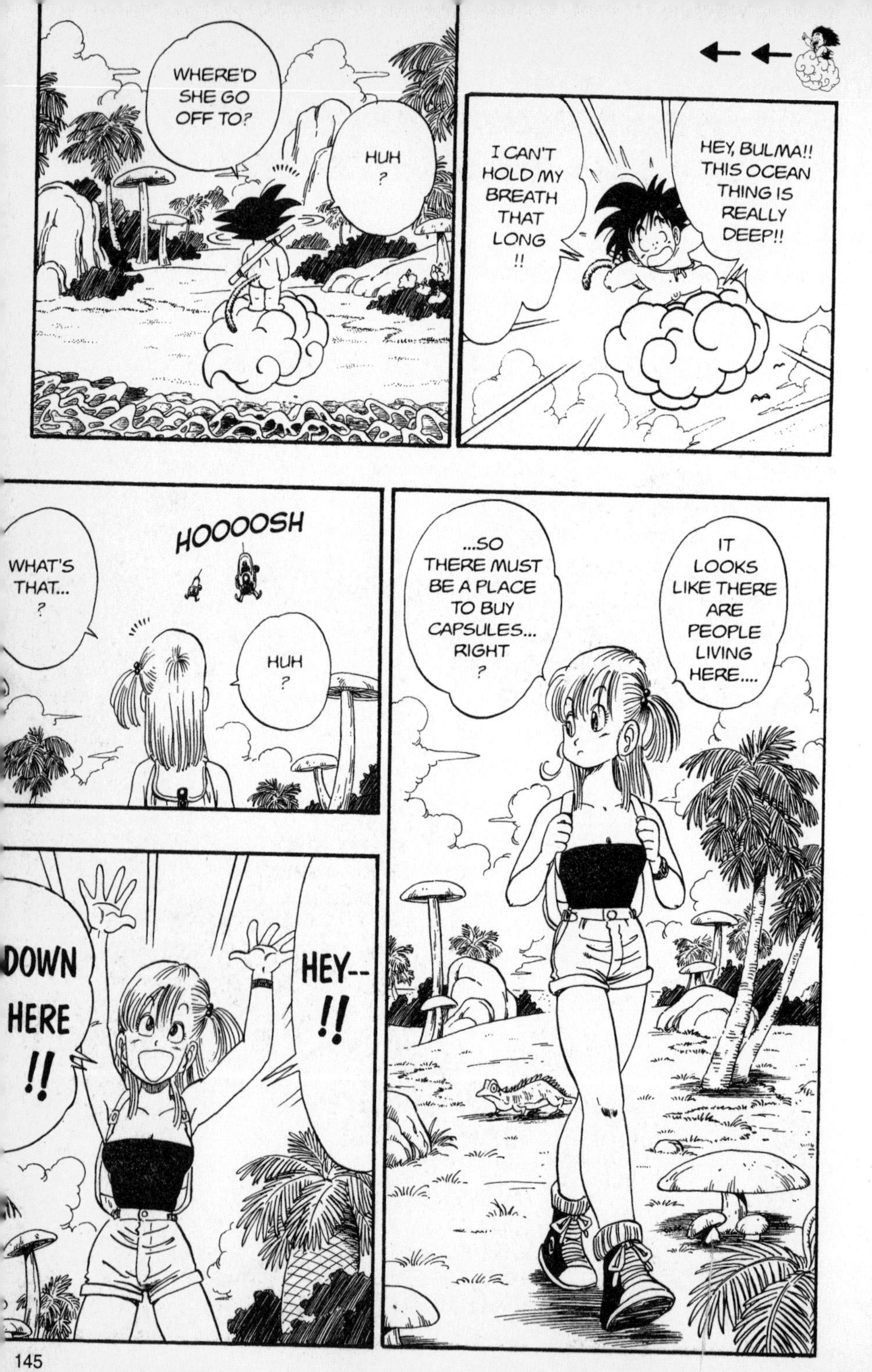
HEY, BULMA!! THIS OCEAN THING IS REALLY DEEP!!
I CAN'T HOLD MY BREATH THAT LONG !!
HUH ?
WHERE'D SHE GO OFF TO?
IT LOOKS LIKE THERE ARE PEOPLE LIVING HERE....
...SO THERE MUST BE A PLACE TO BUY CAPSULES... RIGHT ?
HOOOOSH
HUH ?
WHAT'S THAT... ?
HEY-- !!
DOWN HERE !!

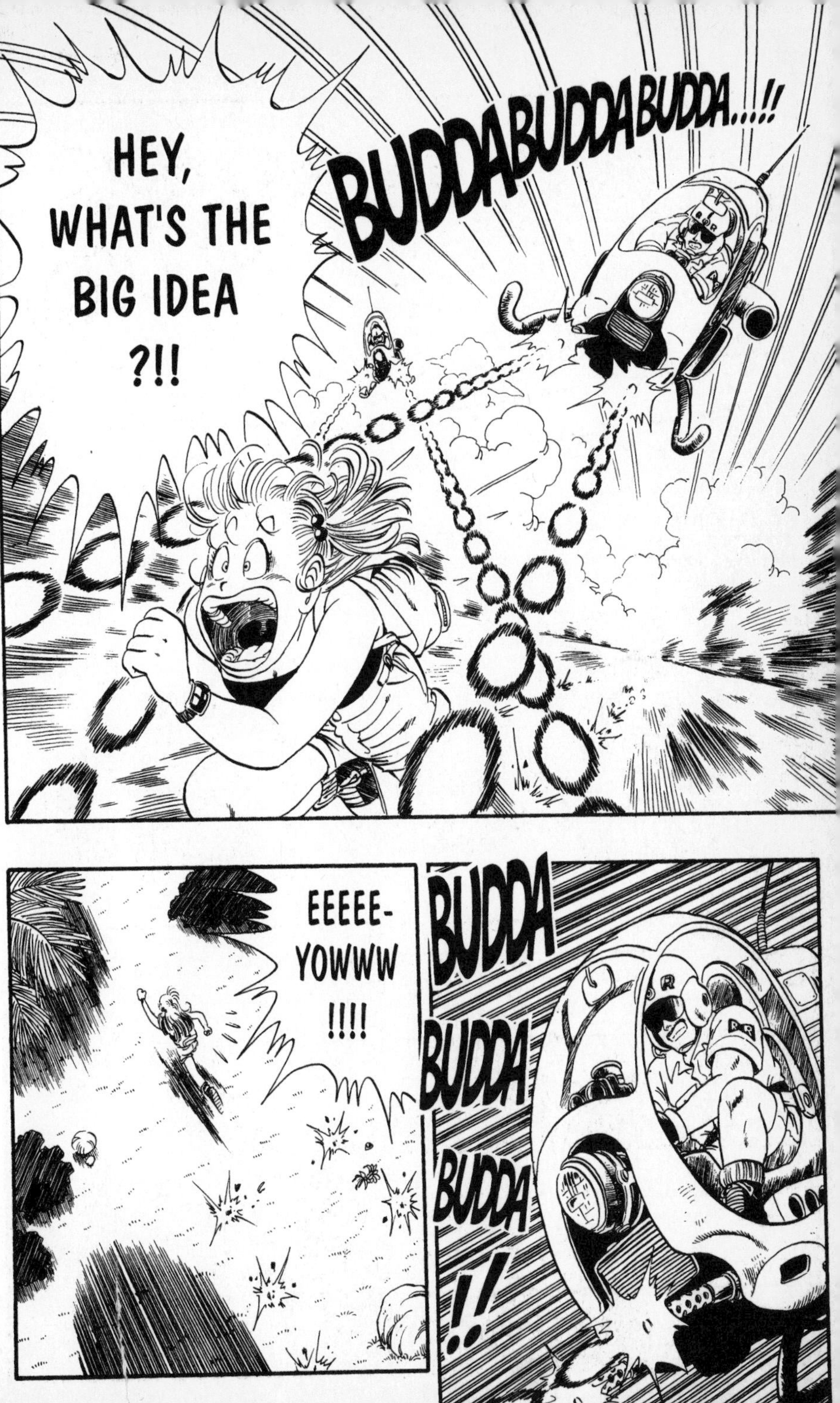
BUDDABUDDABUDDA...!!
HEY, WHAT'S THE BIG IDEA ?!!
BUDDA BUDDA BUDDA !!
EEEEE-YOWWW !!!!

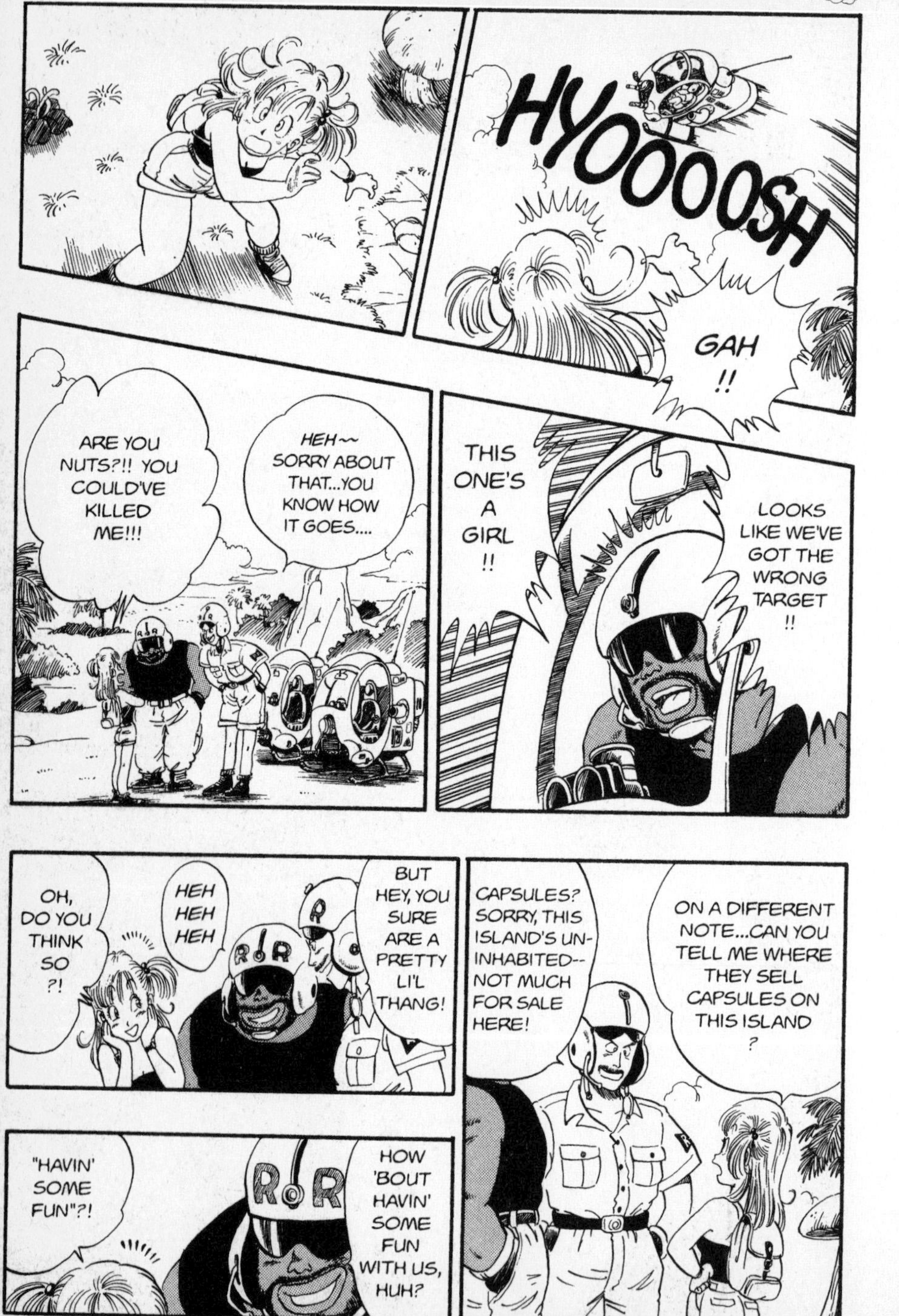
HYOOOOSH
GAH!!
LOOKS LIKE WE'VE GOT THE WRONG TARGET!!
THIS ONE'S A GIRL!!
ARE YOU NUTS?!! YOU COULD'VE KILLED ME!!!
HEH~ SORRY ABOUT THAT...YOU KNOW HOW IT GOES....
ON A DIFFERENT NOTE...CAN YOU TELL ME WHERE THEY SELL CAPSULES ON THIS ISLAND?
CAPSULES? SORRY, THIS ISLAND'S UN-INHABITED--NOT MUCH FOR SALE HERE!
BUT HEY, YOU SURE ARE A PRETTY LI'L THANG!
HEH HEH HEH
OH, DO YOU THINK SO?!
HOW 'BOUT HAVIN' SOME FUN WITH US, HUH?
"HAVIN' SOME FUN"?!

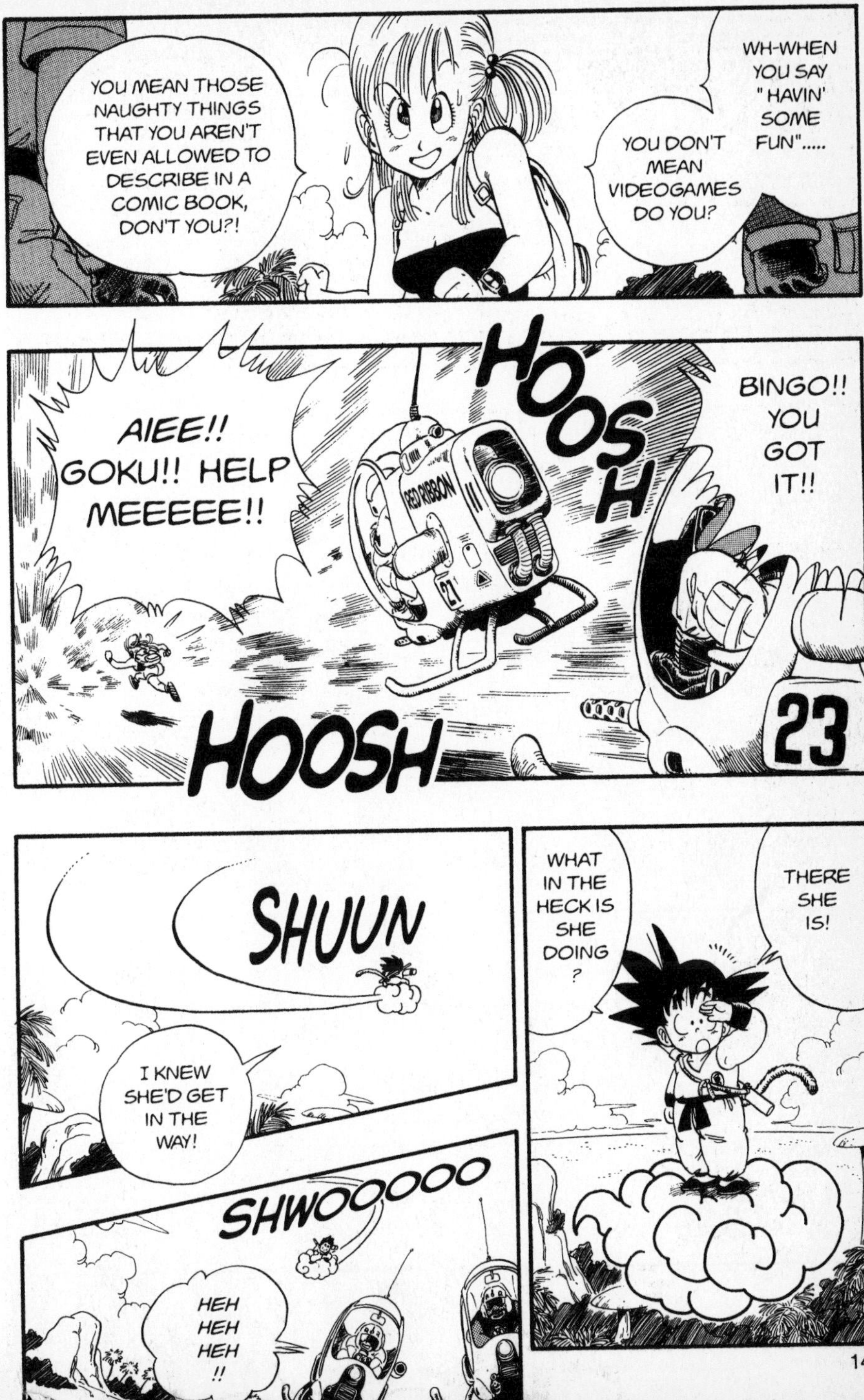

WH-WHEN YOU SAY "HAVIN' SOME FUN".....
YOU DON'T MEAN VIDEOGAMES DO YOU?
YOU MEAN THOSE NAUGHTY THINGS THAT YOU AREN'T EVEN ALLOWED TO DESCRIBE IN A COMIC BOOK, DON'T YOU?!
BINGO!! YOU GOT IT!!
HOOSH
RED RIBBON
27
AIEE!! GOKU!! HELP MEEEEEE!!
23
HOOSH
THERE SHE IS!
WHAT IN THE HECK IS SHE DOING?
SHUUN
I KNEW SHE'D GET IN THE WAY!
SHWOOOOOO
HEH HEH HEH!!

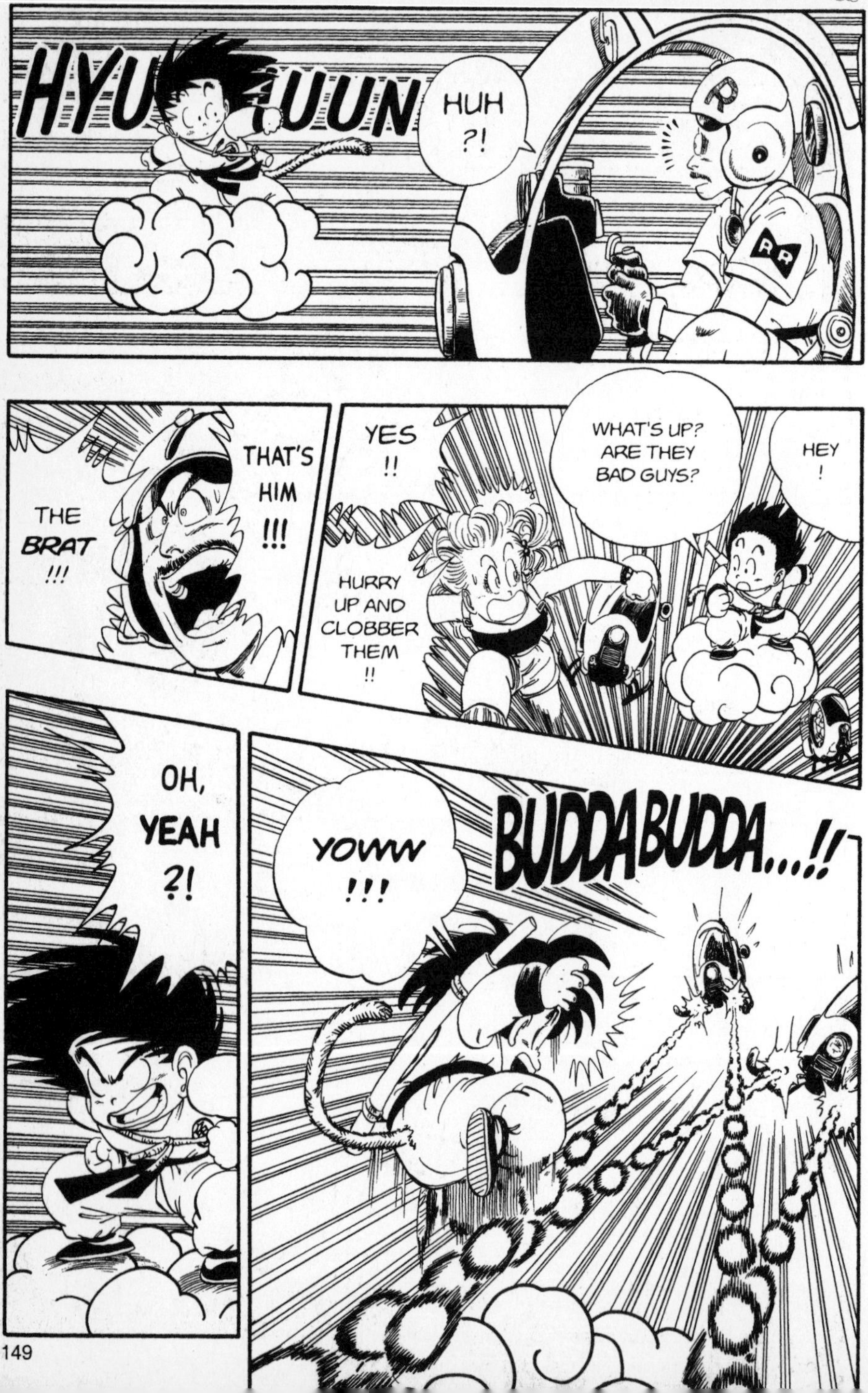
HYUUUN
HUH ?!
HEY !
WHAT'S UP? ARE THEY BAD GUYS?
YES !!
HURRY UP AND CLOBBER THEM !!
THAT'S HIM !!!
THE *BRAT* !!!
BUDDABUDDA...!!
YOWW !!!
OH, YEAH ?!

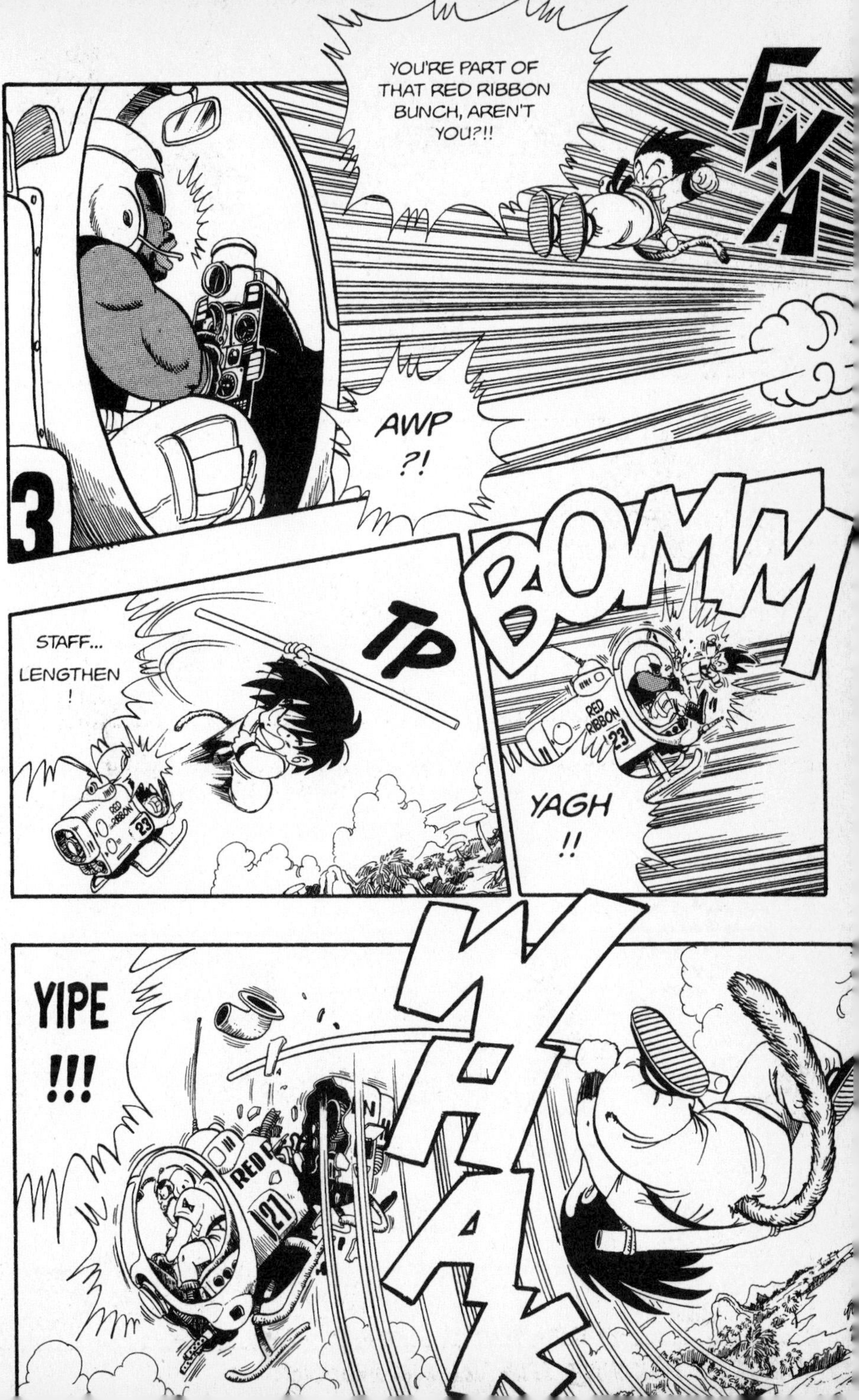
YOU'RE PART OF THAT RED RIBBON BUNCH, AREN'T YOU?!!
FWA
AWP ?!
BOMM
YAGH !!
TP
STAFF... LENGTHEN !
WHAK
YIPE !!!

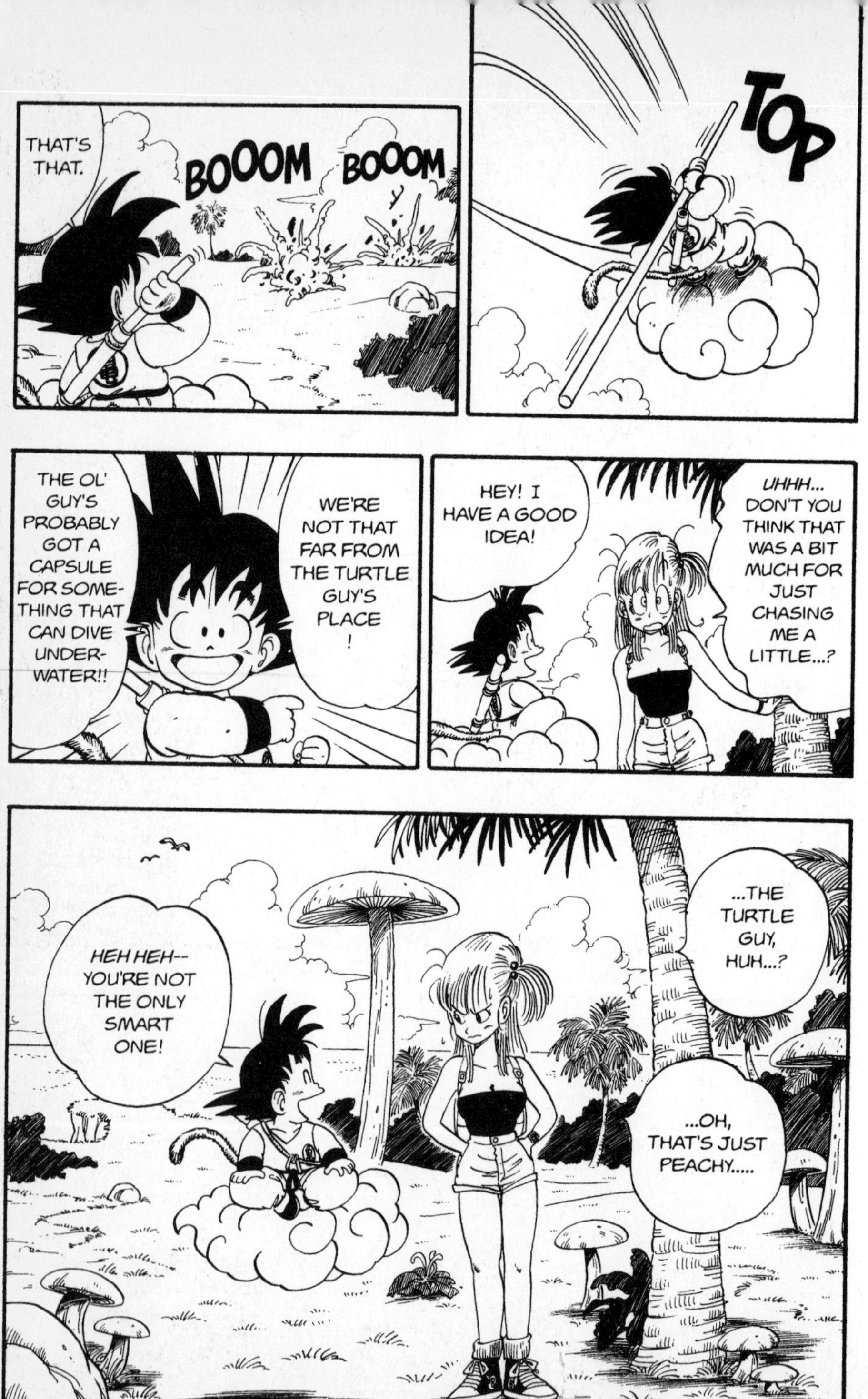
TOP
THAT'S THAT.
BOOOM
BOOOM
UHHH... DON'T YOU THINK THAT WAS A BIT MUCH FOR JUST CHASING ME A LITTLE...?
HEY! I HAVE A GOOD IDEA!
WE'RE NOT THAT FAR FROM THE TURTLE GUY'S PLACE!
THE OL' GUY'S PROBABLY GOT A CAPSULE FOR SOME-THING THAT CAN DIVE UNDER-WATER!!
HEH HEH-- YOU'RE NOT THE ONLY SMART ONE!
...THE TURTLE GUY, HUH...?
...OH, THAT'S JUST PEACHY.....

NEXT: Finding the Turtle House!

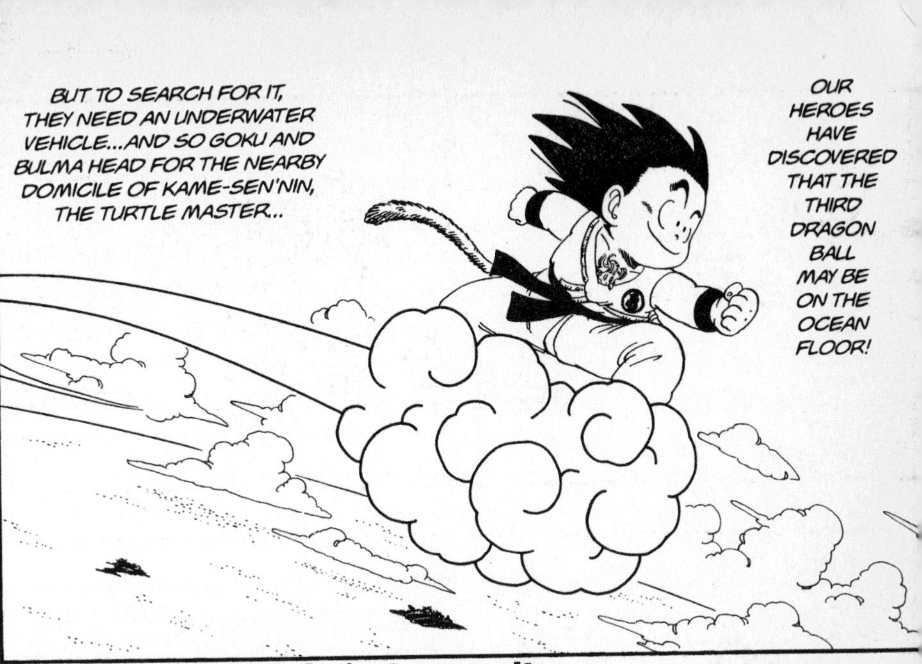
OUR HEROES HAVE DISCOVERED THAT THE THIRD DRAGON BALL MAY BE ON THE OCEAN FLOOR!
BUT TO SEARCH FOR IT, THEY NEED AN UNDERWATER VEHICLE...AND SO GOKU AND BULMA HEAD FOR THE NEARBY DOMICILE OF KAME-SEN'NIN, THE TURTLE MASTER...

Tale 71 • The Turtle is Spotted!

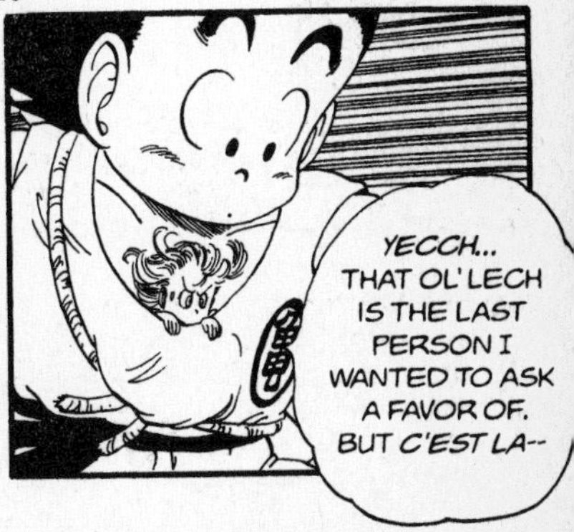
YECCH... THAT OL' LECH IS THE LAST PERSON I WANTED TO ASK A FAVOR OF. BUT C'EST LA--

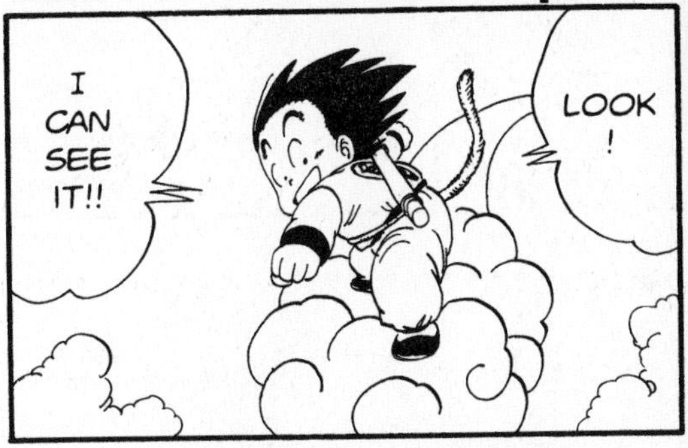
LOOK!
I CAN SEE IT!!

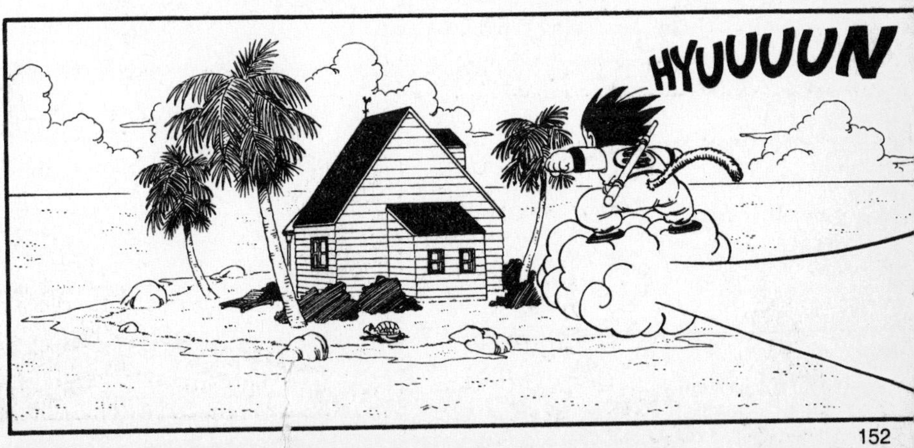
HYUUUUN

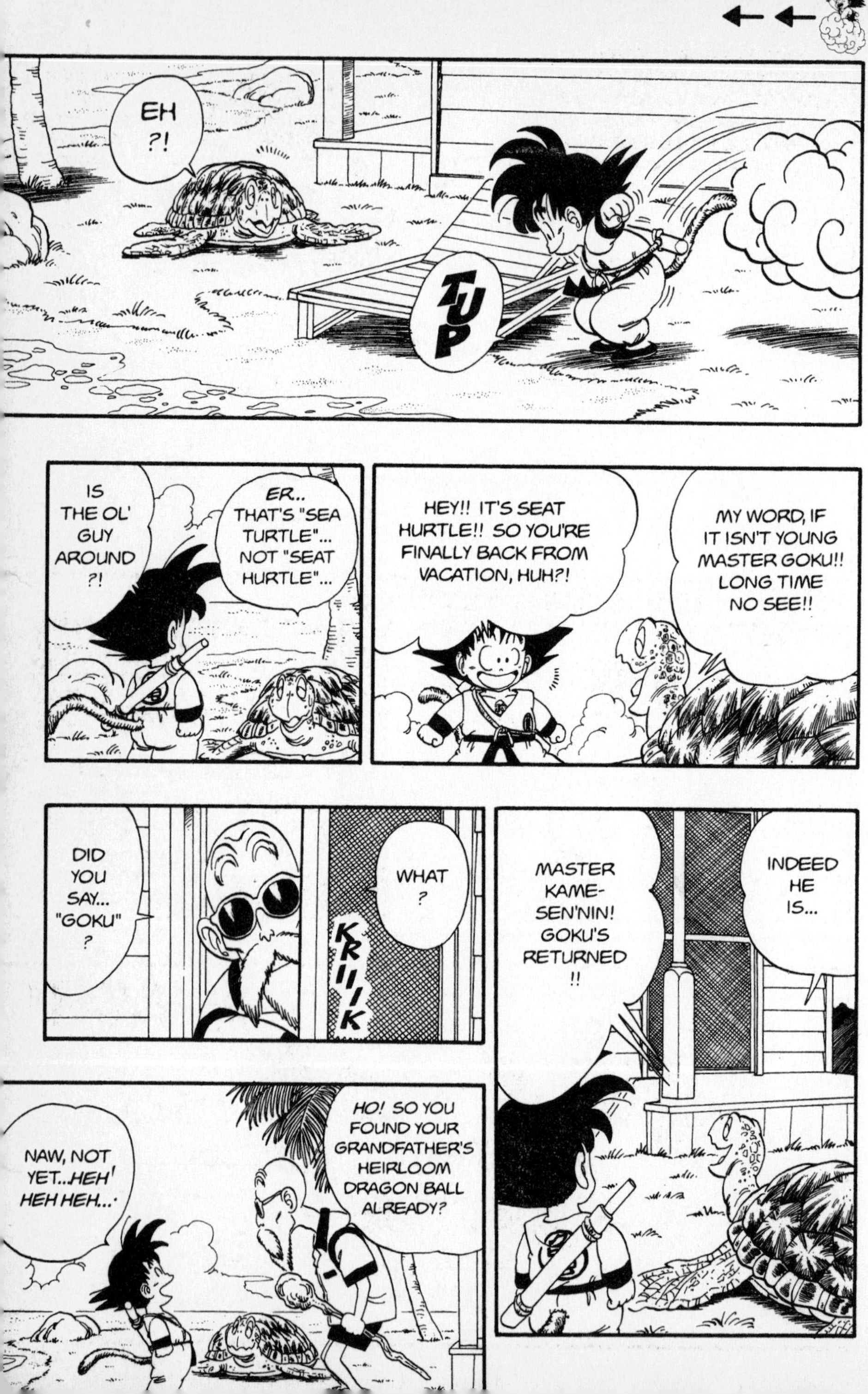
EH ?!
TUP
MY WORD, IF IT ISN'T YOUNG MASTER GOKU!! LONG TIME NO SEE!!
HEY!! IT'S SEAT HURTLE!! SO YOU'RE FINALLY BACK FROM VACATION, HUH?!
ER... THAT'S "SEA TURTLE"... NOT "SEAT HURTLE"...
IS THE OL' GUY AROUND ?!
INDEED HE IS...
MASTER KAME-SEN'NIN! GOKU'S RETURNED !!
WHAT ?
KRIIIK
DID YOU SAY... "GOKU" ?
HO! SO YOU FOUND YOUR GRANDFATHER'S HEIRLOOM DRAGON BALL ALREADY?
NAW, NOT YET...HEH HEH HEH...

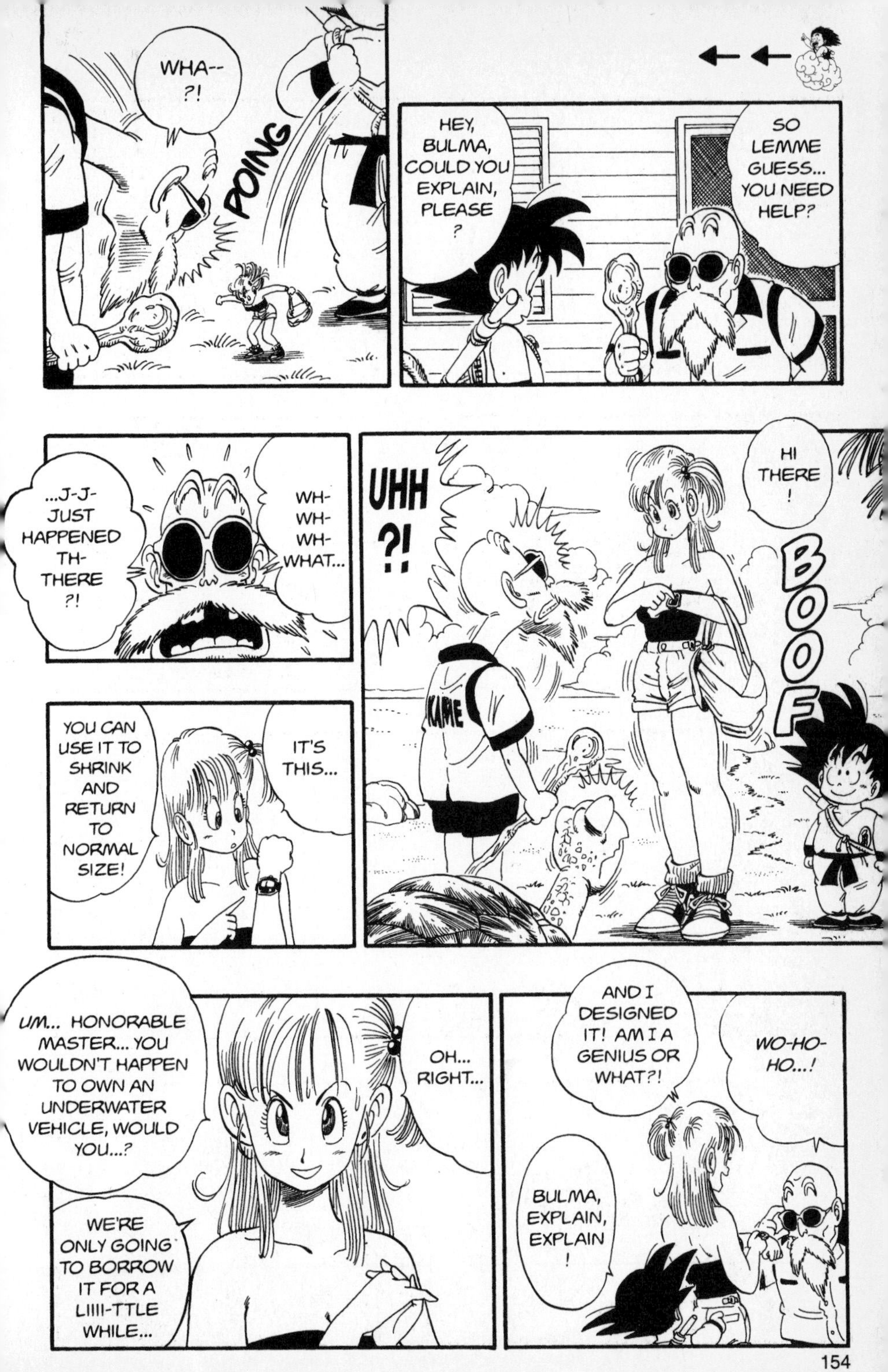

SO LEMME GUESS... YOU NEED HELP?
HEY, BULMA, COULD YOU EXPLAIN, PLEASE ?
WHA-- ?!
POING
HI THERE !
BOOOF
UHH ?!
KAME
WH-WH-WH-WHAT...
...J-J-JUST HAPPENED TH-THERE ?!
IT'S THIS...
YOU CAN USE IT TO SHRINK AND RETURN TO NORMAL SIZE!
WO-HO-HO...!
AND I DESIGNED IT! AM I A GENIUS OR WHAT?!
BULMA, EXPLAIN, EXPLAIN !
OH... RIGHT...
UM... HONORABLE MASTER... YOU WOULDN'T HAPPEN TO OWN AN UNDERWATER VEHICLE, WOULD YOU...?
WE'RE ONLY GOING TO BORROW IT FOR A LIIII-TTLE WHILE...

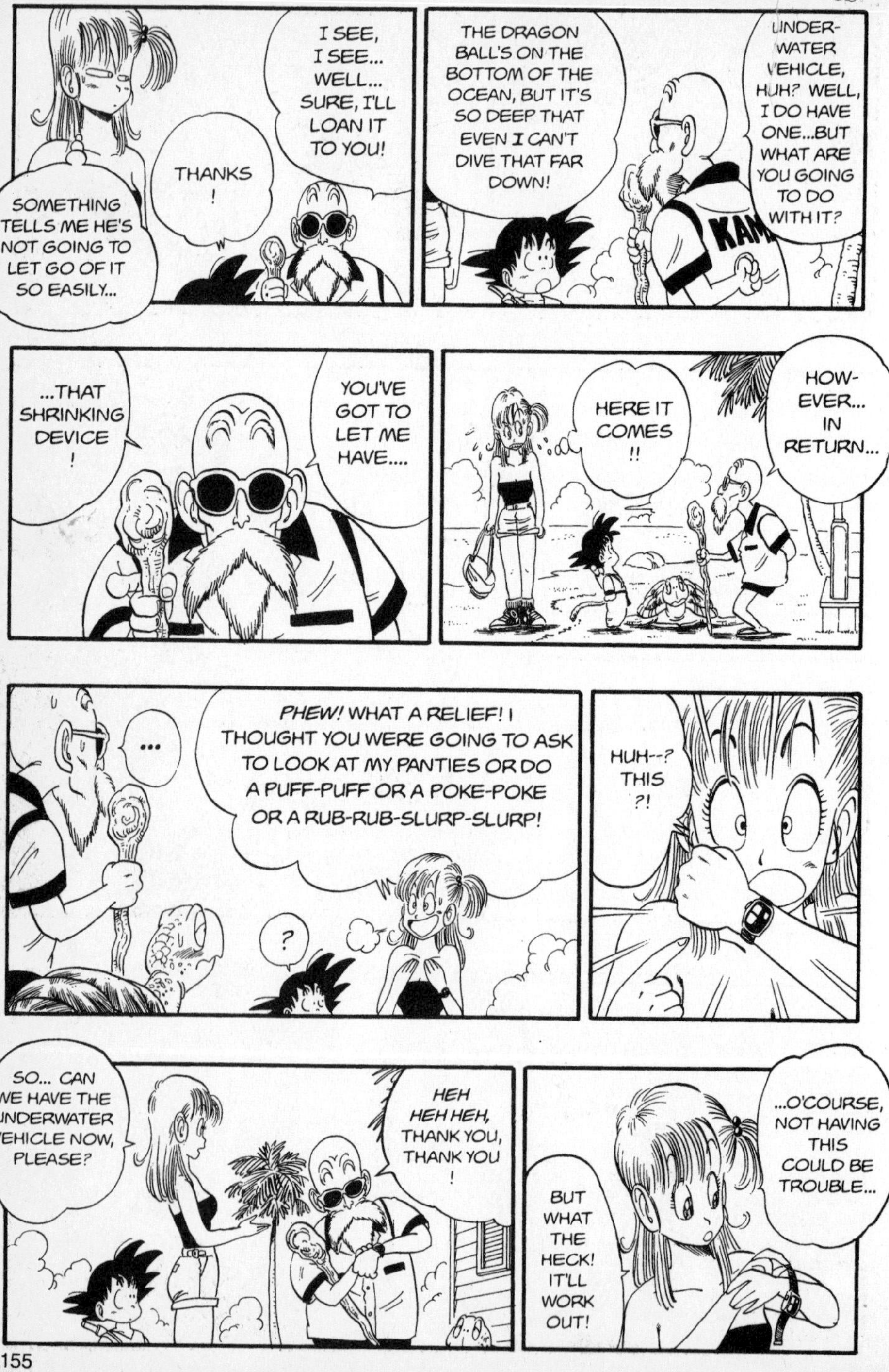
UNDER-WATER VEHICLE, HUH? WELL, I DO HAVE ONE...BUT WHAT ARE YOU GOING TO DO WITH IT?
THE DRAGON BALL'S ON THE BOTTOM OF THE OCEAN, BUT IT'S SO DEEP THAT EVEN *I* CAN'T DIVE THAT FAR DOWN!
KAM
I SEE, I SEE... WELL... SURE, I'LL LOAN IT TO YOU!
THANKS !
SOMETHING TELLS ME HE'S NOT GOING TO LET GO OF IT SO EASILY...
HOW-EVER... IN RETURN...
HERE IT COMES !!
YOU'VE GOT TO LET ME HAVE....
...THAT SHRINKING DEVICE !
HUH--? THIS ?!
...
PHEW! WHAT A RELIEF! I THOUGHT YOU WERE GOING TO ASK TO LOOK AT MY PANTIES OR DO A PUFF-PUFF OR A POKE-POKE OR A RUB-RUB-SLURP-SLURP!
?
...O'COURSE, NOT HAVING THIS COULD BE TROUBLE...
BUT WHAT THE HECK! IT'LL WORK OUT!
SO... CAN WE HAVE THE UNDERWATER VEHICLE NOW, PLEASE?
HEH HEH HEH, THANK YOU, THANK YOU !

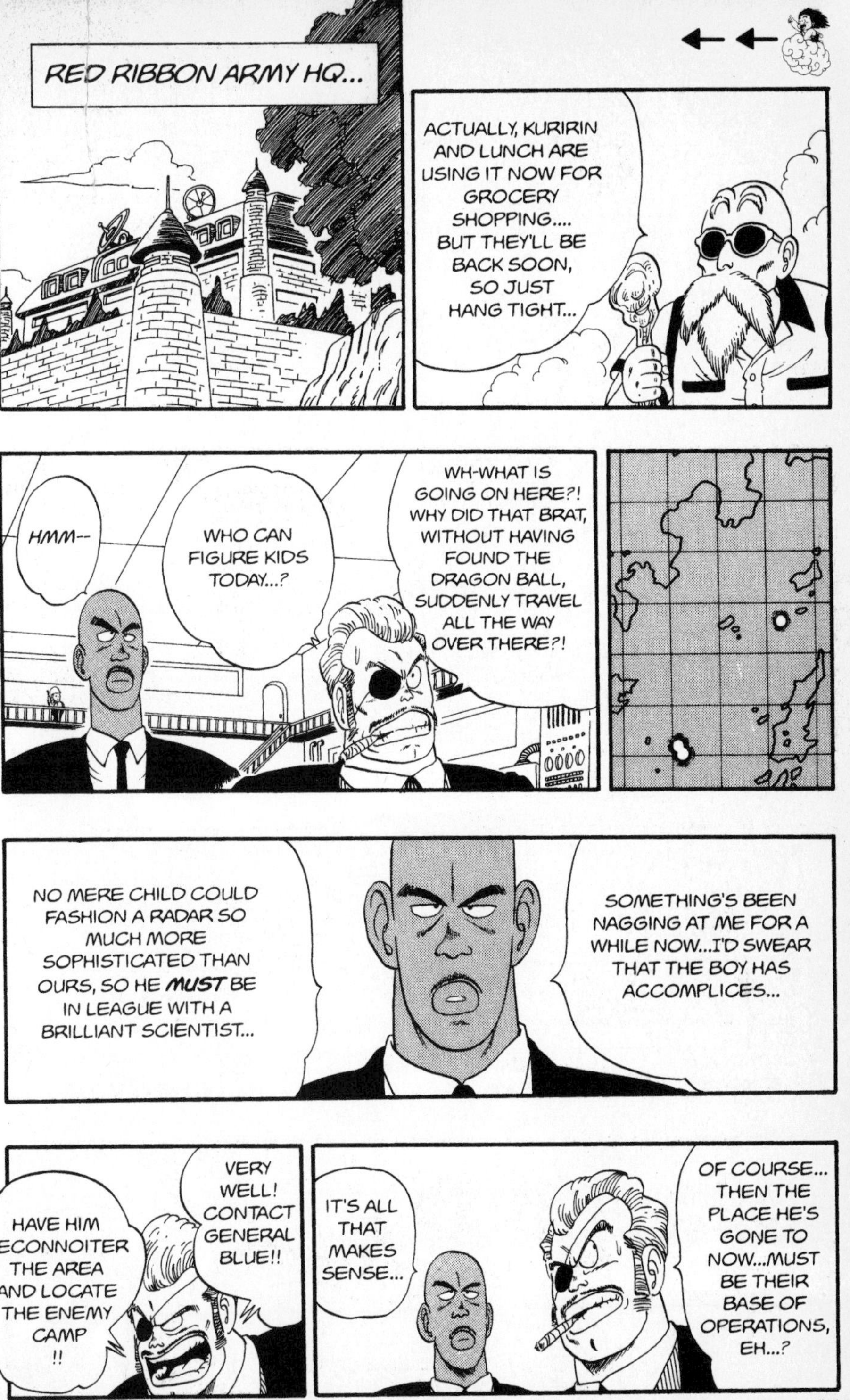
ACTUALLY, KURIRIN AND LUNCH ARE USING IT NOW FOR GROCERY SHOPPING.... BUT THEY'LL BE BACK SOON, SO JUST HANG TIGHT...
RED RIBBON ARMY HQ...
WH-WHAT IS GOING ON HERE?! WHY DID THAT BRAT, WITHOUT HAVING FOUND THE DRAGON BALL, SUDDENLY TRAVEL ALL THE WAY OVER THERE?!
WHO CAN FIGURE KIDS TODAY...?
HMM--
SOMETHING'S BEEN NAGGING AT ME FOR A WHILE NOW...I'D SWEAR THAT THE BOY HAS ACCOMPLICES...
NO MERE CHILD COULD FASHION A RADAR SO MUCH MORE SOPHISTICATED THAN OURS, SO HE *MUST* BE IN LEAGUE WITH A BRILLIANT SCIENTIST...
OF COURSE... THEN THE PLACE HE'S GONE TO NOW...MUST BE THEIR BASE OF OPERATIONS, EH...?
IT'S ALL THAT MAKES SENSE...
VERY WELL! CONTACT GENERAL BLUE!!
HAVE HIM RECONNOITER THE AREA AND LOCATE THE ENEMY CAMP !!

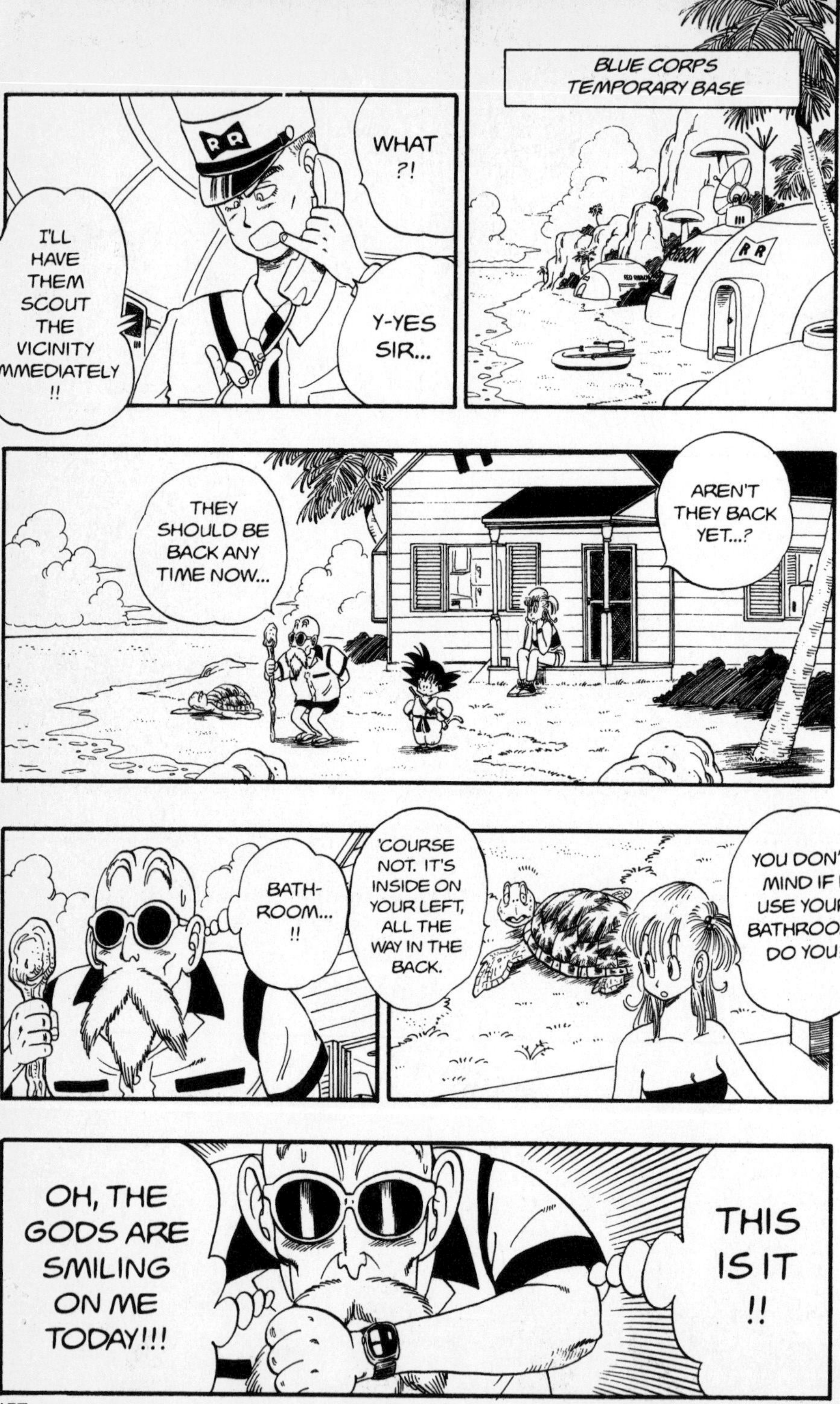
BLUE CORPS TEMPORARY BASE
WHAT ?!
Y-YES SIR...
I'LL HAVE THEM SCOUT THE VICINITY IMMEDIATELY !!
AREN'T THEY BACK YET...?
THEY SHOULD BE BACK ANY TIME NOW...
YOU DON'T MIND IF I USE YOUR BATHROOM, DO YOU?
'COURSE NOT. IT'S INSIDE ON YOUR LEFT, ALL THE WAY IN THE BACK.
BATH-ROOM... !!
THIS IS IT !!
OH, THE GODS ARE SMILING ON ME TODAY!!!

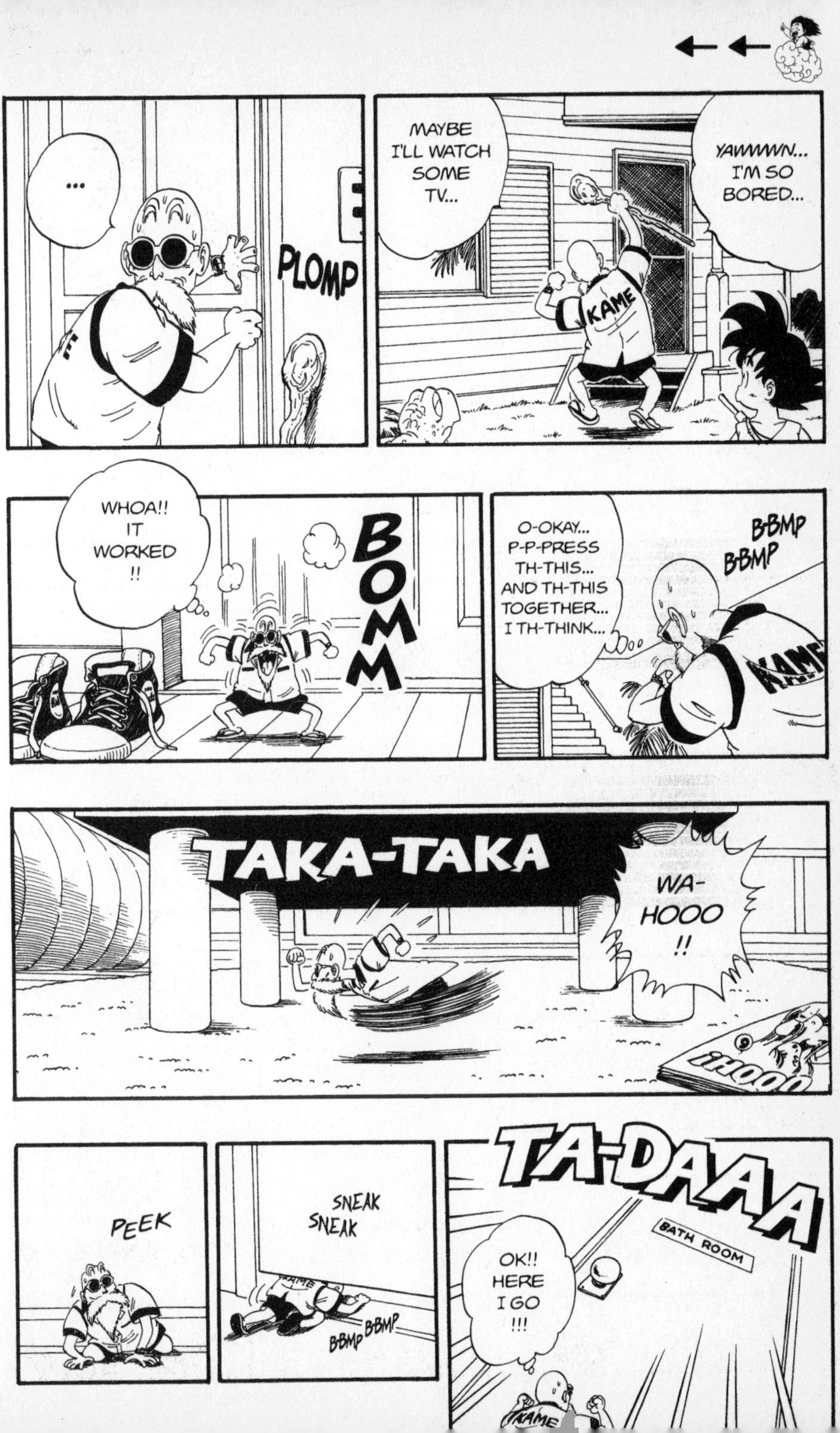
YAWWWN... I'M SO BORED...
MAYBE I'LL WATCH SOME TV...
...
PLOMP
O-OKAY... P-P-PRESS TH-THIS... AND TH-THIS TOGETHER... I TH-THINK...
B-BMP B-BMP
BOMM
WHOA!! IT WORKED !!
WA-HOOO !!
TAKA-TAKA
TA-DAAA
BATH ROOM
OK!! HERE I GO !!!
SNEAK SNEAK
B-BMP B-BMP
PEEK

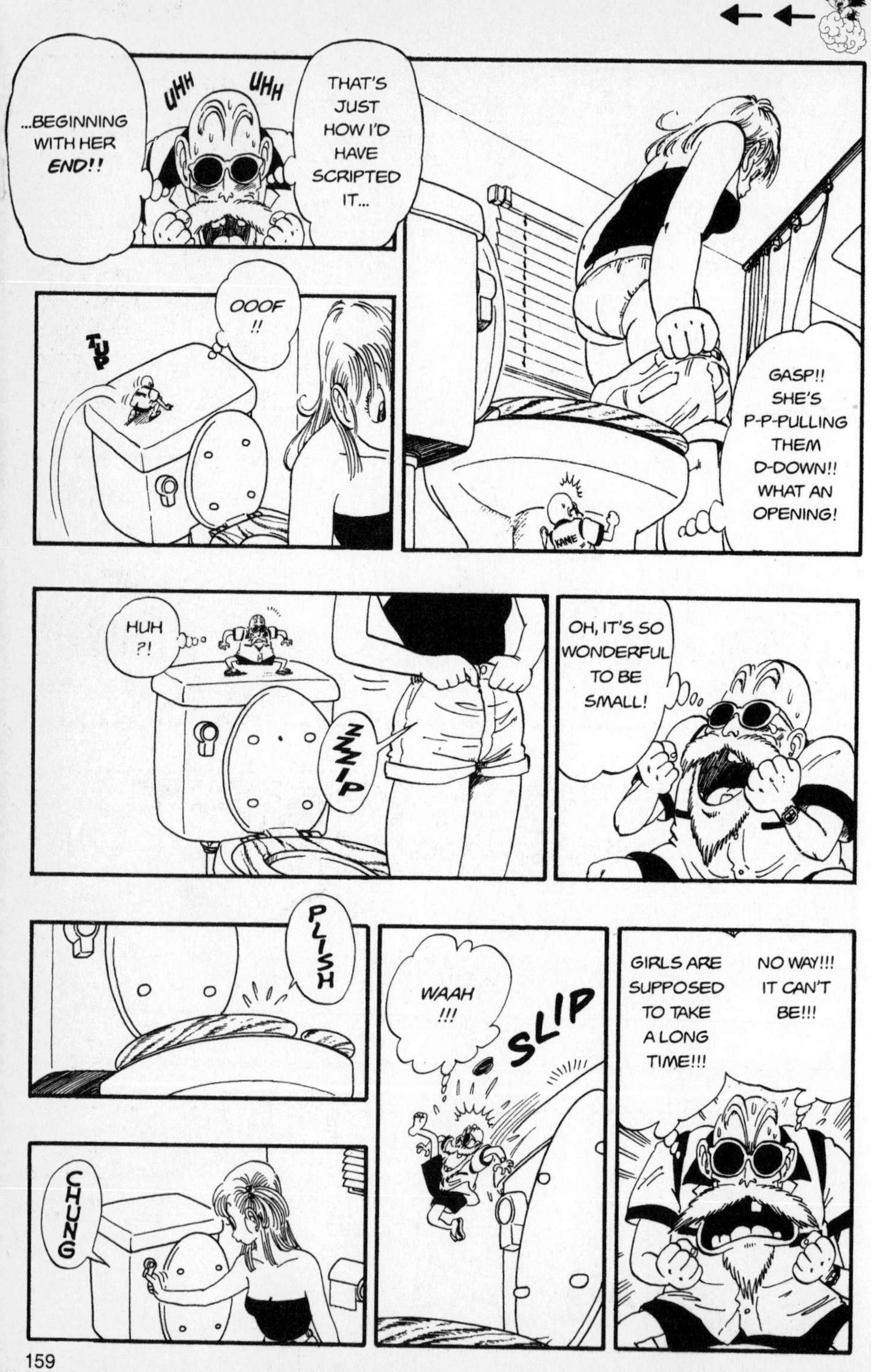
GASP!! SHE'S P-P-PULLING THEM D-DOWN!! WHAT AN OPENING!
KAME
THAT'S JUST HOW I'D HAVE SCRIPTED IT...
UHH UHH
...BEGINNING WITH HER END!!
OOOF !!
TUP
OH, IT'S SO WONDERFUL TO BE SMALL!
HUH ?!
ZZZIP
NO WAY!!! IT CAN'T BE!!!
GIRLS ARE SUPPOSED TO TAKE A LONG TIME!!!
WAAH !!!
SLIP
PLISH
CHUNG

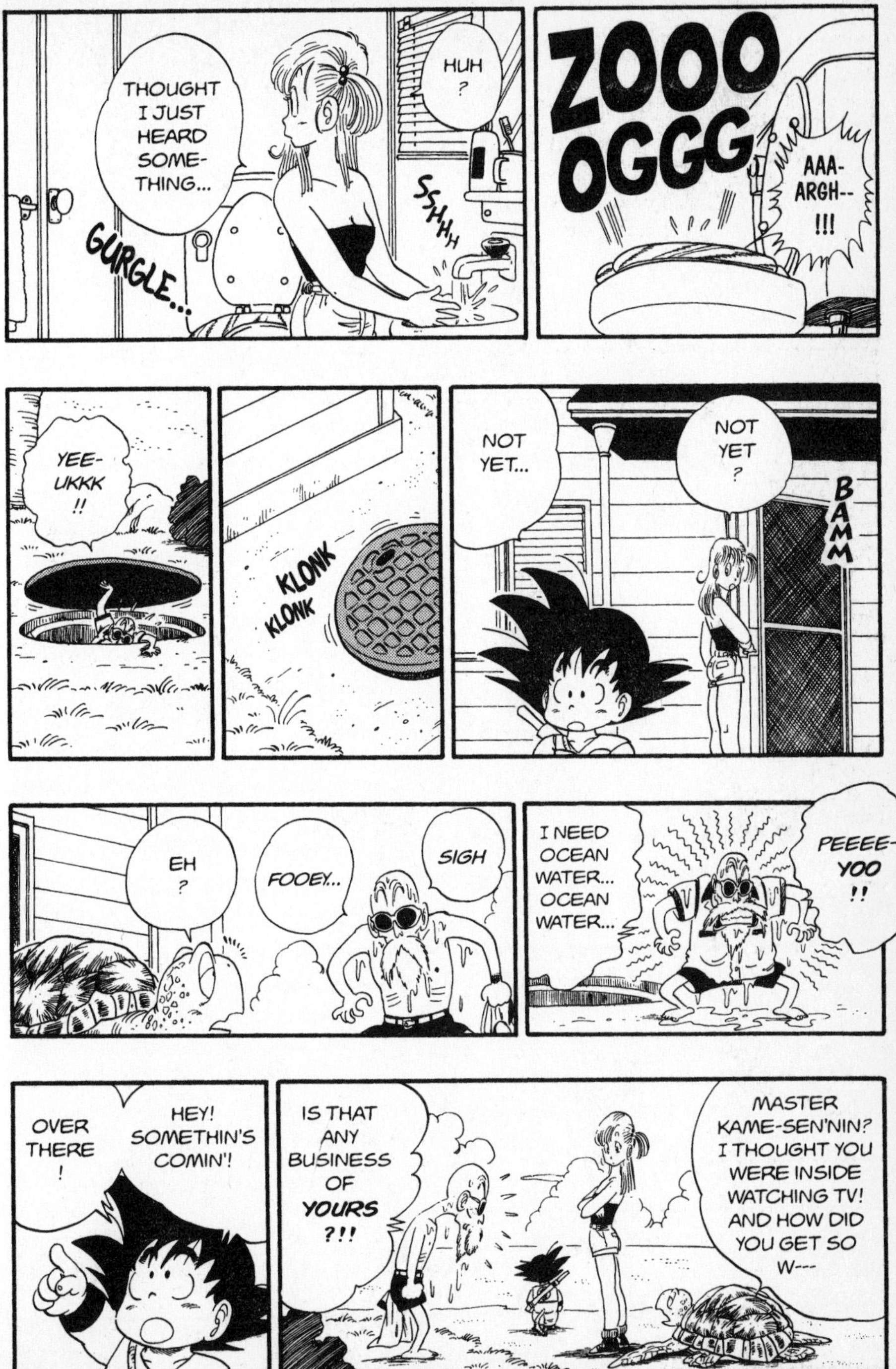
ZOOO OGGG
AAA-ARGH--!!!
HUH ?
THOUGHT I JUST HEARD SOME-THING...
SSHHH
GURGLE...
NOT YET ?
BAMM
NOT YET...
KLONK KLONK
YEE-UKKK !!
PEEEE-*YOO* !!
I NEED OCEAN WATER... OCEAN WATER...
SIGH
FOOEY...
EH ?
MASTER KAME-SEN'NIN? I THOUGHT YOU WERE INSIDE WATCHING TV! AND HOW DID YOU GET SO W---
IS THAT ANY BUSINESS OF *YOURS* ?!!
HEY! SOMETHIN'S COMIN'!
OVER THERE !

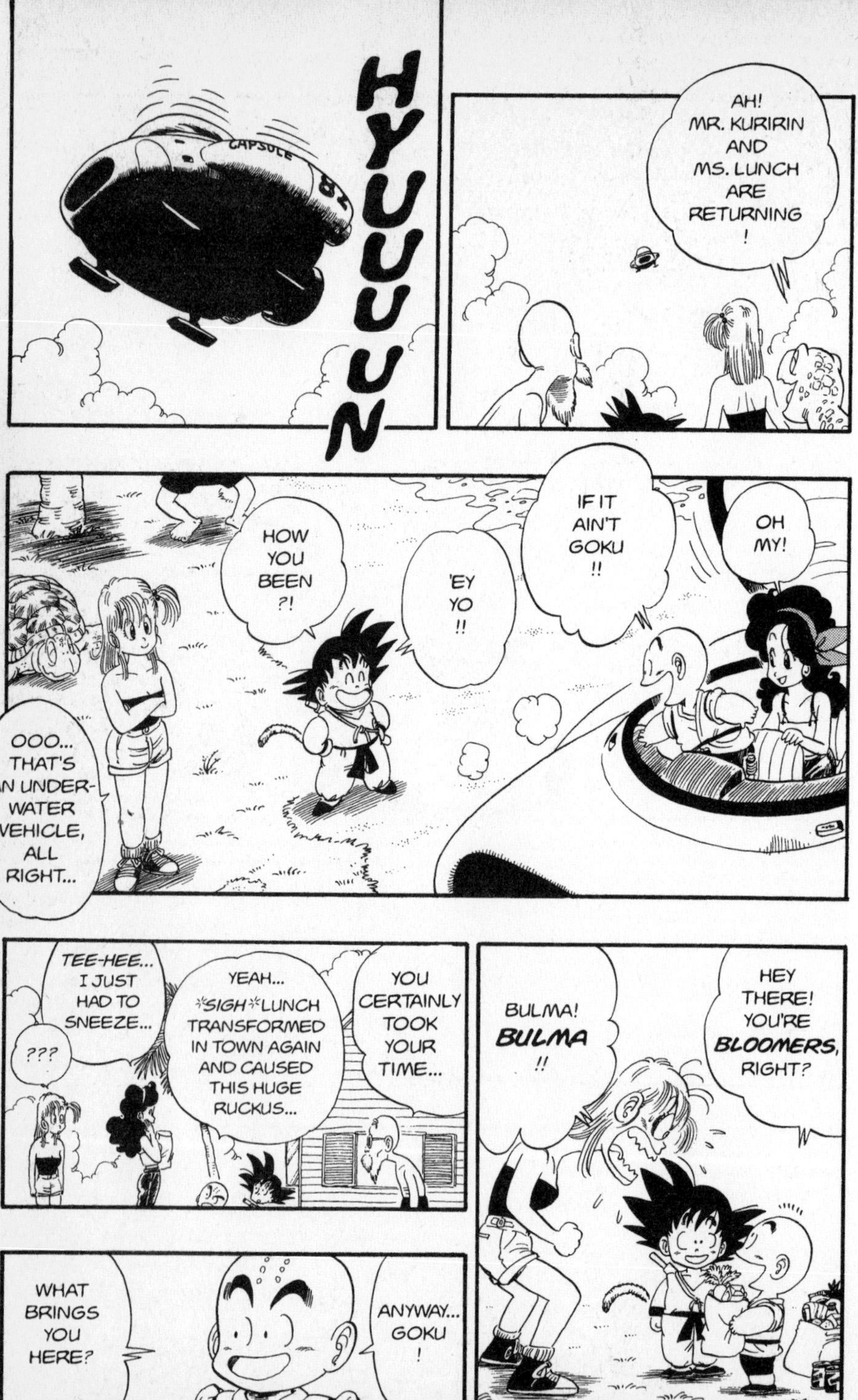
AH! MR. KURIRIN AND MS. LUNCH ARE RETURNING !
HYUUUUN
CAPSULE
OH MY!
IF IT AIN'T GOKU !!
'EY YO !!
HOW YOU BEEN ?!
OOO... THAT'S AN UNDER-WATER VEHICLE, ALL RIGHT...
HEY THERE! YOU'RE BLOOMERS, RIGHT?
BULMA! BULMA !!
YOU CERTAINLY TOOK YOUR TIME...
YEAH... *SIGH* LUNCH TRANSFORMED IN TOWN AGAIN AND CAUSED THIS HUGE RUCKUS...
TEE-HEE... I JUST HAD TO SNEEZE...
???
ANYWAY... GOKU !
WHAT BRINGS YOU HERE?

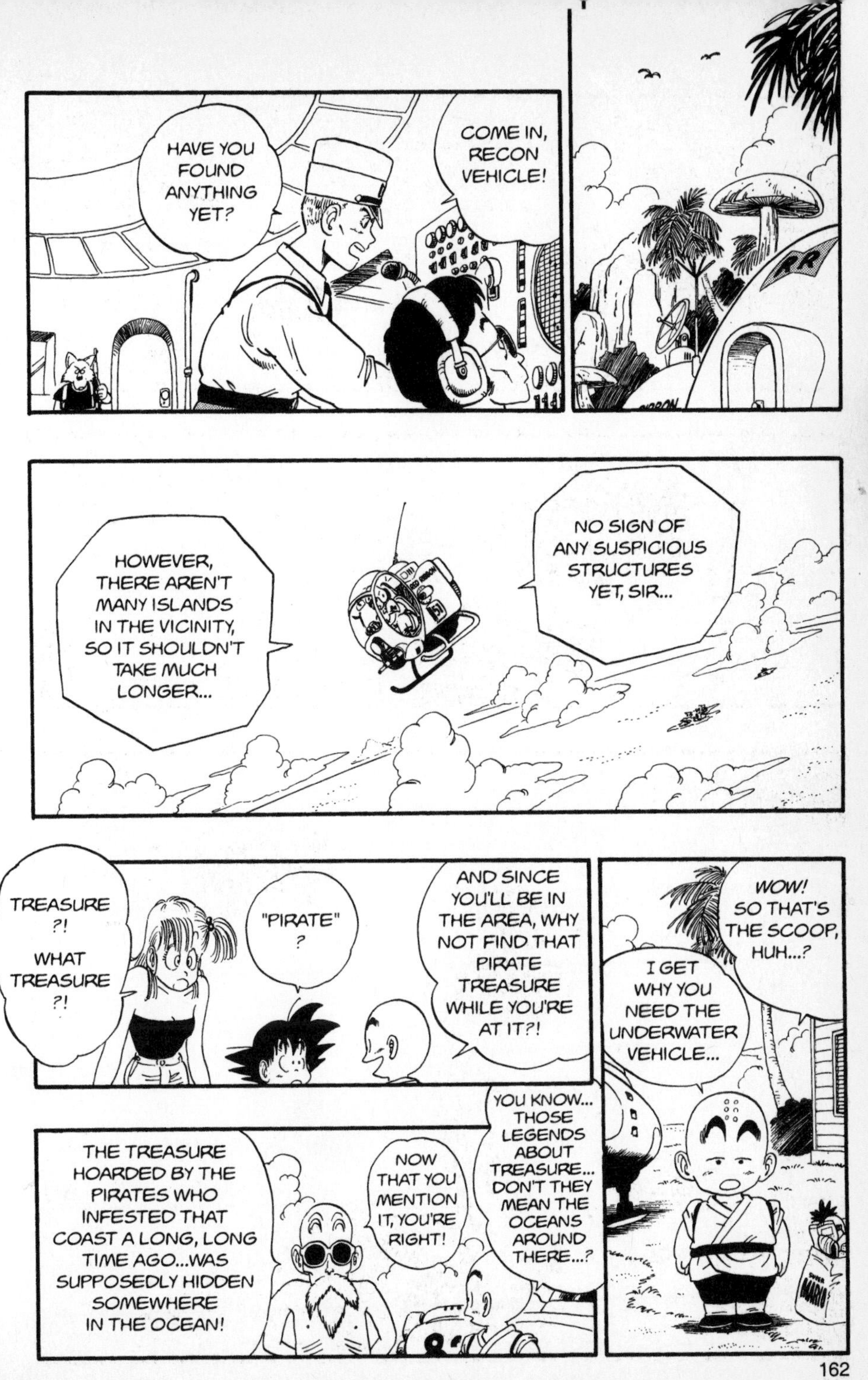
COME IN, RECON VEHICLE!
HAVE YOU FOUND ANYTHING YET?
NO SIGN OF ANY SUSPICIOUS STRUCTURES YET, SIR...
HOWEVER, THERE AREN'T MANY ISLANDS IN THE VICINITY, SO IT SHOULDN'T TAKE MUCH LONGER...
WOW! SO THAT'S THE SCOOP, HUH...?
I GET WHY YOU NEED THE UNDERWATER VEHICLE...
AND SINCE YOU'LL BE IN THE AREA, WHY NOT FIND THAT PIRATE TREASURE WHILE YOU'RE AT IT?!
"PIRATE" ?
TREASURE ?! WHAT TREASURE ?!
YOU KNOW... THOSE LEGENDS ABOUT TREASURE... DON'T THEY MEAN THE OCEANS AROUND THERE...?
NOW THAT YOU MENTION IT, YOU'RE RIGHT!
THE TREASURE HOARDED BY THE PIRATES WHO INFESTED THAT COAST A LONG, LONG TIME AGO...WAS SUPPOSEDLY HIDDEN SOMEWHERE IN THE OCEAN!

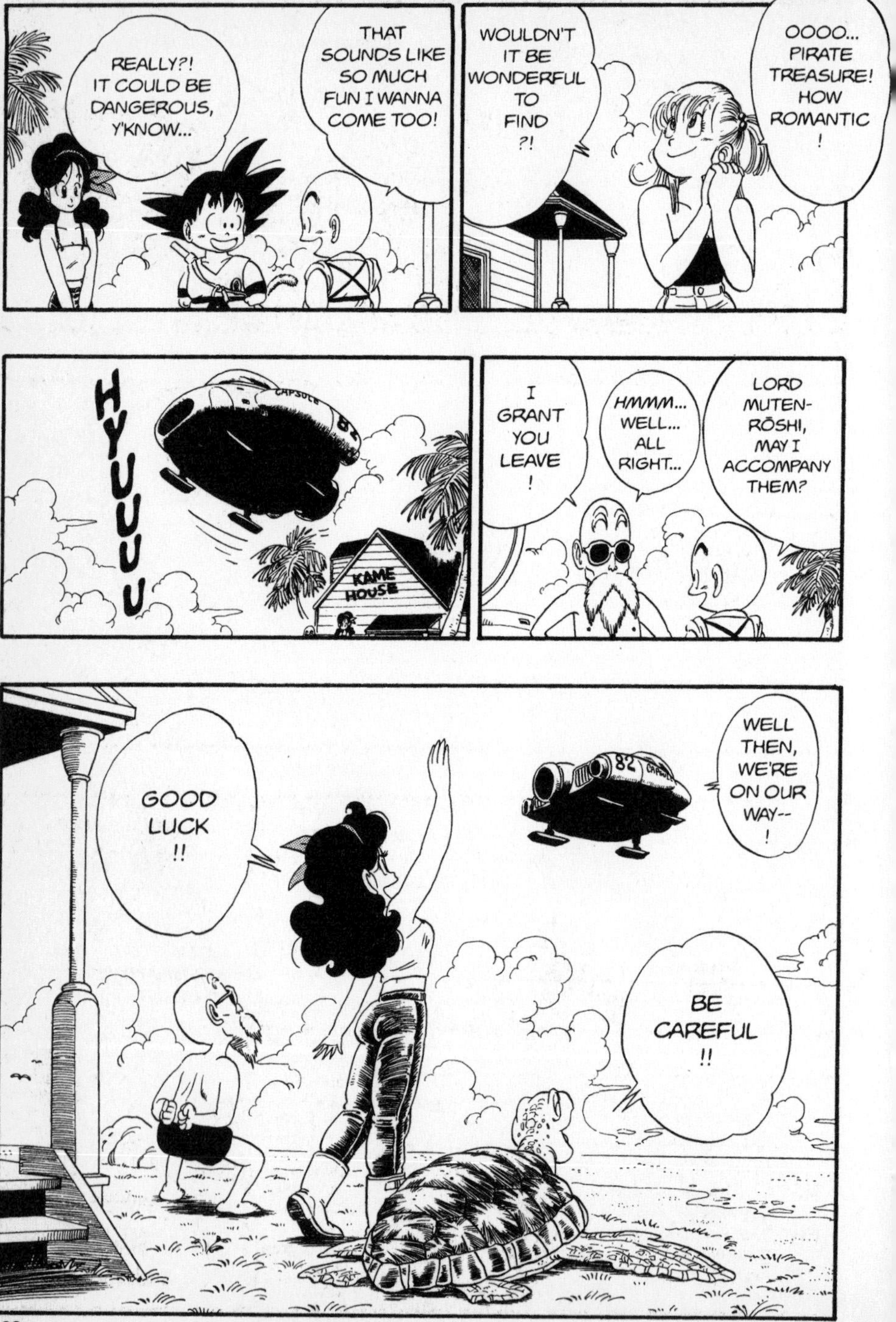
OOOO... PIRATE TREASURE! HOW ROMANTIC!
WOULDN'T IT BE WONDERFUL TO FIND?!
THAT SOUNDS LIKE SO MUCH FUN I WANNA COME TOO!
REALLY?! IT COULD BE DANGEROUS, Y'KNOW...
LORD MUTEN-RŌSHI, MAY I ACCOMPANY THEM?
HMMM... WELL... ALL RIGHT...
I GRANT YOU LEAVE!
HYUUUU
CAPSULE 82
KAME HOUSE
WELL THEN, WE'RE ON OUR WAY--!
82 CAPSULE
GOOD LUCK!!
BE CAREFUL!!

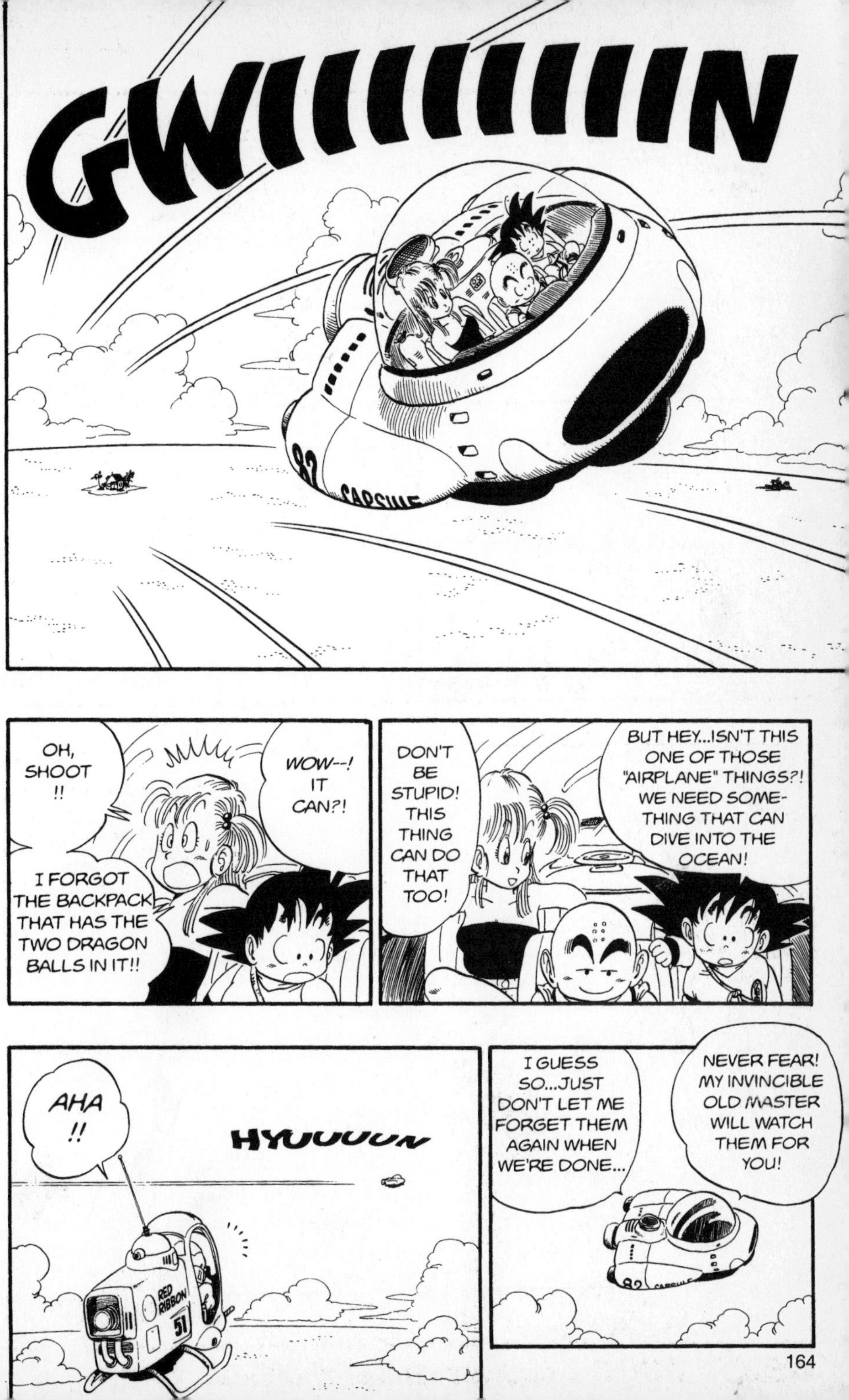
GWIIIIIIIIN
82 CAPSULE
BUT HEY...ISN'T THIS ONE OF THOSE "AIRPLANE" THINGS?! WE NEED SOME-THING THAT CAN DIVE INTO THE OCEAN!
DON'T BE STUPID! THIS THING CAN DO THAT TOO!
WOW--! IT CAN?!
OH, SHOOT !!
I FORGOT THE BACKPACK THAT HAS THE TWO DRAGON BALLS IN IT!!
NEVER FEAR! MY INVINCIBLE OLD MASTER WILL WATCH THEM FOR YOU!
I GUESS SO...JUST DON'T LET ME FORGET THEM AGAIN WHEN WE'RE DONE...
HYUUUUN
AHA !!
RED RIBBON 51

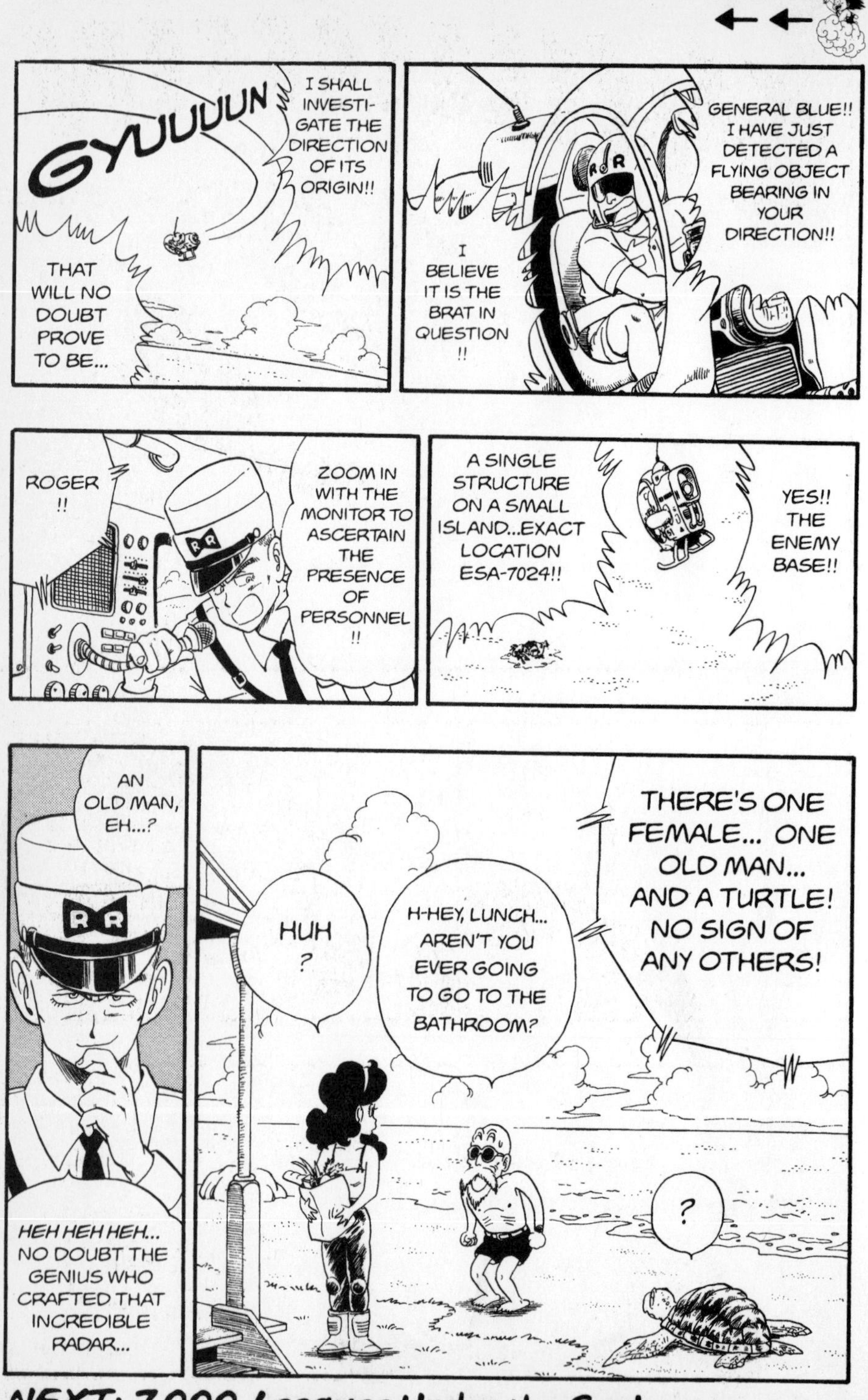
GENERAL BLUE!! I HAVE JUST DETECTED A FLYING OBJECT BEARING IN YOUR DIRECTION!!
I BELIEVE IT IS THE BRAT IN QUESTION!!
I SHALL INVESTI-GATE THE DIRECTION OF ITS ORIGIN!!
GYUUUUN
THAT WILL NO DOUBT PROVE TO BE...
YES!! THE ENEMY BASE!!
A SINGLE STRUCTURE ON A SMALL ISLAND...EXACT LOCATION ESA-7024!!
ZOOM IN WITH THE MONITOR TO ASCERTAIN THE PRESENCE OF PERSONNEL!!
ROGER!!
THERE'S ONE FEMALE... ONE OLD MAN... AND A TURTLE! NO SIGN OF ANY OTHERS!
H-HEY, LUNCH... AREN'T YOU EVER GOING TO GO TO THE BATHROOM?
HUH?
?
AN OLD MAN, EH...?
HEH HEH HEH... NO DOUBT THE GENIUS WHO CRAFTED THAT INCREDIBLE RADAR...

NEXT: 7,000 Leagues Under the Sea!

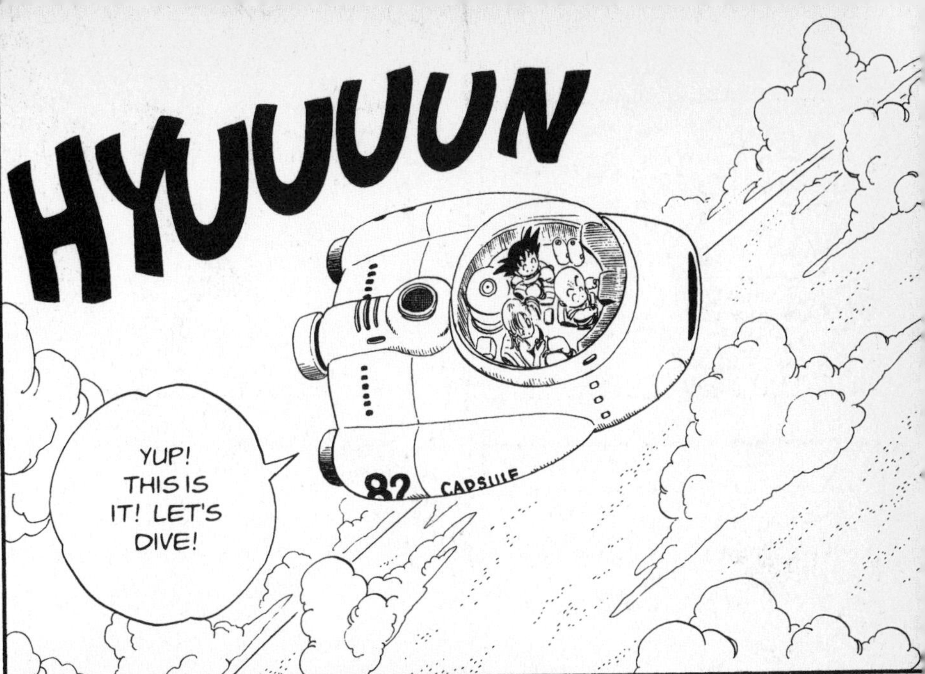
HYUUUUN
YUP! THIS IS IT! LET'S DIVE!
82 CAPSULE

Tale 72 • The Blue Meanies

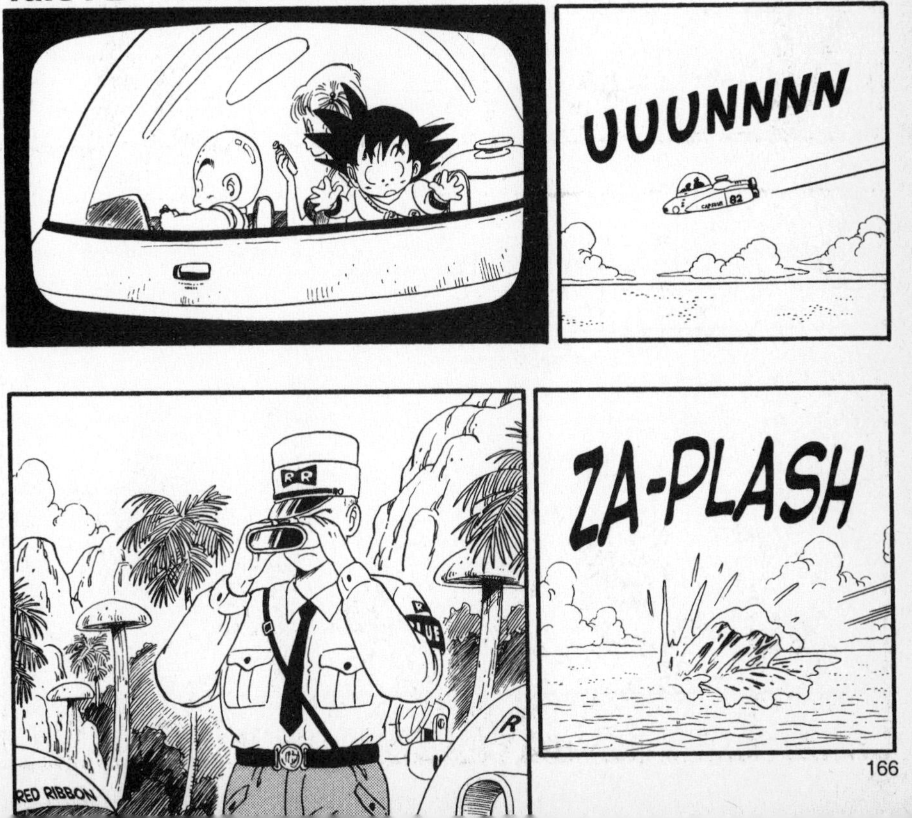
UUUNNNN
ZA-PLASH
RED RIBBON

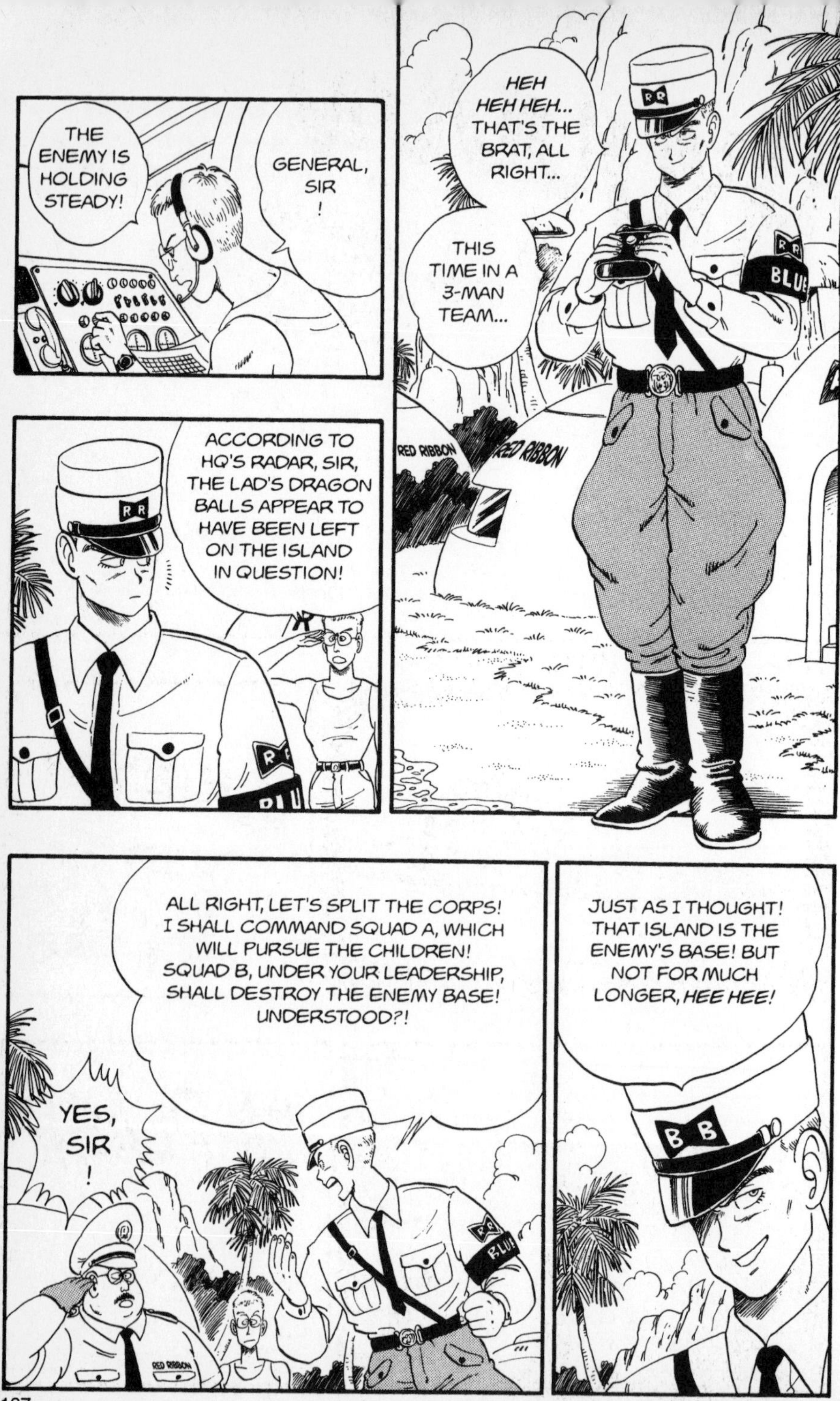
HEH HEH HEH... THAT'S THE BRAT, ALL RIGHT...
THIS TIME IN A 3-MAN TEAM...
GENERAL, SIR!
THE ENEMY IS HOLDING STEADY!
ACCORDING TO HQ'S RADAR, SIR, THE LAD'S DRAGON BALLS APPEAR TO HAVE BEEN LEFT ON THE ISLAND IN QUESTION!
JUST AS I THOUGHT! THAT ISLAND IS THE ENEMY'S BASE! BUT NOT FOR MUCH LONGER, *HEE HEE!*
ALL RIGHT, LET'S SPLIT THE CORPS! I SHALL COMMAND SQUAD A, WHICH WILL PURSUE THE CHILDREN! SQUAD B, UNDER YOUR LEADERSHIP, SHALL DESTROY THE ENEMY BASE! UNDERSTOOD?!
YES, SIR!

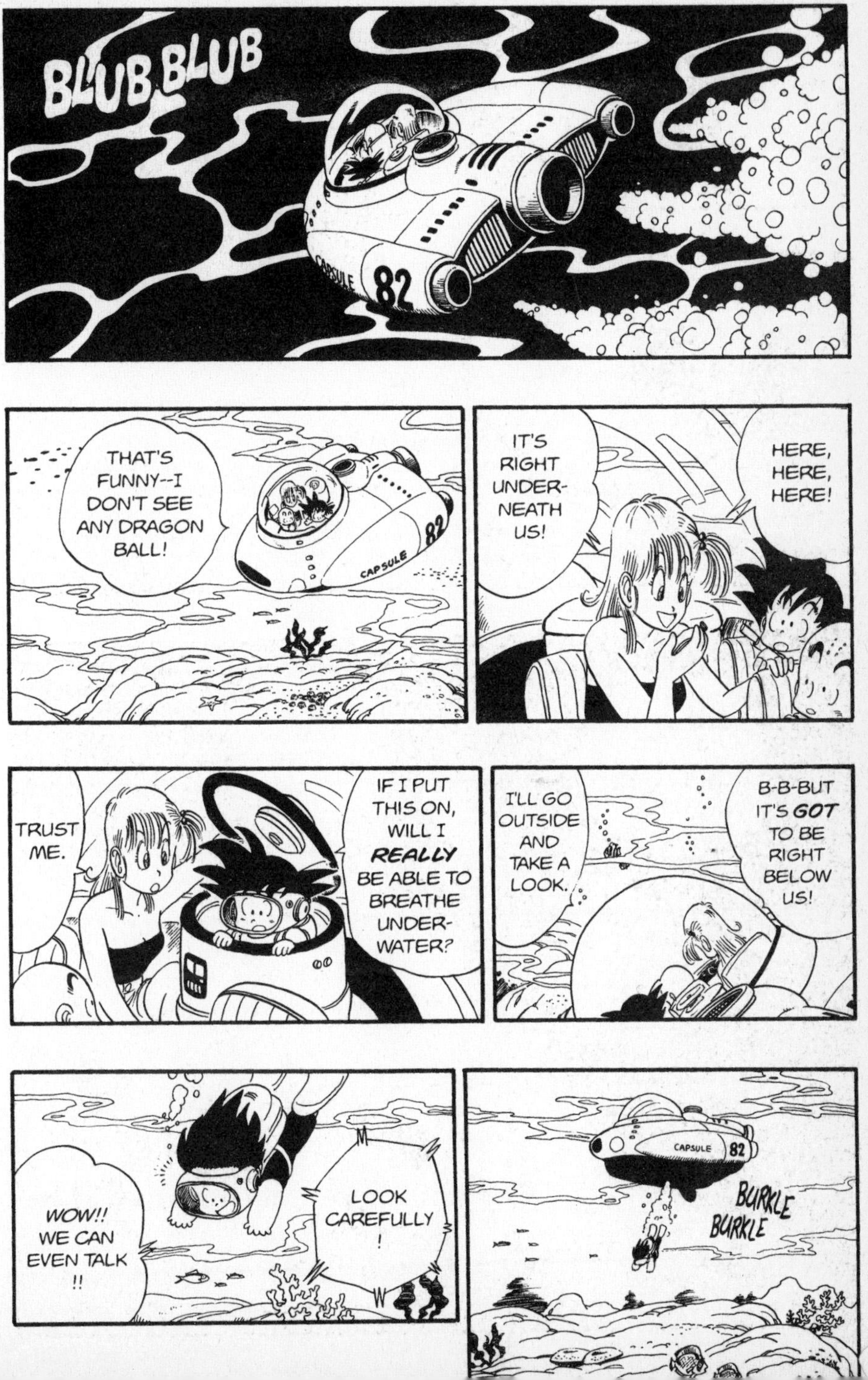
BLUB BLUB
CAPSULE 82
HERE, HERE, HERE!
IT'S RIGHT UNDERNEATH US!
THAT'S FUNNY--I DON'T SEE ANY DRAGON BALL!
B-B-BUT IT'S *GOT* TO BE RIGHT BELOW US!
I'LL GO OUTSIDE AND TAKE A LOOK.
IF I PUT THIS ON, WILL I *REALLY* BE ABLE TO BREATHE UNDERWATER?
TRUST ME.
BURKLE BURKLE
LOOK CAREFULLY!
WOW!! WE CAN EVEN TALK!!

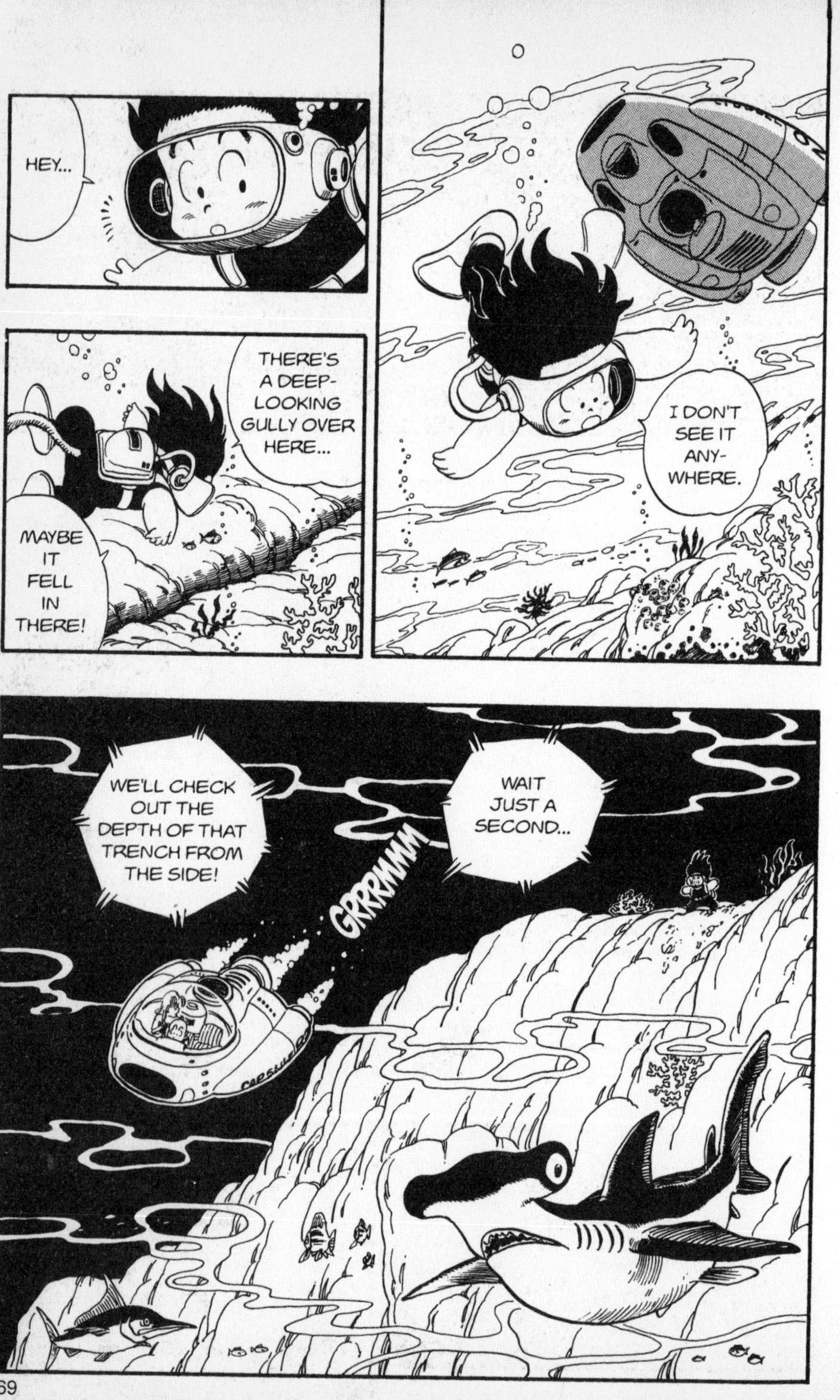
I DON'T SEE IT ANY-WHERE.
HEY...
THERE'S A DEEP-LOOKING GULLY OVER HERE...
MAYBE IT FELL IN THERE!
WAIT JUST A SECOND...
WE'LL CHECK OUT THE DEPTH OF THAT TRENCH FROM THE SIDE!
GRRRMMM

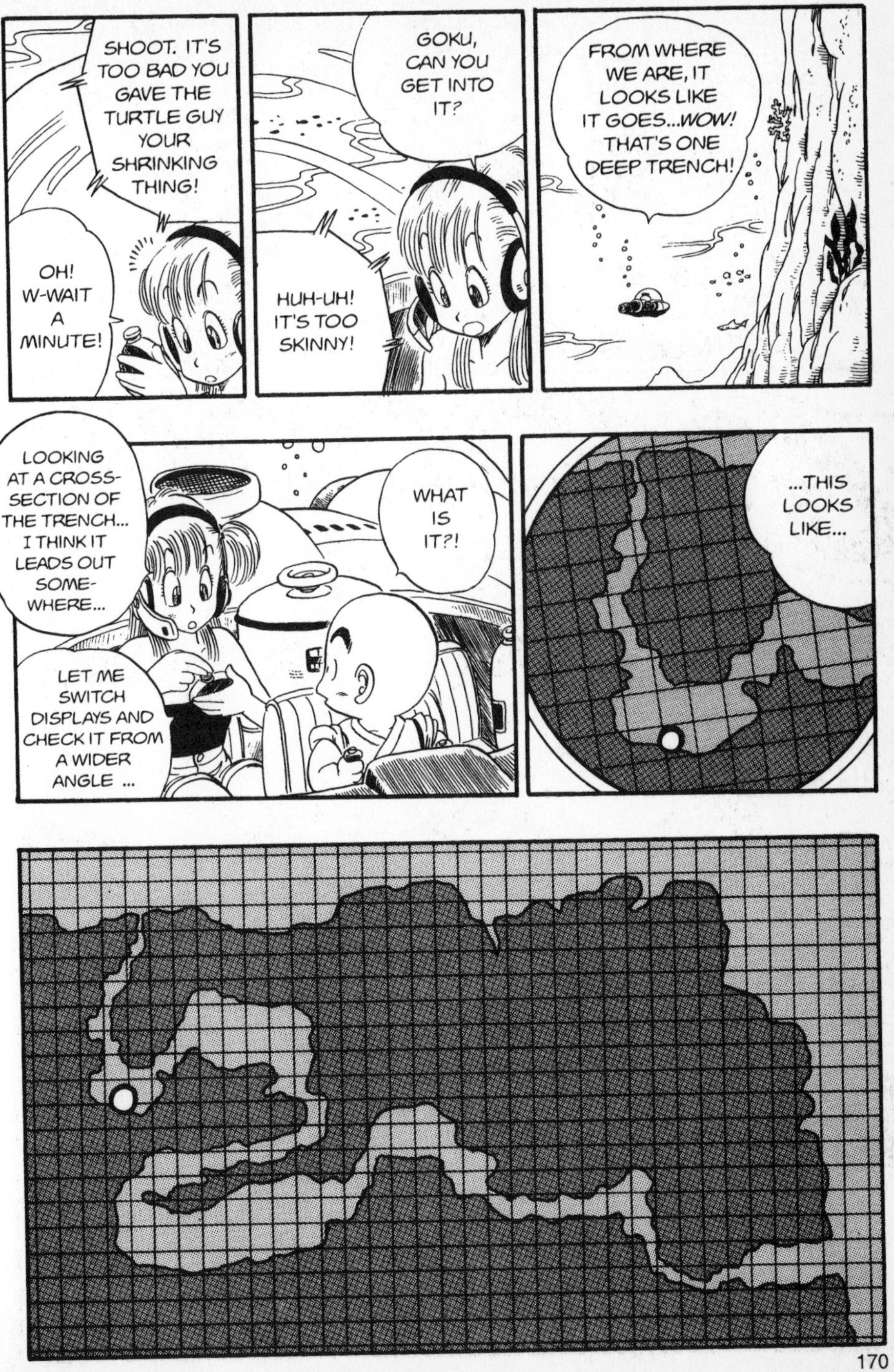
FROM WHERE WE ARE, IT LOOKS LIKE IT GOES...*WOW!* THAT'S ONE DEEP TRENCH!
GOKU, CAN YOU GET INTO IT?
HUH-UH! IT'S TOO SKINNY!
SHOOT. IT'S TOO BAD YOU GAVE THE TURTLE GUY YOUR SHRINKING THING!
OH! W-WAIT A MINUTE!
...THIS LOOKS LIKE...
WHAT IS IT?!
LOOKING AT A CROSS-SECTION OF THE TRENCH... I THINK IT LEADS OUT SOME-WHERE...
LET ME SWITCH DISPLAYS AND CHECK IT FROM A WIDER ANGLE ...

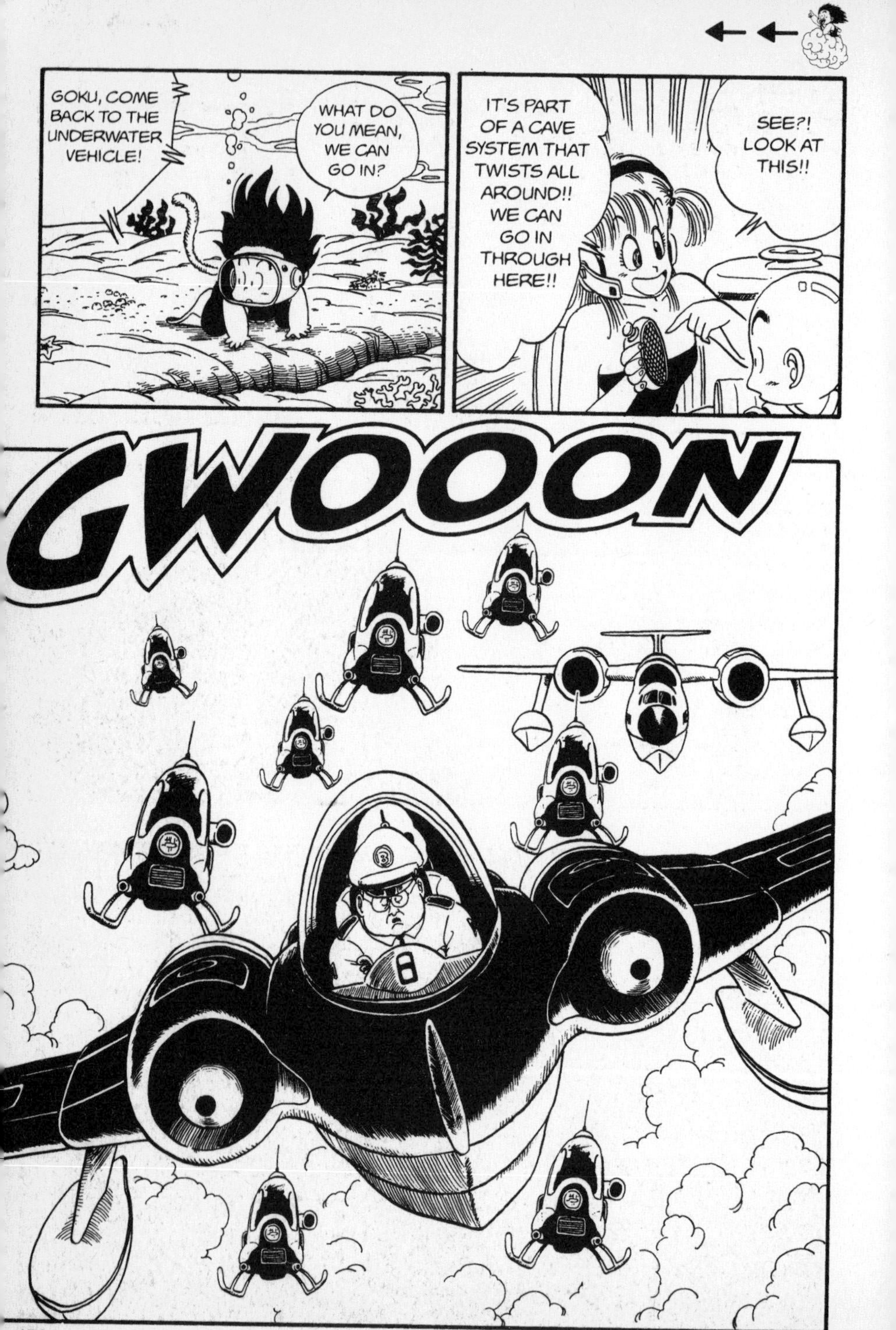
SEE?! LOOK AT THIS!!
IT'S PART OF A CAVE SYSTEM THAT TWISTS ALL AROUND!! WE CAN GO IN THROUGH HERE!!
WHAT DO YOU MEAN, WE CAN GO IN?
GOKU, COME BACK TO THE UNDERWATER VEHICLE!
GWOOON

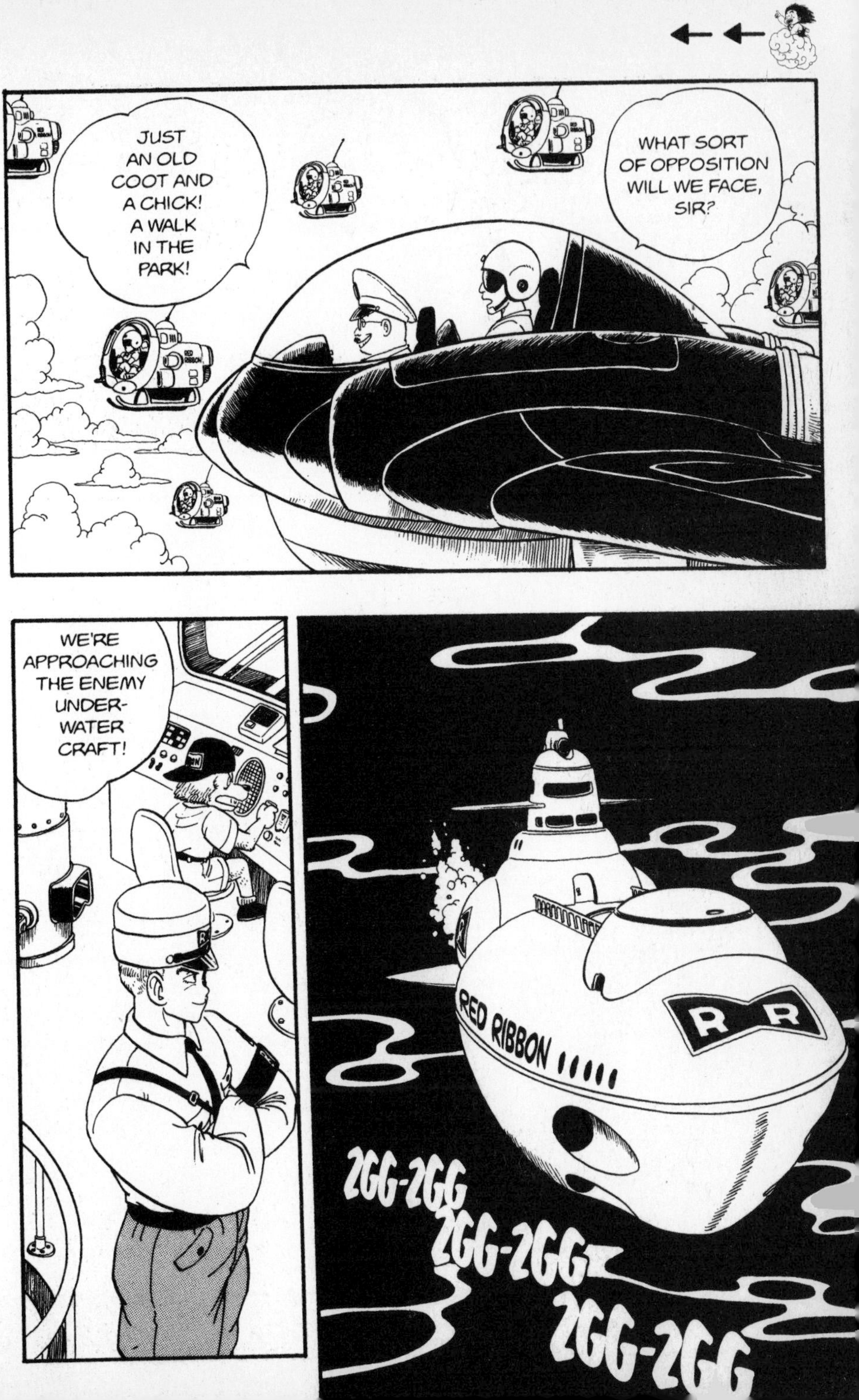
WHAT SORT OF OPPOSITION WILL WE FACE, SIR?
JUST AN OLD COOT AND A CHICK! A WALK IN THE PARK!
RED RIBBON
ZGG-ZGG
ZGG-ZGG
ZGG-ZGG
WE'RE APPROACHING THE ENEMY UNDER-WATER CRAFT!

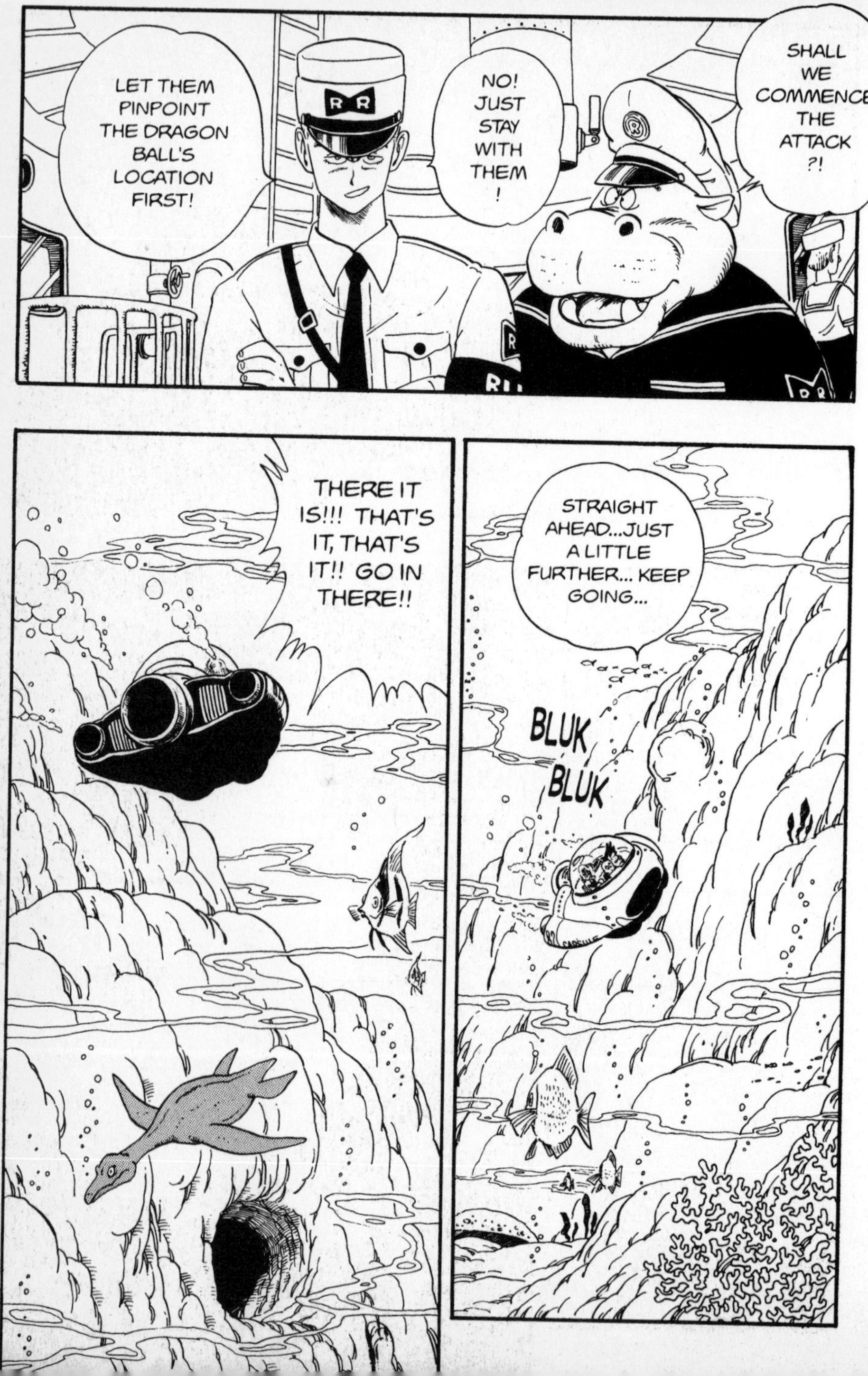
SHALL WE COMMENCE THE ATTACK?!
NO! JUST STAY WITH THEM!
LET THEM PINPOINT THE DRAGON BALL'S LOCATION FIRST!
STRAIGHT AHEAD...JUST A LITTLE FURTHER... KEEP GOING...
BLUK BLUK
THERE IT IS!!! THAT'S IT, THAT'S IT!! GO IN THERE!!

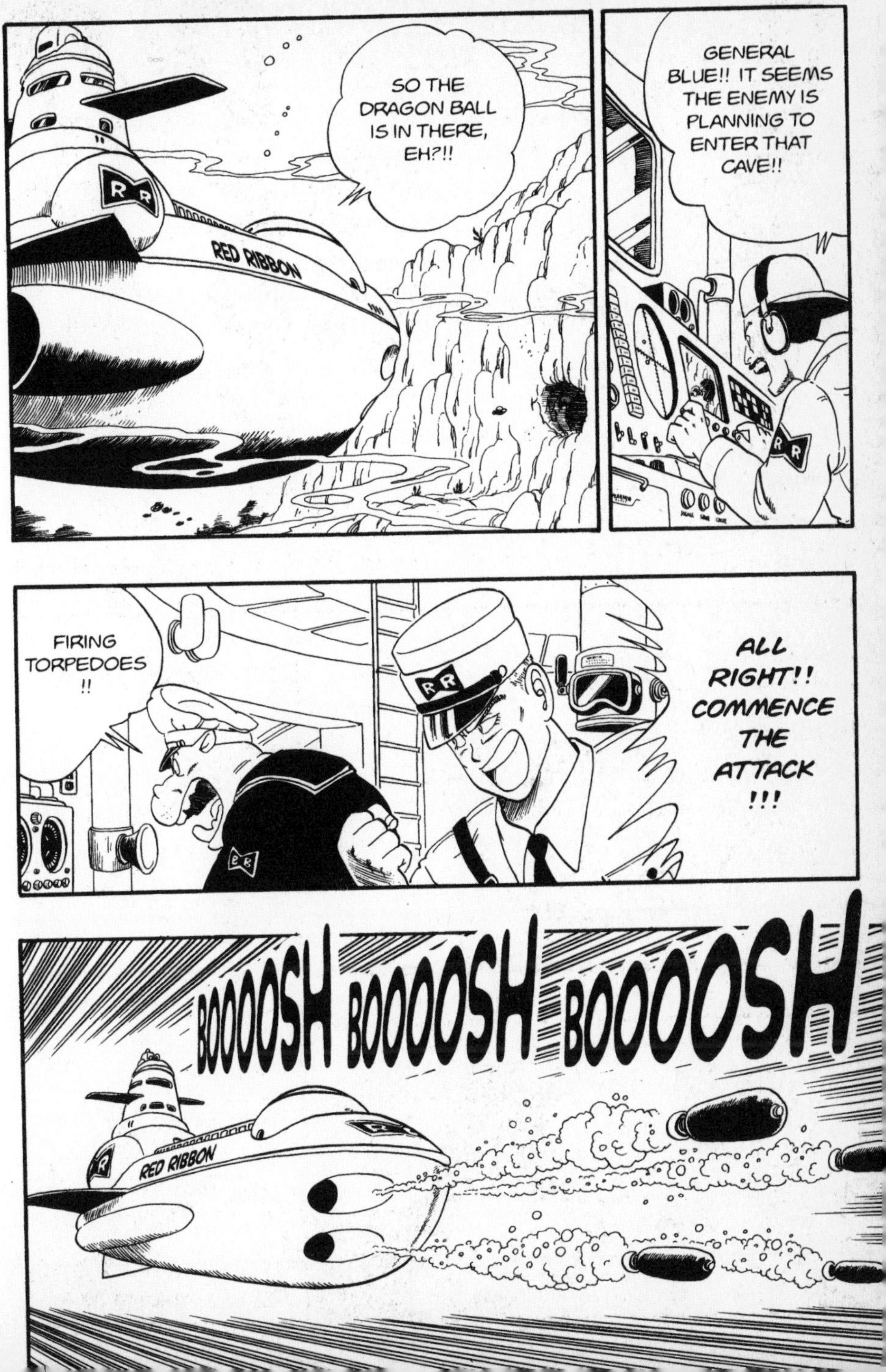
GENERAL BLUE!! IT SEEMS THE ENEMY IS PLANNING TO ENTER THAT CAVE!!
SO THE DRAGON BALL IS IN THERE, EH?!!
ALL RIGHT!! COMMENCE THE ATTACK !!!
FIRING TORPEDOES !!
RED RIBBON
BOOOOSH BOOOOSH BOOOOSH

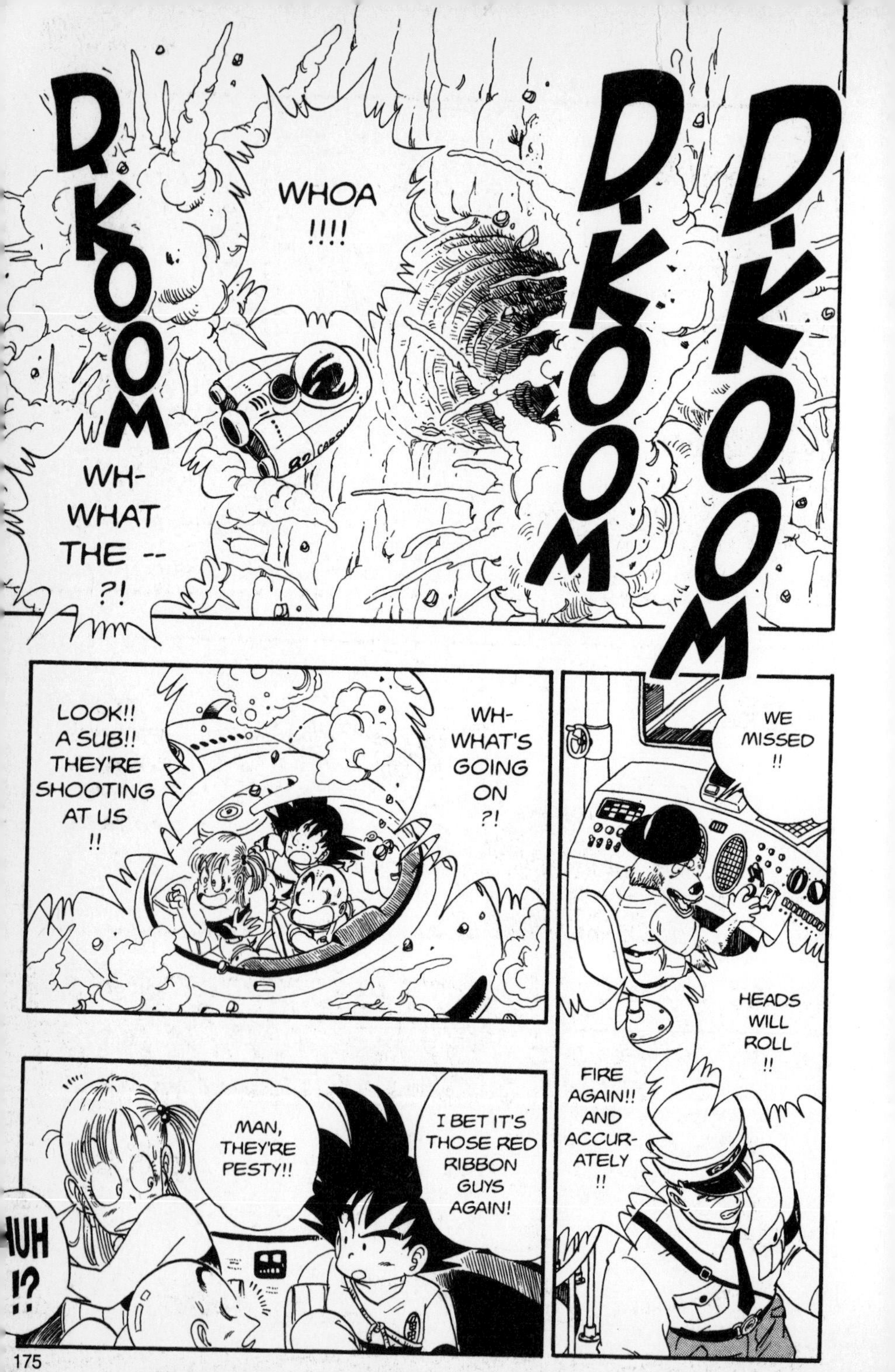
D-KOOM
D-KOOM
WHOA !!!!
D-KOOM
WH- WHAT THE -- ?!
WE MISSED !!
HEADS WILL ROLL !!
FIRE AGAIN!! AND ACCUR-ATELY !!
WH- WHAT'S GOING ON ?!
LOOK!! A SUB!! THEY'RE SHOOTING AT US !!
I BET IT'S THOSE RED RIBBON GUYS AGAIN!
MAN, THEY'RE PESTY!!
HUH !?

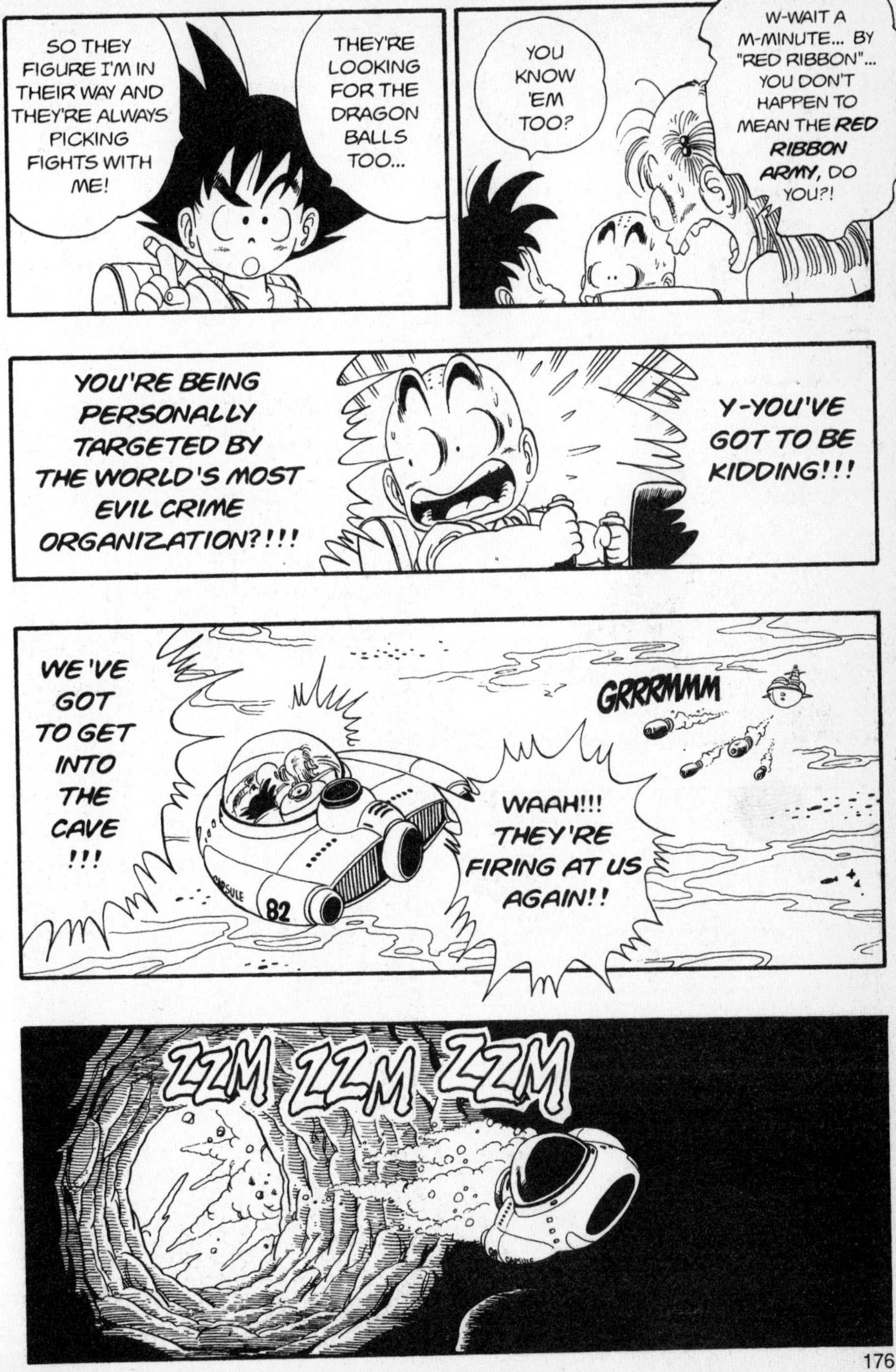
W-WAIT A M-MINUTE... BY "RED RIBBON"... YOU DON'T HAPPEN TO MEAN THE **RED RIBBON ARMY**, DO YOU?!
YOU KNOW 'EM TOO?
THEY'RE LOOKING FOR THE DRAGON BALLS TOO...
SO THEY FIGURE I'M IN THEIR WAY AND THEY'RE ALWAYS PICKING FIGHTS WITH ME!
Y-YOU'VE GOT TO BE KIDDING!!!
YOU'RE BEING PERSONALLY TARGETED BY THE WORLD'S MOST EVIL CRIME ORGANIZATION?!!!
GRRRMMM
WAAH!!! THEY'RE FIRING AT US AGAIN!!
WE'VE GOT TO GET INTO THE CAVE!!!
82
CAPSULE
ZZM ZZM ZZM

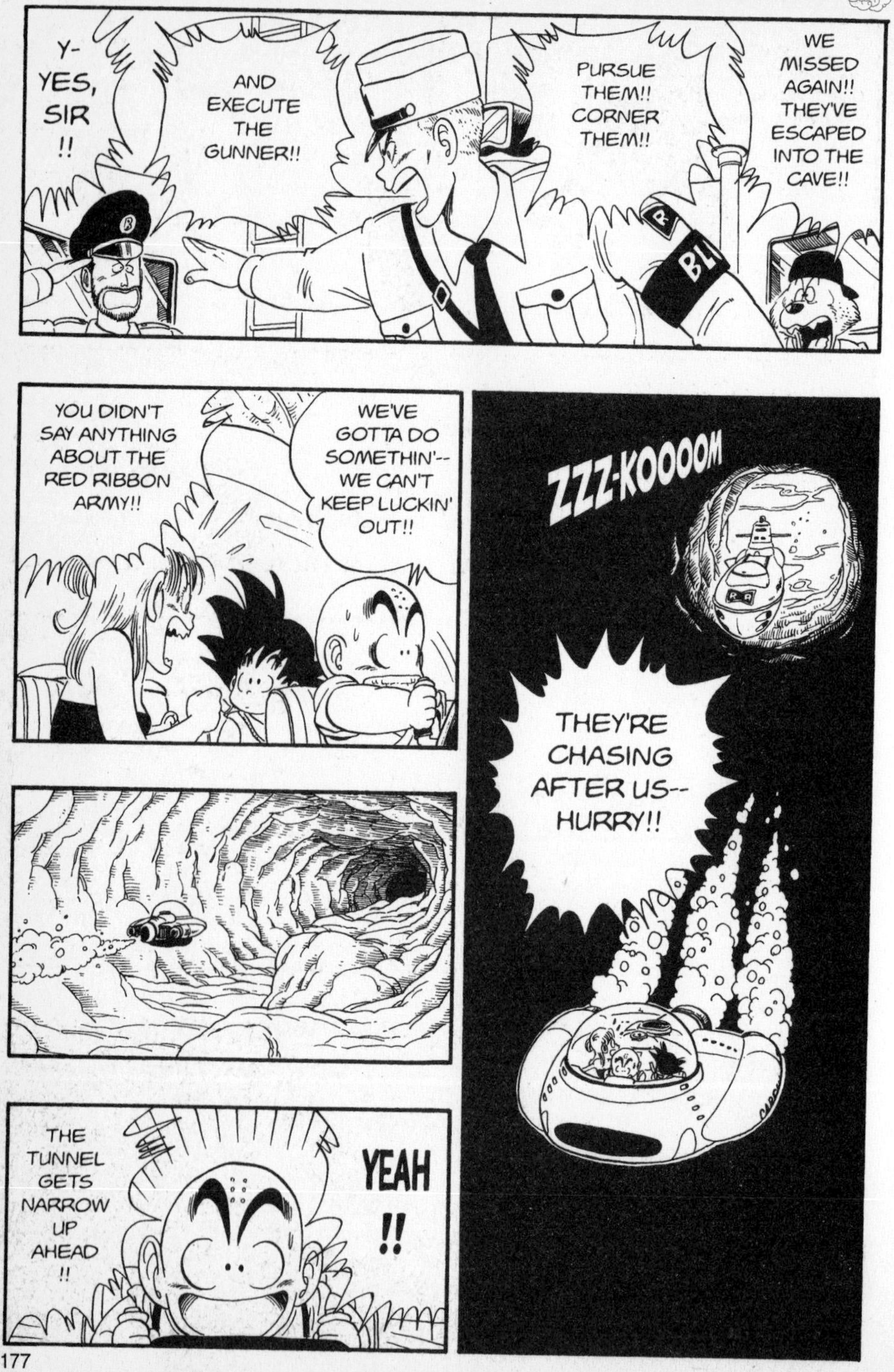
WE MISSED AGAIN!! THEY'VE ESCAPED INTO THE CAVE!!
PURSUE THEM!! CORNER THEM!!
AND EXECUTE THE GUNNER!!
Y-YES, SIR!!
ZZZ-KOOOOM
THEY'RE CHASING AFTER US--HURRY!!
WE'VE GOTTA DO SOMETHIN'--WE CAN'T KEEP LUCKIN' OUT!!
YOU DIDN'T SAY ANYTHING ABOUT THE RED RIBBON ARMY!!
YEAH!!
THE TUNNEL GETS NARROW UP AHEAD!!

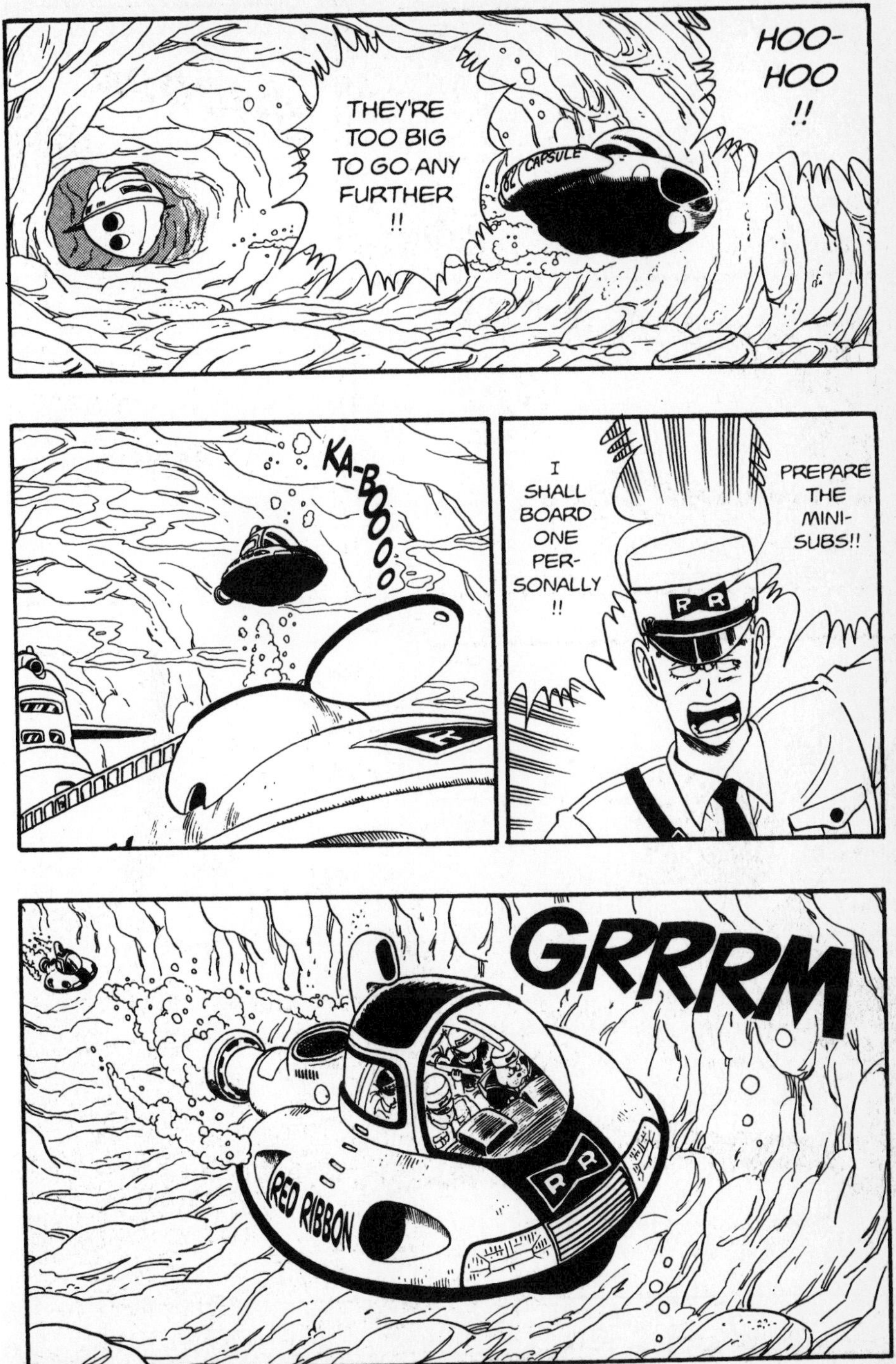
HOO-HOO!!
THEY'RE TOO BIG TO GO ANY FURTHER!!
CAPSULE
PREPARE THE MINI-SUBS!!
I SHALL BOARD ONE PERSONALLY!!
KA-BOOOOOO
GRRRM
RED RIBBON

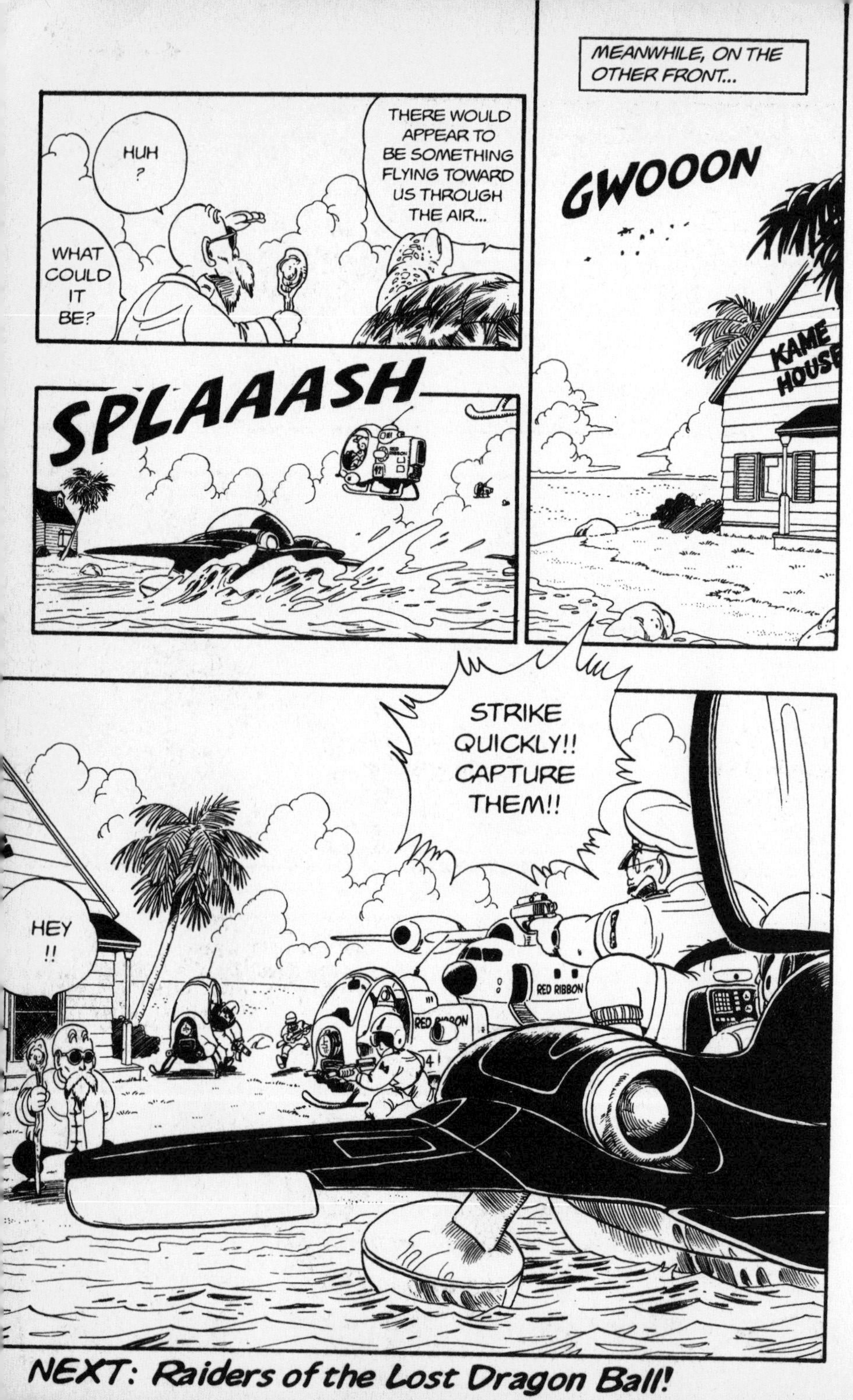
MEANWHILE, ON THE OTHER FRONT...
GWOOON
KAME HOUSE
THERE WOULD APPEAR TO BE SOMETHING FLYING TOWARD US THROUGH THE AIR...
HUH ?
WHAT COULD IT BE?
SPLAAASH
RED RIBBON
STRIKE QUICKLY!! CAPTURE THEM!!
RED RIBBON
RED RIBBON
HEY !!

NEXT: Raiders of the Lost Dragon Ball!

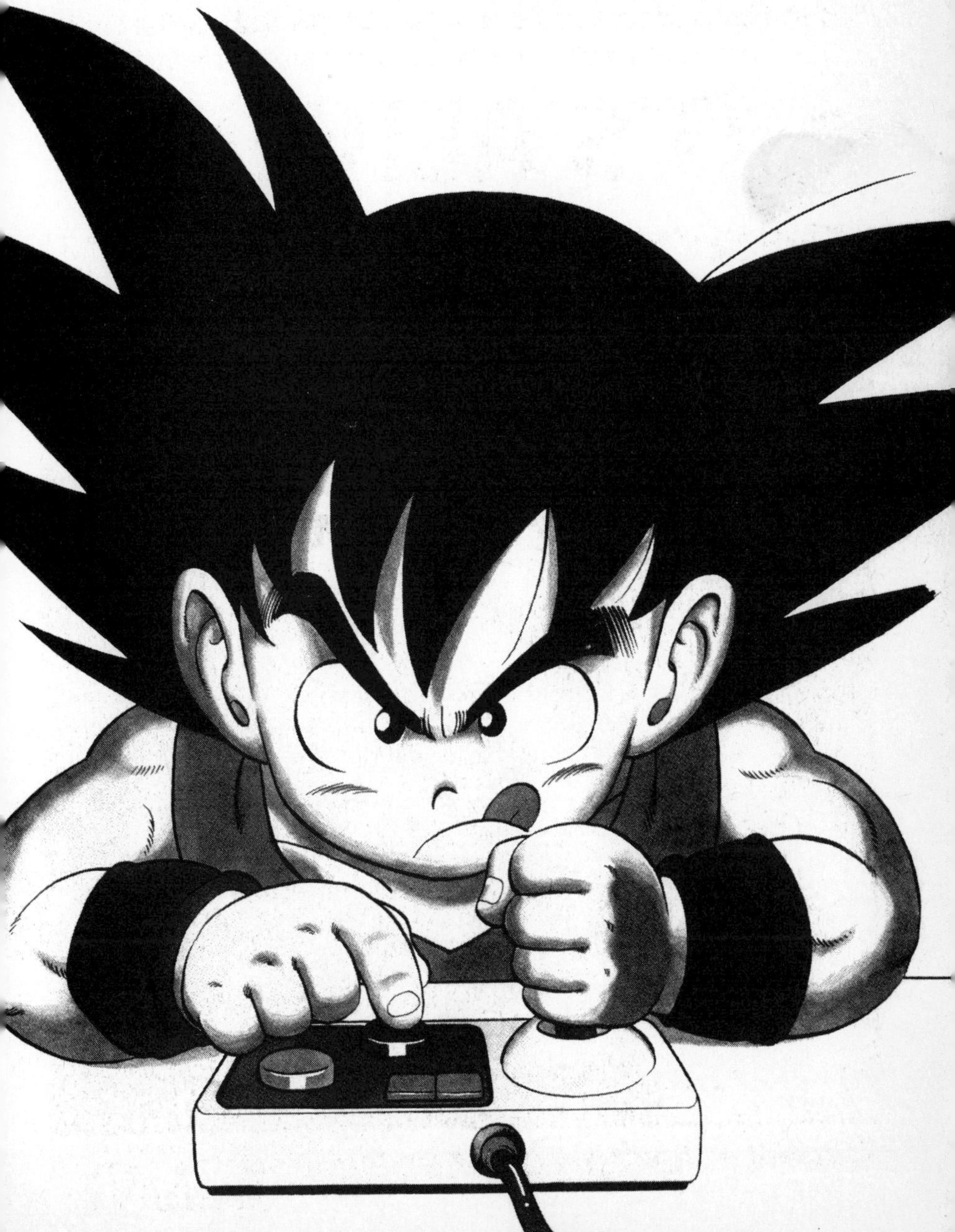

Title Page Gallery

Here are all the chapter title pages which were used when **Dragon Ball** **Vol. 6** was originally published in Japan in **Shônen Jump** magazine. Some were previously published in Viz's **Dragon Ball** monthly comic series; some have never before been seen in America!

IT'S ALIVE!!!

THE SHOCKING MECHANICAL MAN!!!

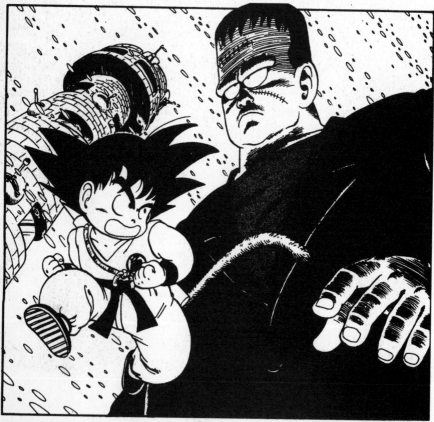

Tale 63 • Mechanical Man No.8

Akira Toriyama

鳥山明

ドラゴンボール

DRAGON BALL

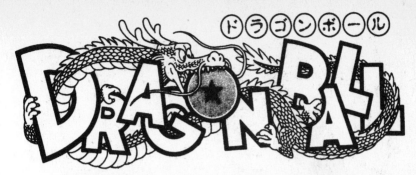

HEY! WHAT AM I DOING IN THAT BOX?

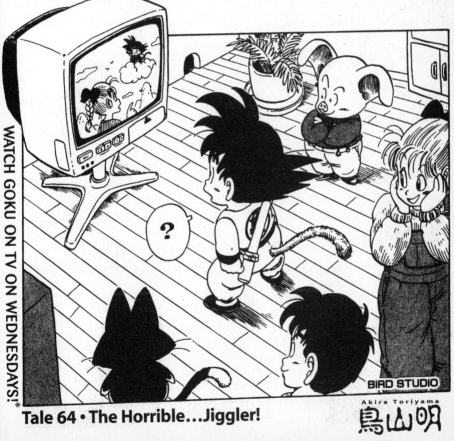

?
BIRD STUDIO

WATCH GOKU ON TV ON WEDNESDAYS!*

Tale 64 • The Horrible...Jiggler!

Akira Toriyama
鳥山明

* In Japan, the Dragon Ball TV series originally played every Wednesday at 7 PM.

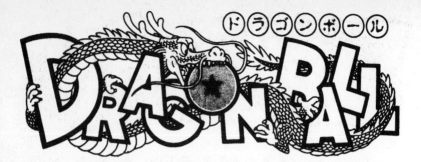

ドラゴンボール

CAN NO MOVE DEFEAT…THE JIGGLER?!?

Tale 65 • How to Unjiggle a Jiggler

Akira Toriyama
鳥山明 BIRD STUDIO

IF I HAVE TO LOSE, AT LEAST GET MY NAME RIGHT!

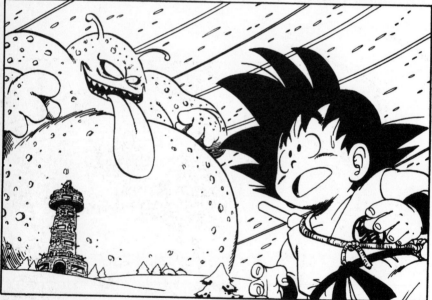

OOPS! I MADE A MISTAKE!

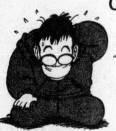

In two earlier issues, I accidentally referred to General White as “General Silver!” I didn’t notice it until a lot of people wrote in about it (including my editor)…luckily it was fixed for the American version! But still…I’M SORRY!

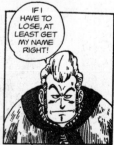

ドラゴンボール

DRAGON BALL

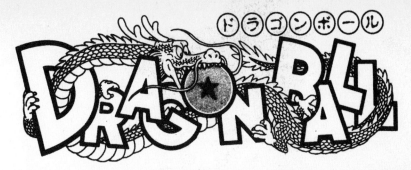

YOU'LL HAVE MANY MORE ADVENTURES!

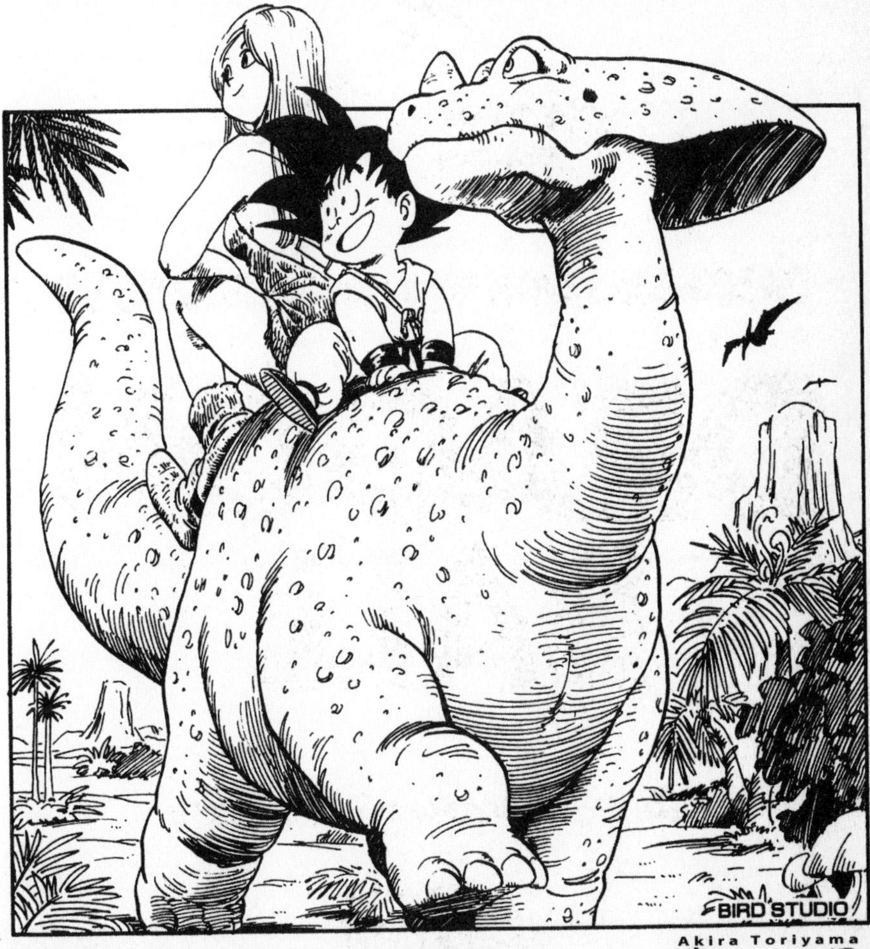
BIRD STUDIO

Akira Toriyama
鳥山明

Tale 67 • Go West, Young Goku...

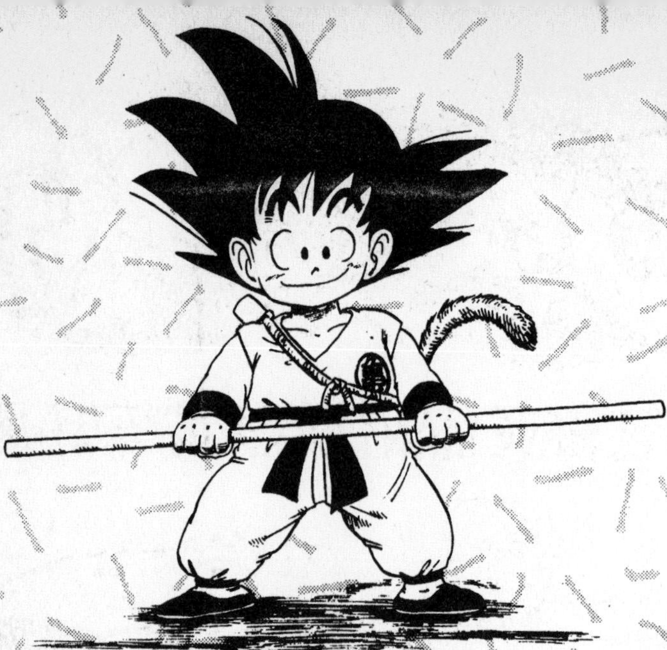

I'M SON GOKU, WITH MY NYOIBÔ AND KINTO'UN

DRAGON BALL

Tale 68 • Monkey in the City

Akira Toriyama
鳥山明
BIRD STUDIO

ドラゴンボール

DRAGON BALL

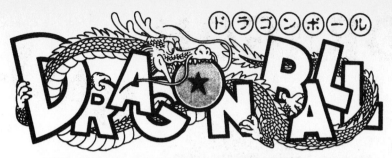

RETURN OF THE DRAGON BALL DYNAMIC DUO!

Tale 69 • Bulma and Goku

CAPSULE CORP.
67

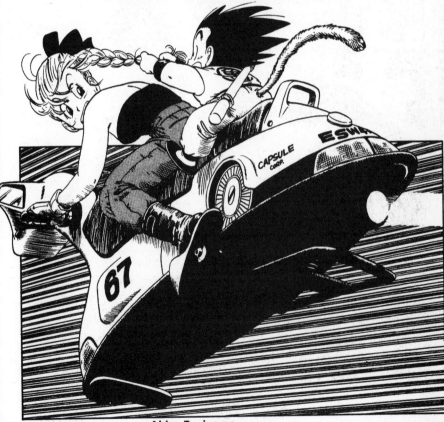

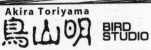

Akira Toriyama
鳥山明 BIRD STUDIO

DRAGON BALL

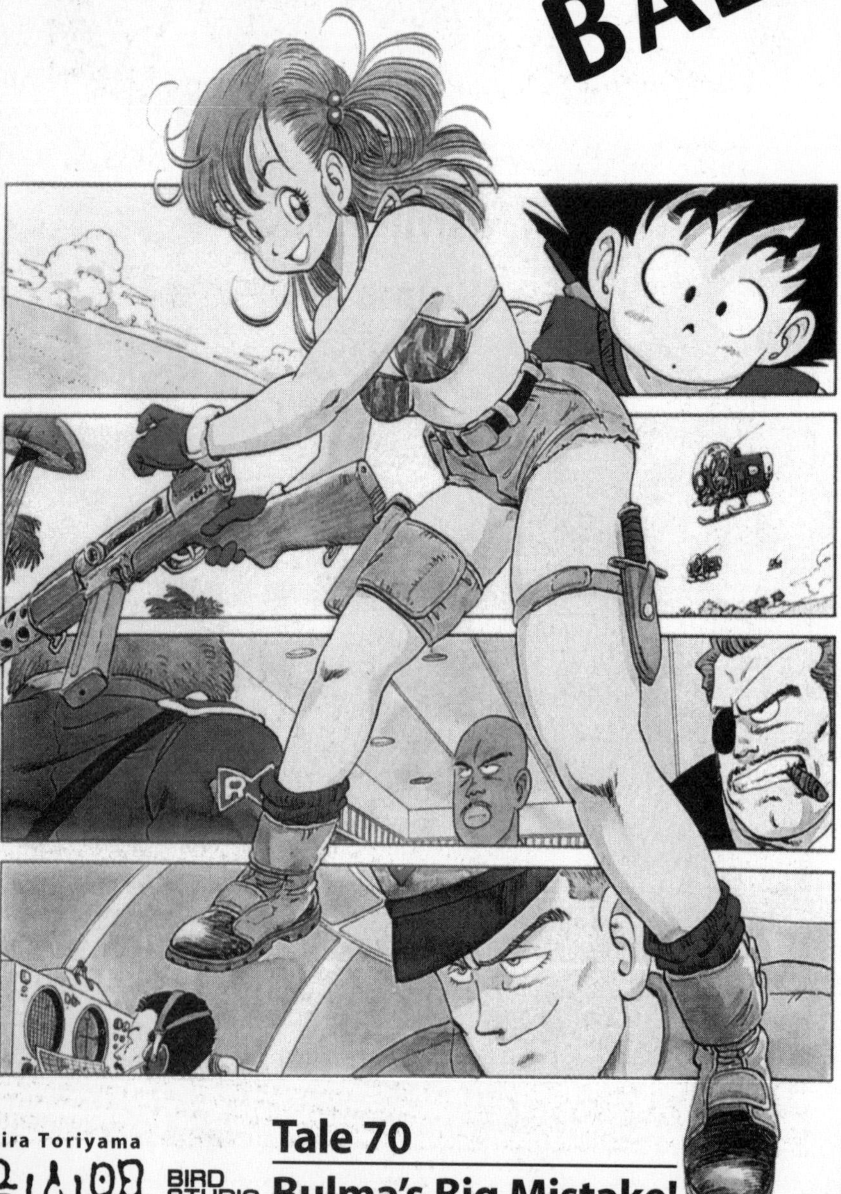

ALL RIGHT! LET'S GET THAT THIRD DRAGON BALL!

Tale 70
Bulma's Big Mistake!

Akira Toriyama
鳥山明
BIRD STUDIO

ドラゴンボール

DRAGON BALL

HE'S BACK AND HE'S BAD!

Akira Toriyama
鳥山明
BIRD STUDIO

Tale 71 • The Turtle is Spotted!

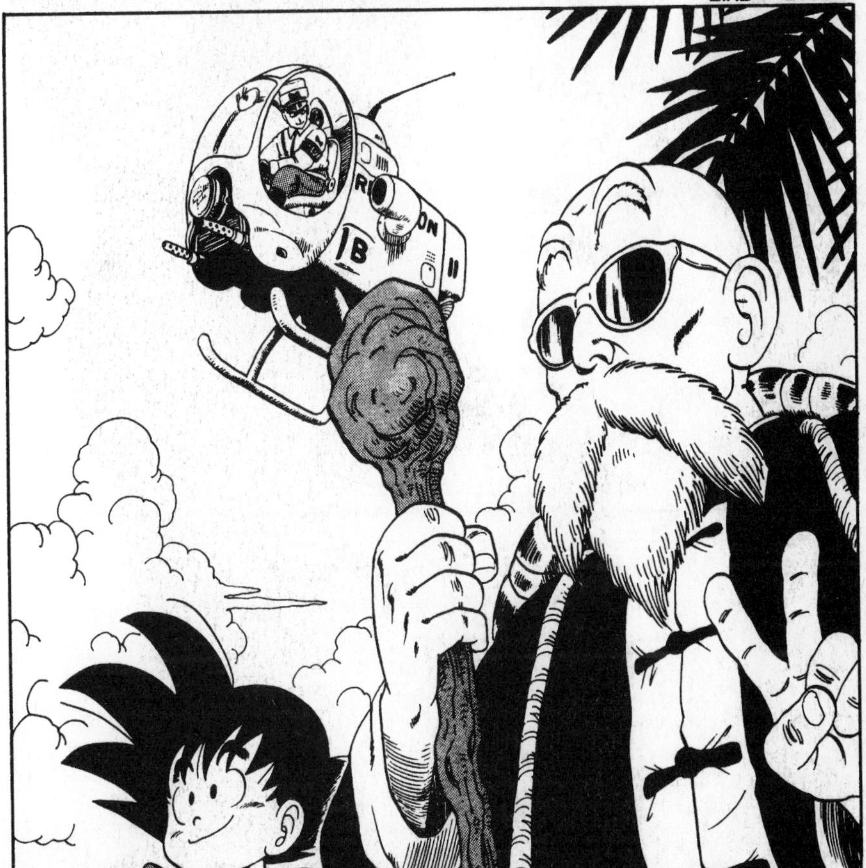

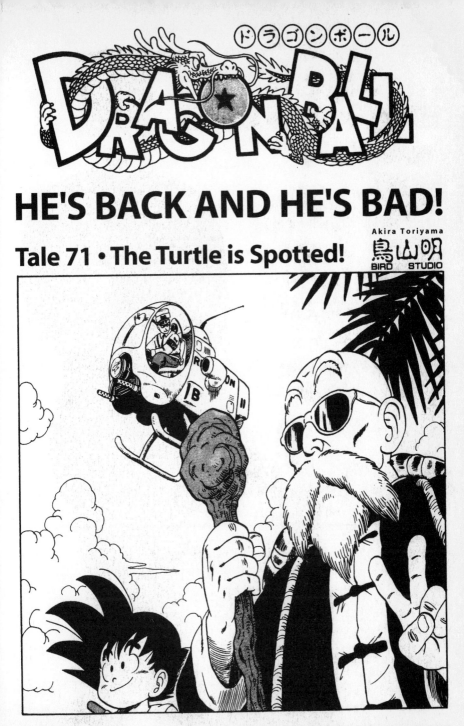

KAME-SEN'NIN...STRONGER AND SLEAZIER THAN EVER!!!

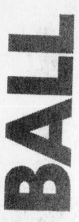

DRAGON BALL

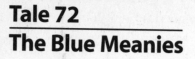

Tale 72
The Blue Meanies

JUST 'CUZ
YOU'RE
LITTLE
DOESN'T
MEAN
YOU'RE
WEAK!

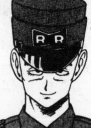

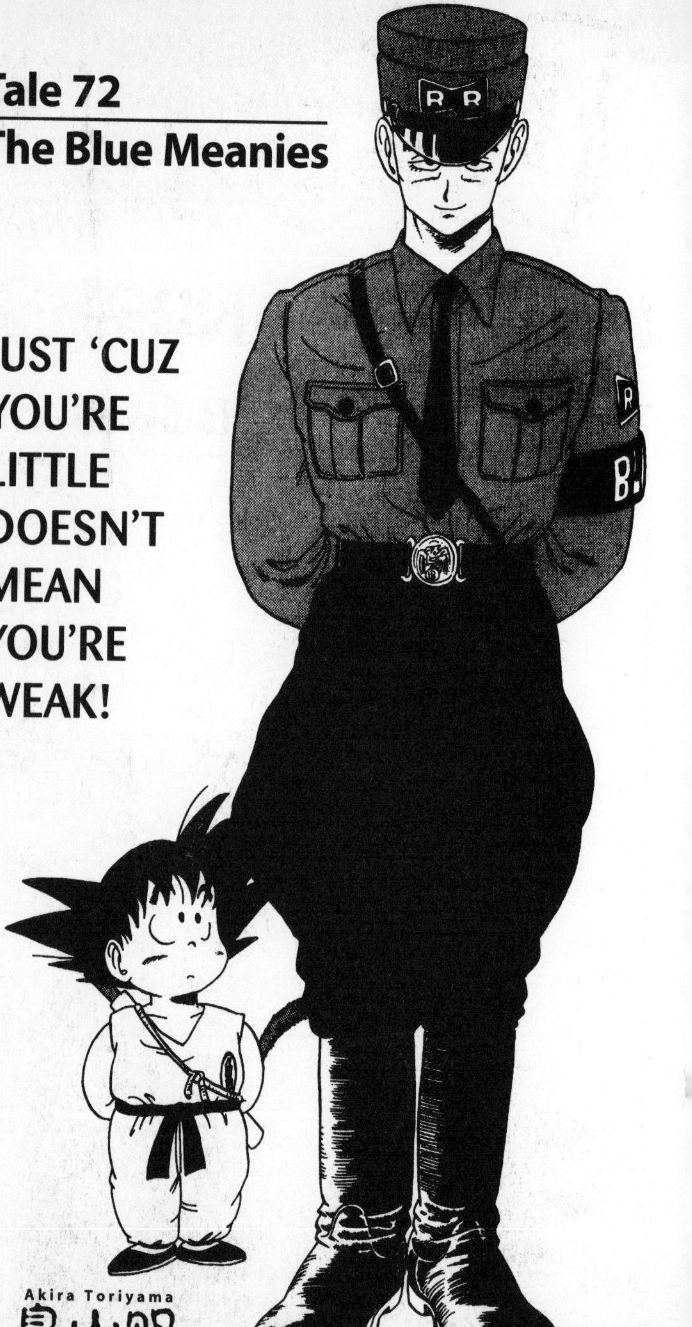

Akira Toriyama
鳥山明
BIRD STUDIO

DRAGON BALL

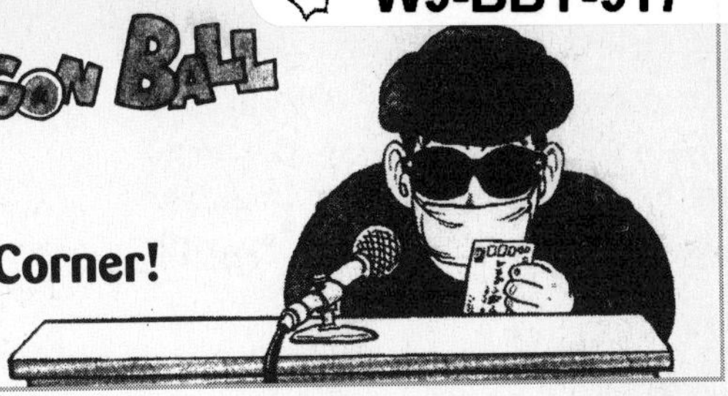

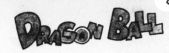

Akira Toriyama's "ASK ME ANYTHING" Corner!

That's right! These are actual questions asked by Japanese **Dragon Ball** readers and answered by Akira Toriyama! (Sorry, Toriyama is too busy to do these sessions nowadays.)

Q. On the spines of the **Dragon Ball** graphic novels, so far you've drawn a Dragon Ball with one star for every volume of the series. What will you do if the series goes over seven volumes?

Tatsuhira Koike
Saitama Prefecture

A. You're right! The spines with the drawings of the dragon and the Dragon Balls will end after the seventh volume. I am wondering myself what to do from the eighth volume on.

Q. I like Pu'ar. I told my brother that Pu'ar is a cat and he told me that Pu'ar is a mouse. Who is right?

Nobukatsu Sekigawa
Kanagawa Prefecture

A. Actually, Pu'ar is neither a cat nor a mouse, but I draw him a little bit like a cat.

Q. Over New Year's break, I made a stamp using your characters [see below]. Nine months from now, I am planning on using the dragon from **Dragon Ball** to make my New Year's greeting cards.

Kimio Nagasaki
Shizuoka Prefecture

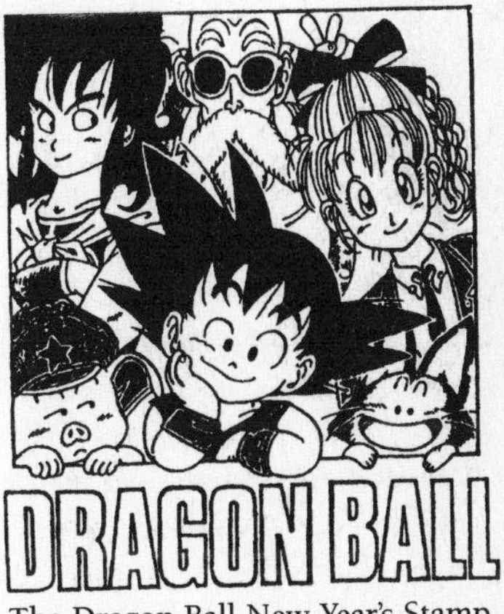
DRAGON BALL

The Dragon Ball New Year's Stamp

A. This is a great stamp! I imagine it took quite a lot of work. I am really impressed. I look forward to seeing your dragon cards, please send me one when you're finished.